S0-AQN-885

FROM GEORGE WASHINGTON TO COL. ELIAS DAYTON
26.7.1777

"The necessity of procuring good intelligence is apparent & need not be further urged—All that remains for me to add is, that you keep the whole matter as Secret as possible. For upon Secrecy, Success depends in Most Enterprizes of the Kind, and for want of it, they are generally defeated, however well planned and promising a favorable issue.

I am Sir
Yr. Most Obed. Sev."

THE BALLANTINE ESPIONAGE/INTELLIGENCE LIBRARY

is the first cohesive collection of true chronicles of the greatest, most important, and most intriguing events in the history of international espionage and intelligence gathering. The series offers astonishing new information for the professional and an exciting introduction for the uninitiated. The books delve deeply into the people, events, and techniques of modern espionage—the puzzles, wiles, ruthlessness, romance, and secrets of this endlessly fascinating world.

Written by eyewitnesses or experts, they read "like fiction." But they are undeniably more powerful, because they are *true . . .*

⦿ ESPIONAGE/INTELLIGENCE LIBRARY ⦿

THE
AMERICAN
BLACK
CHAMBER

HERBERT O. YARDLEY

WITH AN INTRODUCTION BY DAVID KAHN

ESPIONAGE ★ INTELLIGENCE ★ LIBRARY

BB

BALLANTINE BOOKS • NEW YORK

Coyright, 1931, © 1981 by Herbert O. Yardley
Introduction Copyright © 1981 by David Kahn

All rights reserved under International and Pan-American
Copyright Conventions. Published in the United States by
Ballantine Books, a division of Random House, Inc., New
York, and simultaneously in Canada by Random House of
Canada, Limited, Toronto, Canada.

Library of Congress Catalog Card Number: 81-66359

ISBN 0-345-29867-5

Manufactured in the United States of America

First Ballantine Books Edition: September 1981

to
The Personnel of MI-8 and The American Black Chamber
and to
Our Skilful Antagonists,
The Foreign Cryptographers,
Who still remain behind the Curtain of Secret Diplomacy

The publisher gratefully acknowledges
the assistance and inspiration of
Edna R. Yardley, a fine cryptographer

Contents

Introduction

WHEN I was a boy of 13, newly interested in the fascinating world of secret writing, *The American Black Chamber* was my grail. Other books alluded to it; every bibliography listed it. Yet I could not find it in my school library or at the Great Neck Library, and I did not know where else to look. Finally, an advertisement in *The New York Times Book Review* led me to a company that sought out-of-print books, The Seven Bookhunters, I think. To my amazement and delight, within a few weeks the firm actually offered it to me, at the then rather steep price of $12.50, and I snatched it up.

I devoured it. It was one of the most thrilling books I had ever read. For in recounting the story of America's first code-breaking organization, which he had founded and led to one success after another, Herbert O. Yardley proved to be a natural storyteller.

He peoples his pages with diplomats, spies, shy code-breakers. He races from one astonishing case to the next. He can catch the mood of an episode, indeed of the whole clandestine system, in a memorable image. A photostat operator, reproducing a letter in secret ink that can lead to a spy's execution, has a "face the color of death under the dim green lights." A schoolgirl picks her way through the Fifth Avenue crowds at dusk to a rendezvous with a German agent in St. Patrick's Cathedral. An official whispers to him, "The Spanish code?" Moreover, his stories are revelations: Yardley was disclosing the hidden reasons why things had happened as they did.

Yet a darkness hovers around the edges of this book. It must be part of the mystery that obscures all occult sciences.

Despite the sunniness of much of the book, the darkness is never dispelled. This shadow, together with the book's readability, its disclosures, its mysteries, have made it a classic of intelligence literature. Erle Stanley Gardner, the best-selling mystery writer, called *The American Black Chamber* "one of the most interesting books I have ever read."

Herbert Osborne Yardley came to Washington in 1913 at 23 as a $900-a-year telegrapher and code clerk for the State Department. He had been born April 13, 1890, in Worthington, Indiana, and had grown up in that small Midwestern town—president of his high-school class, editor of the school paper, captain of the football team. His mother died when he was 16, and from his father, a railroad agent, he learned telegraphy. This gave him his first job, as a telegrapher for several railroads. Meanwhile, from the owner and card players at Monty's Place, a Worthington saloon, he learned poker, which became a lifelong passion. Short, balding, witty, a marvelous raconteur, with what one acquaintance called "a dynamo of concentrated intellectual power in his head" and a way of talking that expressed utter conviction, he exercised a strong attraction upon many of those who knew him.

Yardley opens his book with an unforgettable word picture of the State Department code room in tranquil pre–World War I Washington. Codes, ciphers, their solution, and the power that the resultant knowledge gave governments fired his imagination, and he determined to devote his life to it. With America's entry into World War I, he got his chance. He tells how he was commissioned a lieutenant in military intelligence and created and organized its Cipher Bureau, its eighth section, MI-8. Though individuals had broken foreign codes for the government since the American Revolution, no organization like this had ever existed in the United States before. MI-8 soon discovered spy letters written in invisible ink, solved German diplomatic codes and ciphers, and found specialists to read obscure German shorthand systems.

Near the end of hostilities, Yardley went to Europe and met with French, British, and American Expeditionary Force cryptologists, staying on for a tour of duty during the peace conference. Ten days after it opened, the army intelligence head was cabling Washington that "I consider the establishment of MI-8 on a peacetime basis most essential." On May 16, 1919, Yardley submitted a plan for a "permanent organization for code and cipher investigation and attack." The need for the United States to continue to obtain the valuable intelligence it had obtained during the war from cryptanalysis was persuasive, and three days later the army chief of staff approved it and the acting secretary of state brown-penciled an "O.K." on the memorandum. America had its first permanent code-breaking agency.

Yardley took a handful of people, most from MI-8, to New York, and by July had begun the operations of what was officially called the Cipher Bureau. His first major assignment was to break the codes of Japan, with whom tension was high owing to Japanese expansion—in particular their receiving as mandates islands along the ocean route to China, Japan, and the Philippines, and their naval shipbuilding program.

The Cipher Bureau succeeded. In what is probably the most dramatic single moment in the whole literature of cryptology, Yardley tells how the solution came to him one night "out of the darkness." His heart stood still and he tumbled out of bed then ran to his office on the floor below, where he confirmed that his vision had been correct. The solution led, several months later, to a remarkable American diplomatic coup. With the knowledge, gained through intercepts, of how much the Japanese negotiators at the Washington Disarmament Conference of 1921 to 1922 would yield if pressed, the United States squeezed Japan to accept less capital-ship tonnage than Japan had wished: the famous 5:5:3 ratio between Britain, the United States, and Japan.

In the years that followed, Yardley's Cipher Bureau, which was under the joint jurisdiction of the State and War Departments, solved the codes of 20 nations. But financial support dwindled as the 1920s proceeded and the fear and memory of war receded. The staff shrank; some members worked only part-time. In November, 1928, Herbert Hoover was elected president. He named as his secretary of state a political New York lawyer with experience in government and in international affairs, Henry L. Stimson. Yardley waited until Stimson had been in office a few months, then sent him the solutions of an important series of messages. Stimson was shocked. He regarded it as a violation of the principle of trust on which he conducted both his personal affairs and the nation's foreign policy.

As he said later, "Gentlemen do not read each other's mail." He withdrew all State Department funds from the Cipher Bureau. Since these constituted its major support, their loss effectively closed the office. The agency had cost the State Department $230,404 and the War Department $98,808.49—just under a third of a million dollars for a decade of cryptanalysis.

Two days before the formal closing on October 31, 1929, the stock market crashed. Yardley, out of a job, went back to Worthington, after having lost money in real estate in Queens, New York, where he had lived. Broke, unable to get a loan from an old MI-8 friend, Chicago University professor John Manly, he decided in desperation to make some money to feed his wife and son, Jack, by telling the story of his cryptologic work. The Bobbs-Merrill Company of Indianapolis agreed to publish it; excerpts would appear in *The Saturday Evening Post*, the leading magazine of its day. He described the composition in a letter to the MI-8 friend in the spring of 1931:

> I hadn't done any real work for so long that I told Bye, my agent, and the Sat Eve Post that I would need some one else to write the stuff. I showed a few things to Bye and Costain, the latter editor of POST, and both told me to go to work myself. I sat for days before a typewriter, helpless. Oh, I pecked away a bit, and gradually under the encouragement of Bye I got a bit of confidence. Then Bobbs-Merrill advanced me $1000 on outline. Then there was a call to rush the book. I began to work in shifts, working a few hours, sleeping a few hours, going out of my room only to buy some eggs, bread, coffee and cans of tomatoe juice. Jesus, the stuff I turned out. Sometimes only a thousand words, but often as many as 10,000 a day. As the chapters appeared, I took them to Bye who read them and offered criticism. Anyway I completed the book and boiled down parts of it for the articles [that ran in *The Saturday Evening Post*] all in 7 weeks.

The American Black Chamber was published on June 1, 1931. It was an instant success. It immediately became the most famous book on cryptology ever published till then. Yardley's vigorous and pungent style, his narrative skill, and the total novelty of his revelations—people knew about spies, but few had heard of codes before—fixed the book instantly in the popular mind. Reviews were unanimously good. Critic W. A. Rogers, in a commendatory review, summed up the prevailing opinion: "I think it the most sensational contribution to the secret history of the war, as well as the immediate post-war period, which has yet been written by an American. Its deliberate indiscretions exceed any to be found in the recent memoirs of European secret agents." Its advertisements claimed it was a best seller. William Allen White, the Kansas journalist and sage, called it "the most important book of the season." It sold 17,931 copies—a remarkable figure. A British edition added 5,480, and there were French, Swedish, an unauthorized Chinese, and Japanese translations.

But the positive views of the public were matched by a corresponding negative view in official circles. Though American officials smoothly denied to inquiring reporters that an agency such as Yardley's had existed, beneath this bland surface they were infuriated. Yardley had, they felt with considerable justice, violated his trust. Some damage was probably apparent almost at once, for at least some of the nations named as having their codes broken must have changed them. One of them was Japan. It was there, as might be expected, that sales skyrocketed. On a per-capita basis, sales in Japan of 33,119 copies were almost four times better than in the United States. A tremendous furor erupted over it. The Tokyo *Nichi Nichi,* one of the most influential papers in Japan, published a long article in which everyone tried to save face by throwing blame on the Foreign Ministry. The episode impelled Japan to improve her codes and ciphers, and it so imprinted itself on Japanese consciousness that, 10 years later, shortly before Pearl Harbor, the foreign minister had *The American Black Chamber* in his mind when he asked his cable chief whether Japan's diplomatic cryptosystems were then secure.

The cable chief assured the minister that "This time, it's all right." In fact, it was not. American army and navy cryptanalysts had solved a difficult new Japanese cryptosystem, a cipher machine the Americans called PURPLE. Though its solution caused the Americans a great deal more work than that of earlier systems would have, in the end it might have yielded greater results than the solution of simpler systems. For the Japanese reposed such absolute trust in PURPLE that they never changed it during the war, when it became a major source of Allied intelligence on Axis intentions, while they might have changed lesser systems from time to time, causing the cryptanalysts to lose out. This of course is speculation, but the point is that Yardley's revelations may not have been the unmitigated disaster that many claimed they were.

The publication of *The American Black Chamber* catapulted Yardley to fame. He capitalized on it as much as he could. He gave lectures. He wrote articles. He tried to sell a secret ink. And he decided to utilize the two boxes of secret documents he had taken with him when the Cipher Bureau closed to expand the central story of the book—how the solution of Japanese codes had led to the American diplomatic victory at the Washington Disarmament Conference of 1921–22.

But he did not want to write it himself. Probably he realized that the cream had been skimmed off this project. So he turned the papers over to a young journalist. She did little more than select several hundred of the most pertinent Japanese diplomatic intercepts out of the 5,000 Yardley had and connect them with an outline history of the conference. But it was suffocatingly dull—she had none of Yardley's remarkable literary gifts. Moreover, the manuscript was seized by the government from a prospective publisher on the grounds that it violated a statute prohibiting agents of the government from appropriating secret documents. It was never published. One lasting result came from it, however. The government passed a law that would prevent publication of any material that had once been prepared in any official diplomatic code; it lies today on the statute books as Section 952 of Title 18, United States Code.

Four days after it passed, on June 10, 1933, the Bobbs-Merrill Company petitioned the State Department for approval to carry out a 1931 contract with Blue Ribbon Books to reprint 15,000 copies of *The American Black Chamber*. Evidently, it was seeking State Department protection against a possible Justice Department prosecution. But State declined. This was the source of a persistent legend that the government had suppressed *The American Black Chamber*, though of course State's refusal had no effect on the thousands of copies already printed and awaiting distribution.

Meanwhile, Yardley continued writing. Two novels came from his pen—*The Red Sun of Nippon* and *The Blonde Countess*. Metro-Goldwyn-Mayer adapted the latter into its movie *Rendezvous,* starring William Powell, Rosalind Russell, and Cesar Romero. It premiered in New York on October 25, 1935, with *The New York Times* calling it "a lively and amusing melodrama." A book of puzzle cryptograms also appeared with Yardley's name both in the title —*Yardleygrams*—and as author, but in fact was ghosted by a friend, Clem Koukol, a telephone-company engineer.

Yardley also dabbled in real estate in Queens, where he was living, until in 1938 he got a call to go to China to solve codes for Chiang Kai-shek, then leading China's fight against Japanese aggression. He went, living in soggy, bombed, heroic Chungking, and successfully solving low-level tactical Japanese army systems—two- and three-digit codes and *kata kana* transpositions—which sometimes revealed the secrets of Japanese troop movements. After almost two years, weary, 40 pounds lighter, lonely, he returned to America—and almost immediately got a call to set up a code-breaking agency for Canada. This he did, starting in the middle of 1941, establishing what was officially called the Examination Unit of the Department of External Affairs on the second floor of a brand-new brick building with a wind-tunnel under it in an isolated area about three or four miles outside Ottawa. He and his handful of experts mostly solved the transposition ciphers of German agents in South America.

Thereafter, Yardley lived in Washington, engaged in a variety of businesses and war work—a restaurant at 13th and H Streets, Northwest, rationing-practices investigator for the wartime Office of Price Administration, another novel, *Crows Are Black Everywhere,* written with a former instructor, office work in a federal housing agency, general contracting in Silver Spring, Maryland. For a short time, he supervised the selling of kitchen appliances while living in Washington, D.C. Yardley was employed by the Housing Administration when he retired from government service. In 1956, he wrote *The Education of a Poker Player,* in which, between stories of how he learned that game in Indiana and played it in China, he offered tips on how to win at it. The book was an immediate success and, more than 20 years later, was still in print and selling.

A month before its actual publication, he suffered a stroke. Eight months later, he had another attack, went into a coma for eight days, and at 12:45 P.M. on August 7,

1958, died in his home in Silver Spring. He was buried with military honors in Arlington National Cemetery. But to many, Herbert Yardley is not dead. In his books, he lives still.

—David Kahn

Foreword

IN the written history of the world there is not so much as a glimpse behind the heavy curtains that enshroud the background of secret diplomacy. The background? The Black Chamber. The Cryptographic Bureau, where specialists pore over cipher telegrams of foreign governments, where chemists forge diplomatic seals and photograph letters of foreign plenipotentiaries.

It is my aim to unfold in a simple dispassionate way the intimate details of a secret organization that I fostered for the American Government; an organization which, at its height of power, employed one hundred and sixty-five men and women. I created the bureau and directed its mysterious activities, until, at the end of twelve years, a new Secretary of State ordered the door of the Black Chamber closed and bolted.

In a period of twelve years, this Secretary was the first diplomatist who, though well aware that all great powers have their Black Chambers, had the courage—or was it naïveté?—to announce that diplomatic correspondence must be inviolate, thus renouncing the secret practises of the American Cryptographic Bureau. Now that the Black Chamber has been destroyed there is no valid reason for witholding its secrets.

We shall hear the words of England, France, the Vatican, Japan, Mexico, Cuba, Spain, Nicaragua, Peru, Brazil and many others.

We see the safe of a Minister opened, his code book photographed.

A lovely girl dances with a Secretary of an Embassy.

She flatters him. They become confidential. He is indiscreet —we learn the nature of his code book.

A diplomatic seal is carefully forged. Experts skilfully open the letter and photograph the contents.

Months of labor to decipher another code. Fifty typists feverishly type elaborate frequency tables over which cryptographers strain their eyes for a key that will unravel the mystery.

A letter intercepted. Chemists at work with glass tubes and strange chemicals. Faint characters appear, a sentence ... a paragraph ... then another—designs on the Panama Canal! A beautiful woman arrested and cast into prison. She confesses and dies.

A jumble of letters; they are deciphered. A secret trial and sentence of death.

A sensational telegram. The Attorney-General and the Secretary of State stumble over each other to be the first to reach the President—like school-children running to their teacher with an apple to bribe her favors.

The first Armament Conference is in session. Here will be determined the naval strengths of the Great Powers. Couriers rush from the Black Chamber to Washington, carrying decipherments of the latest secret code telegrams of foreign governments. The Black Chamber is closely guarded. We are showered with honors. The Secretary of War pins the Distinguished Service Medal on my lapel and winks at me.

CHAPTER I

The State Department
Code Room

THE secret activities of the American Black Chamber, which I directed, ceased in 1929, sixteen years after I arrived at the Department of State as a young telegraph operator. At that time I knew exactly nothing about the solution of the diplomatic codes and ciphers of foreign nations. No one else in this country knew much.

Washington in 1913 seemed a quiet prosaic city, but I was soon to learn that the Code Room held pages of history rivaling the great intrigues of the past. This spacious room with its high ceiling overlooked the southern White House grounds. By lifting my eyes from my work I could see a tennis game in progress where a few years earlier President Roosevelt and his tennis Cabinet had played each day.

Along one side of the room ran a long oak telegraph table with its stuttering resonators and sounders; cabinets containing copies of current telegrams almost blocked the entrance. In the center sprawled two enormous flat-topped desks shoved together, about which a few code clerks thumbed code books and scribbled rapidly, pausing now and then to light cigarettes. The pounding of typewriters specially constructed to make fifteen copies of a telegram mingled with the muffled click of the telegraph instruments. The walls were covered with old-fashioned closed cupboards filled with bound copies of telegrams from and to consular and diplomatic posts throughout the world. In the corner stood a huge safe, its thick doors slightly ajar.

There was an air of good-fellowship in the room and

I was soon at home. However, I was mystified at the casual attitudes of these overworked code clerks. Daily history passed through their hands in one long stream and they thought less of it than of the baseball scores. The murder of Madero, the shelling of Vera Cruz, the rumblings of a threatening World War—these merely meant more telegrams, longer hours—nothing else.

But when I was shifted to night duty I found myself in a different atmosphere. Minor officials and sometimes the Secretary himself made the Code Room a loafing-place. Many officials, including members of our diplomatic corps, the specialists on South American, European, Near Eastern and Far Eastern affairs, often dropped in to look over the telegrams, and now and then, when wine had flowed freely at some diplomatic function, to argue for hours about the Secretary's "damn fool" policies. One in particular, the hardest-drinking but the shrewdest of the lot, always came in to read the latest dispatches from Mexico City before going home. Having finished, he never failed, in his solemn way, to ask me whether a certain word was spelled with a *c* or a *k*.

Seeing the cut of their smart clothes and hearing tales of their amorous experiences in foreign capitals impressed my country mind, but I detected no signs of greatness in any of them and in my lowly place of code clerk and telegraph operator, I held them in amused contempt. Later, when I was to meet them as an equal, my early impressions were confirmed: good-natured, jolly, smartly dressed pigmies, strutting around with affected European mannerisms.

The Chief of the Latin American Division was an entirely different type, neither a politician nor a member of the diplomatic corps. He had received his training by hard knocks in South America instead of in the drawing-rooms of European courts. He seemed little interested in drawing-rooms and in amorous intrigues. Instead he preferred to hold the strings that made the armies, generals and presidents of South and Central America dance at his bidding. Whether he was wise or not, I do not know, but he was a strong man and the author of American "dollar diplomacy." Bryan, when he was appointed Secretary of State, kicked him out for this policy. From that day I never heard the words "dollar diplomacy," nor on the other hand did I observe any change in policy, although I read a great deal about it in the newspapers.

2

This man, when at leisure, loved to think aloud. I cultivated his friendship and looked forward to his next tale of intrigue. He gave me approximate dates, and when he had gone I pulled down the dusty bound volumes of copies of telegrams to read there the authentic record of his machinations. There too I found the thrilling stories of the seizure of the Panama Canal, the Venezuelan incident when America was on the verge of war with England, and other great moments of American nationalism. I was again sitting on a flour barrel in the village bakery, listening to intrigues of the vivid past as recited by the baker, an exiled German nobleman.

Were our diplomatic codes safe from prying eyes? Who knew? From the pages of history I had had glimpses of the decipherer who could unravel military and diplomatic cipher telegrams. Other countries must have cryptographers. Why did America have no bureau for the reading of secret diplomatic code and cipher telegrams of foreign governments?

As I asked myself this question I knew that I had the answer to my eager young mind which was searching for a purpose in life. I would devote my life to cryptography. Perhaps I too, like the foreign cryptographer, could open the secrets of the capitals of the world. I now began a methodical plan to prepare myself.

I quickly devoured all the books on cryptography that could be found in the Congressional Library. These were interesting but of no practical value. Next I searched Edgar Allan Poe's letters for a glimpse of the scientific treatment of cryptography. These were full of vague boasts of his skill—nothing more. Today, looking at cryptography from a scientific point of view, for the American Black Chamber has never had an equal, I know that Poe merely floundered around in the dark and did not understand the great underlying principles.

At last I found the American Army pamphlet on the solution of military ciphers. This pamphlet was used as a text-book for a course in cipher solution at the Signal Corps School at Fort Leavenworth. The book was full of methods for the solution of various types. The only trouble was that the types of cipher it explained were so simple that any bright schoolboy could solve them without a book of instructions. I was at the end of the trail.

It was obvious I would have to do my own pioneer work. I began at once. Due to friendly connections previously established, I had no difficulty in obtaining copies of code and cipher communications dispatched by various embassies in Washington. Progress was slow, for the clerical work incidental to the solution of messages is enormous. (Later I was to have fifty typists busy making elaborate frequency tables.) Some I solved and some I did not. But I was learning a new science, with no beaten path to follow.

One night, business being quiet, I was working on the solution of a cipher when I heard the cable office in New York tell the White House telegraph operator (we used the same wire to New York) that he had five hundred code words from Colonel House to the President. As the telegram flashed over the wire I made a copy. This would be good material to work on, for surely the President and his trusted agent would be using a difficult code.

Imagine my amazement when I was able to solve the message in less than two hours! I had little respect for the doings of the great—I dealt with them every day and was too close for worship—but this was incredible. Colonel House was in Germany. He had just seen the Emperor. This message had passed over British cables and we already knew that a copy of every cable went to the Code Bureau in the British Navy.

Colonel House must be the Allies' best informant! No need to send spies into Germany when they have Colonel House's reports of interviews with the Emperor, Princes, Generals, leading industrial leaders. And movements for peace! Is it possible that a man sits in the White House, dreaming, picturing himself a maker of history, an international statesman, a mediator of peace, and sends his agents out with schoolboy ciphers? Is this the cause of his failures?

I am trembling with my great secret but what can I do with it? I can inform my superiors. But what then? The President holds advice in contempt. Besides, this would put him in a very bad light, and adverse criticism he will not tolerate. He would have some one's head and that head would be mine for presuming to read his secret dispatches. I have other uses for my head. I touched a match to the sheets of paper and destroyed the ashes. Let the President and his confidential agent continue their comedy.

The President seems to have had a penchant for schoolboy ciphers. While I was organizing the American Black Chamber, directly after America entered the World War, the President sent a mission into Russia, headed by another

4

of his favorites, George Creel. By this time all code messages filed with the cable companies came to me in a routine manner, and so simple to solve were the American Mission's secret dispatches that they were used as elementary examples in the training of student cryptographers.

For months now, I had been working on the solution of the American diplomatic code, which progressed slowly but surely. The clerical work incidental to its solution was uninspiring but unfortunately necessary. Aside from this I was making notes as I slowly chiseled out words here and there, for it was my aim to write an exhaustive treatise on this problem and hand it to my superior. I shall not explain my methods. To do so would reveal the character of the State Department code book which of course can not be done. Further on we shall follow the scientific analysis and solution of the codes and ciphers of foreign governments.

During these years from 1913 to 1917 many faces passed before me. Among them Mr. Lansing, who was later Secretary of State, stands out vividly. Immaculately dressed, gray hair, a short mustache, and the blank face of a faro dealer. In a deuces-wild poker game, I mused, he should hold his own with even Mont Mull, or at least with Salty East, our two village poker sharks. Had Secretary Lansing not been tied to a tyrant schoolmaster and represented in London by an Anglophile, history might well have been changed.

It is not my aim to write the musings of a mouse as he gazes at his King and his King's noblemen, but having mentioned Ambassador Page, I must continue for a few more lines. A favorite argument of the historians of the late war, in absolving Germany of any guilt, is that nowhere in the German archives have they found incriminating documents. Does this prove that they did not exist? Not at all. I am satisfied that Secretary Bryan's tailor had at one time a small portion of the American diplomatic archives, for the Secretary's favorite habit was to stuff original telegrams into the tail of his coat and forget them. Years later I was to hear of thousands of documents being destroyed. I have myself, at the orders of my immediate superior, who received his instructions direct from the Secretary of State, destroyed all trace of many of Ambassador Page's secret dispatches. These were not even seen by the President. Later, while in London, I learned that some of the Ambassador's ravings were too hot even to leave the Embassy and were destroyed by a member of the staff instead of being dispatched to Washington. Had one of these telegrams reached the President there would have been no *Life and Letters of Walter H. Page*. So much for history and state papers.

Secretary Bryan came in often at night and I grew to look forward to these moments. His deep resonant voice charmed me, and his good nature was infectious, though I, like all others, laughed at the ridiculous figure he made as Secretary of State. Now and then he would dictate an answer to an urgent message and the next day sign another with directly opposite instructions. If the spirit moved him he would stop at a telegraph office and file a message to some ambassador not in code but in plain language. The next day an inquiry would come in, reading: "Just received uncoded undated telegram signed Bryan. Advise if authentic." He sent a telegram of congratulation to Henry Lane Wilson, American Minister to Mexico. President Wilson was not on the best of terms with Minister Wilson, and when he saw the telegram he was outraged. The next day Secretary Bryan cabled that the message was an error and must be canceled. He was the despair of the whole State Department but his kindness made everybody love him, even though they laughed behind his back.

One writer, who should know better, accuses him of referring to the Japanese Ambassador in some such words as "show that little monkey in." Heywood Broun wrote that this seemed unbelievable. And so it is. It was not Bryan, but a tactless secretary who said this; a youngster who while in college led a demonstration of applause when it looked as if Bryan might be hissed off the platform. Such are the steps to greatness.

Other notables frequented the Code Room of the Department of State. One night half of the Cabinet came in. They wished to witness the deciphering of the message which would tell us whether Mexico would salute our flag. This argument was later to lead to the shelling of Vera Cruz. Zero hour was seven P.M. With such a distinguished audience present, I requested, in the name of the State Department, that the wire from Galveston, Texas, the cable from Galveston to Vera Cruz, the telegraph wire from Vera Cruz to Mexico City, be held open. A few minutes after seven the operator at Galveston said, "Here you are, forty words from Mexico City."

"What is it?" demanded Daniels.

"The message you are waiting for," I replied and turned to my typewriter, beginning to copy.

As the sounder spelled out the code words, Secretary Daniels began in a solemn voice, "Gentlemen, we are now receiving the most vital message ever confronted by this Administration."

I deciphered the message and handed it to them. Mexico refused. They actually turned pale, but had the good sense to run to the President.

All this time my work on the decipherment of the American diplomatic code was slowly progressing. At last I laid some one hundred pages of typewritten exposition before my immediate superior.

"What's this?" he asked.

"Exposition on the 'Solution of American Diplomatic Codes,' " I replied.

"You wrote it?"

"Yes."

"You mean to say our codes are not safe?" He turned to me. "I don't believe it."

"Very well," I answered. "This memorandum represents over one thousand hours of concentrated analysis and tedious detailed labor. It has taken me nearly two years. I merely ask that you read it."

As I left him he gave me a queer desperate glance, for he had compiled this code and the responsibility of secret communications rested upon his shoulders.

Aside from this I had played him a rather mean mysterious trick, and I really believe he imagined I held some occult power. Nearly a year earlier he had changed the combination of the safe which guarded the code books and as he did so had chuckled to himself. That was Saturday, and I was to open up Sunday morning; he failed to tell me the combination and I forgot to ask him for it.

All this I realized as I opened the office door the next morning. He had a clever mind, of sorts, and would not permit us to carry a string of combination figures in our pockets. Instead, we need only remember a name. The telephone figures opposite the name in the telephone book, anagrammed and distorted in a certain way, represented the combination.

Interested in subtle problems of all sorts, I thought it would be great fun if I could open the safe without telephoning for the combination. Aside from this, to use the telephone would require him to come to the office to change the combination again.

I sat down and thought the matter over. What was he laughing about when he changed the combination the day before? He must have used some one's name for a key, some name that made him chuckle. Now the funniest name I could think of at that time was Henry Ford, who had just pushed off on his quarrelsome Peace Mission. "Out of the trenches before Christmas!"

Henry Ford's name was not in the telephone book. I tried the Ford Company's number without success.

I knew I could open the safe if I could only think straight enough, if I could but place myself in my superior's shoes and follow his train of thought. He had smiled. At what? At a name? Something connected with a name? What name was on every one's lips? "Mrs. Galt" suddenly flashed across my mind. President Wilson had just announced their engagement.

I glanced at the telephone number opposite her name and with trembling fingers spun the dial to the safe. In another second the tumbler clicked and the door swung open!

Almost at the same instant the telephone bell rang. It was my superior.

"Yardley, I forgot to give you the combination . . ."

"No need. The safe is open."

"The safe is open!" he yelled. "Who left it open?"

"No one. I just opened it."

"How? I didn't give you the combination."

"No . . . I just fiddled around until I opened it."

I needed to make an impression on my superior in some other way than by hard efficient work. He could be of use to me later for I still held the vision of success before me. A little mystery wouldn't do any harm. I don't know to this day whether he thought me a safecracker or a mind-reader.

A few days after I gave him my one-hundred-page memorandum on the "Solution of American Diplomatic Codes," he called me to his office.

His face was grave as he glanced up at me.

"How long have you been doing this sort of thing?"

"Nearly ever since I was employed here. Over four years now."

He was very deliberate in his speech.

"Who, besides yourself, knows about your memorandum?"

"No one."

"You realize this is very serious."

"Of course."

What was he driving at? I must keep still about those Wilson-House messages. He started to dismiss me, then:

"We already know by our telegrams from London that England maintains a large bureau for solving diplomatic correspondence."

He paused and looked at me again.

"Do you believe they could solve our code?"

Now he must either be talking to himself to bolster up his courage, or flattering me by attributing to me a greater power of analysis than that possessed by experienced English cryptographers. I did not reply at once. I did not wish to belittle my knowledge, nor did I wish to appear vain.

"For the sake of argument," I answered, "I always assume that what is in the power of one man to do is also in the power of another."

"If you had this problem to do over how long would it take?"

"Well," I replied slowly, "with ten assistants I might do it in a month."

"Say no more about this. I shall see what can be done," he said vaguely, and I started away.

"And, Yardley," he called to me, "it was a masterly piece of analysis."

There were rumblings of our entry into the war. I must be patient. Wars always afforded opportunities.

A month later my superior introduced a new method for encoding our secret dispatches. My fingers itched to tear it apart. While I worked at decoding and encoding messages, or spent an hour now and then at the telegraph desk, ways and means of attack on this new problem crept through my brain. It was the first thing I thought of when I awakened, the last when I fell asleep. There were, also, of course, hours of painstaking labor with paper and pencil. Then several weeks later I awoke during the night and the answer flashed as clear as a simple problem in arithmetic.

I got up and went to my typewriter and typed my impressions before they slipped into darkness.

I was at my superior's desk when he came in.

"If you would care to have some one encode a few

messages," I began, "I'm sure I can, within a day or so, hand you a short memorandum on the solution of your new system."

I well knew he held my powers in deep respect, but he did not seem worried at my statement and readily agreed to the challenge. He had cause to be confident, for his system was indeed an ingenious one.

War would be declared within a few days now and telegrams streamed from every corner of the globe. The hours were long and grinding and I had little time or taste for his problem, because, as far as I was concerned, the problem had been solved. Often in the science of cryptography, when a new principle is discovered, there is no need for the actual solution. The principle equals the solution.

Finally, several weeks later, after the declaration of war, I handed my superior the solved messages and a few pages of exposition. He was already prepared for this through several conversations we had had. He seemed content to let the matter drop, assuming the hopeless view that nothing is indecipherable.

I was to learn that the Black Chamber produced the same reaction on all government officials. What we did seemed to them pure legerdemain.

After reading my memorandum, he expressed his admiration and smiled good-naturedly about the matter. Then I told him I wished to leave the State Department; I wished to apply for a commission in the Army. Would he be good enough to write a memorandum expressing my qualifications as a cryptographer?

He replied that he could not very well recommend my release, and besides, I was familiar enough with the Department of State policies to know that the Assistant Secretary of State would never consent.

"Please forget for a moment," I began, trying to control my voice, for I must have this memorandum from him— my future depended upon this—"that I am an employee of the State Department. You and I should understand each other. You yourself were once a clerk. You know and I know that I do not belong in the Code Room. It has taken me four years of sweat to learn what I know. Give me an opportunity. Write this memorandum for me. I'll take care of the Assistant Secretary of State at the proper moment."

"All right, Yardley," he promised, and shook hands with me. "I'll be sorry to see you go."

The next day I had my precious document. I rushed to

the few Army and Navy officers I knew, for letters, all of which ended up with some such phrase as, "Mr. Yardley would, I am sure, conduct himself at all times in a manner becoming an officer and a gentleman." The Army and Navy love the words "officer" and "gentleman."

One more paper and I would spring my plan for a Cipher Bureau upon the unsuspecting War Department. It had the money, it would soon rule America.

It had taken me four years to obtain one document. It would take me ten to get a release from Assistant Secretary Phillips if I did not play my cards carefully. And the War Department would consider no application for commissions without a release.

Secretary Phillips was of the flower of the American diplomatic corps. Wealthy, young, handsome, cultured, suave, ingratiating, a pleasant smile, a low musical voice, a slender athletic figure, inscrutable eyes.

Would I sit down? Would I have a cigarette? He had heard a great deal about me. He must tell the Secretary himself about this prodigy of the Code Room. There would soon be advances in salary. A word here, and who knows?

"Let me see . . . your salary is . . . Well, we shall see. The State Department must take care of its brilliant employees. But the Department must also function, even if there is a war. And how can it function without . . . ?"

It was, of course, a deep regret that a release at this time was unthinkable. Perhaps later.

I was back in the cool corridors again, wiping the perspiration from my forehead. God, what a man! Prodigy —brilliant—get my salary raised—even mention me to the Secretary himself. This was going to be difficult. I must make myself appear so indispensable to the War Department that it would demand my release. A large order indeed. But why not? This huge army would surely need cryptographers.

I was not to go on duty until four P.M., and so had plenty of time to plan my campaign. Inquiries in the right places pointed to Colonel Gibbs, Signal Corps Officer, as the proper person to whom I should present my ideas.

I slowly walked to his office at the other end of the long corridor, outlining what I must say to him. A civilian clerk stopped me before I could get to Colonel Gibbs' desk. What did I want? Wrong office, I guess.

I hung outside in the corridor until the clerk went to lunch, then stole in to Colonel Gibbs' desk which occupied a small room in the suite. He was alone, apparently thinking over some problem of administration.

He raised his head in a gesture of inquiry.

My great moment had arrived. I made an effort to clear my brain and control my voice, which threatened to tremble with excitement. I began to feel my way along. I was an employee in the Department of State, Code Room; I had studied cryptography in a scientific way for over four years. . . . Had it not occurred to him . . . ?

"Have you seen Major Van Deman?" he interrupted.

"No. Who is he?"

"He isn't much of anything right now, but he will be heard from. He's the father of Military Intelligence in the Army. He can use you. Go see him. Tell him I sent you. You will find him at the War College, and let me know what he says."

I started to leave.

"Here, take your papers with you."

I took a street-car to the barracks. The War College sits back about a quarter of a mile beyond the parade grounds. I hurried past the guard who let me by at the mention of Van Deman and in a few moments stood before the father of Military Intelligence.

He was dictating and motioned me to sit down. As far as I could see, his only assistants were a thin-faced Captain and his secretary. Almost overnight this small force was to grow into an efficient organization with thousands of officers, clerks and agents, until its long tentacles circled the earth.

Van Deman's heavily lined face reminded me of Lincoln's. I was soon to love this man for his patience, deep sympathy and human understanding. (America was late in giving him his just honor but he was finally retired a Major-General.) He appeared old and terribly tired, but when he turned his deep eyes toward me I sensed his power.

I had lost my trepidation and began my story in a confident tone. Rapidly outlining my history I gave him details that would convince him of my knowledge of codes and ciphers and their solution.

He was intensely interested and I boldly came to my point. We of the State Department well knew that the Great Powers maintained large staffs for the reading of foreign diplomatic messages. It was immaterial to America whether I or some one else formed such a bureau. But such a bureau must begin to function, and at once. America must know who her friends were and who her enemies. How except by reading the secret messages of foreign governments was she to learn the truth? And on the Western Front, a section of which American troops might well soon occupy, the Germans were directing their maneuvers by wireless telegrams in code and cipher. These messages must be intercepted. Who would attempt to solve them? General Pershing would demand a cryptographic service in France. Who would train cryptographers for this venture?

He picked up my papers and read them rapidly.

"How old are you?"

"Twenty-seven."

"This is a pretty big job you have picked out for yourself. You talk as if you think you can do it."

I made no comment.

He was scribbling a note.

"I like your confidence well enough but not your age. However, take this note to Colonel Gibbs and tell him I said to get your commission through at the earliest possible moment. Can you start Monday?"

I smiled a bit ruefully. "Yes and no. I really should have told you this to begin with. Secretary Phillips refuses to release me."

He waved his hand. "Tell that to Gibbs. Tell him to see Secretary Phillips. That can be arranged."

And arranged it was. An hour later Colonel Gibbs and I were in the Secretary's office.

"Well, Yardley," Secretary Phillips smiled good-humoredly, when Colonel Gibbs had explained his mission, "if the War Department wants you badly enough to come after you, I guess I'll have to let you go."

CHAPTER II

At the War College

It is all very well to talk about forming a Cryptographic Bureau: to organize one is a different matter.

Suppose you were given unlimited authority to build a hospital with five thousand beds. You build the hospital and fill the beds with patients. As far as you know you are the only doctor available. You can't attend the wants of so many patients. The problem is—how would you go about finding more doctors?

My beds were soon filled with patients; the code messages literally rolled into the War College. Only one course of action was possible: let the patients die while doctors, or at least nurses, were trained.

In the name of Van Deman I at once sent cables to London, Paris and Rome, urging that pressure be brought upon our Allies to send cryptographers to Washington competent to teach students in the solution of German military codes and ciphers. Also to send by pouch a few hundred examples of such messages and all available exposition on their solutions.

The reply was that examples of German military code and cipher intercepts together with explanations were in the pouch, but that cryptographic instructors could not be spared.

Cryptographers were indeed at a premium. Later when I was in London studying cryptography with the British, an English Colonel told me that Captain Hitchings, their most brilliant cryptographer, was worth four divisions to the British Army.

Judging from the letters I found in the files of the War College, nearly every one in the United States had dabbled in ciphers. The authors of these letters were either offering their services, or had a new and indecipherable cipher that the government should immediately purchase.

From among the former I quickly selected a few scholars who appeared to have a superficial knowledge of ciphers, and ordered them commissioned.

The spectacle of an eager thin-faced liuetenant, surrounded by a group of scholarly captains, was indeed a noteworthy sight, and I was obliged to submit to a great deal of good-natured raillery. However, they seemed to enjoy my energetic illiteracy, which they kindly termed "native intelligence," and I was amused at their eagerness to master the principles of cryptography. Here was a problem not found in the classroom, and not many of them would succeed. Scholarship, I suddenly discovered, was nothing more than the capacity to absorb learning. These scholars were faced with a quite different problem, for there was not a great deal of learning to absorb. They would be obliged to make their own discoveries. For this reason most of them were dismal failures.

The first of these captains to arrive was Dr. John M. Manly, a small quiet-spoken scholar, who was head of the English Department of the University of Chicago. Fortunately for us, Captain Manly had the rare gift of originality of mind—in cryptography called "cipher brains." He was destined to develop into the most skilful and brilliant of all our cryptographers. It is to Captain Manly that I owe a great measure of the success I achieved as head of the War Department Cipher Bureau.

I had just begun the task of mapping out a course of instruction on the solution of codes and ciphers when my plans were upset by a memorandum from the Assistant Secretary of State to the Chief of Military Intelligence. This communication contained a paraphrase of a cablegram sent from London, setting forth that the British Government considered the War Department's method of coding cablegrams entirely unsafe and a serious menace to secrecy. Moreover, the British reported that the Germans were intercepting all messages which passed through the cables.

The seriousness of this can be seen at once. The people of the United States themselves were allowed to know nothing of the communications between Pershing and the War Department. The successes or failures of the American Army depended on the safeguarding of secret reports and instructions. If the enemy was able to intercept and read these messages, the most intricate stratagems of the Americans were futile. Along the bottom of the ocean, through the cables between the United States and England, pass these secret messages. Close by this cable, at the bottom of the Atlantic, lay German submarines. The cables can not be tapped, but by stretching other wires alongside for a distance of several hundred feet telegraph operators stationed in the submarines can copy the passing messages by induction.

No wonder the memorandum from the Assistant Secretary of State frightened the War Department! The Chief of Staff made a personal request for a prompt report.

Upon investigation, I learned that a copy of the War Department code book had been stolen in Mexico during our punitive expedition in 1916 and that a photograph of this was reported to be in the hands of the German Government. Furthermore, I discovered from actual tests that because of the technical construction of the code, it could be solved within a short time by the interceptors even though they were not in possession of the book.

I prepared my memorandum after this investigation, but I doubt that it was taken very seriously. However, the opinion of the British Government was held in respect and inasmuch as England had reported the unsafety of communications which *must* be kept secret, I was ordered to drop everything and revise the entire system of War Department codes and ciphers.

I promptly chose a man in the State Department Code Room whom I considered best qualified to follow my directions, and tempted him with a commission. I wished him to take immediate charge of a subsection which would compile codes and ciphers. I had no intention of being overwhelmed with the details of this work for I had much else before me. In a very short time the subsection was efficiently functioning with ten clerks assisting the man who had been put in charge. The arrangement was wholly satisfactory for the work was being done well, and I needed to devote no more than an hour each day to reviewing some of the more important details.

This subsection prepared codes, ciphers, tables, etc., for communication with Military Intelligence officers, special agents, Ordnance Department agents, military attachés, General Bliss of the Supreme War Council, the commanding officer of American Forces in London, and General Pershing.

The compilation of codes and ciphers was, by General Orders, a Signal Corps function, but the war revealed the unpreparedness of this department in the United States. How much so is indicated by a talk I had with a higher officer of the Signal Corps who had just been appointed a military attaché to an Allied country. It was not intended that attachés should actually encode and decode their own telegrams, but as part of an intelligence course they were required to have a superficial knowledge of both processes in order that they might appreciate the importance of certain precautions enforced in safeguarding our communications.

When the new attaché, a veteran of the old Army, appeared, I handed him a brochure and rapidly went over some of our methods of secret communication. To appreciate his attitude, the reader should understand that the so-called additive or subtractive method for garbling a code telegram (used during the Spanish-American War) is about effective for maintaining secrecy as the simple substitution cipher which as children we read in Poe's "The Gold Bug."

He listened impatiently, then growled: "That's a lot of nonsense. Whoever heard of going to all that trouble? During the Spanish-American War we didn't do all those things. We just added the figure 1898 to all our figure code words, and the Spaniards never did find out about it."

He outranked me greatly or I might have added that we were not at war with medieval Spain but with twentieth-century Germany, who had gathered the brains of her empire behind the greatest war machine the world had ever seen.

Amazing as it may seem, his attitude was characteristic, even at the Front. One of the young officers whom we had trained confirmed this when he arrived at General Headquarters in France. He had received his instruction and practical experience in my bureau. Having observed the necessity for revising the War Department's communications in this country, he was eager to learn whether the codes and ciphers of General Pershing in use at the Front were safe.

The first thing which this young officer did after arriving in France was to induce his superiors to intercept by wireless our own radio code and cipher messages along the

American sector. These codes and ciphers were used to transmit the most secret and important messages and by those who employed them they were considered safe.

Without any knowledge of the American method of encipherment, the young officer solved these messages within a few hours. The system was wholly inadequate and as a means of insuring secrecy was little more than a farce.

Through decipherments of German intercepted cipher messages, our Cipher Bureau in France knew that the enemy maintained a large staff of skilled cryptographers. All radio messages of the Allies and of the Americans were intercepted and sent to the German Cipher Bureau for attack. If this young American officer, who was still merely a student cryptographer, could solve these messages, the German cryptographers, with their long experience of code and cipher solution, without question had also solved and read these telegrams even more quickly than he. And once the system was broken, the enemy could solve every message as easily as the person to whom it was addressed.

As it happened, the contents of this particular decipherment were so important and their secrecy so imperative that the young officer's memorandum on the matter threw the General Staff into a panic of confusion. From these wireless intercepts he learned the disposition of troops along the St. Mihiel salient, the number and names of our divisions, and, finally, the actual hour at which the great American offensive would be launched. This, then, the enemy knew!

The herculean effort of flattening out the salient, which for four years had formed a huge "pocket" inside the French lines, cutting off communication and stopping railways between Verdun and Toul, was the task of the Americans. And by reading the intercepts, the Germans had already learned in detail, just as easily as this young officer had learned, plans and preparations for the great American offensive. Incredible! No wonder the General Staff was in a panic. In these messages were contained some of the most important stratagems of the World War.

The Germans considered their position in the salient impregnable. General Pershing knew that the enemy had several lines of defense, the second known as the Schroeter Zone, another as the Hindenburg Line or Kriemhilde Position. What was to happen to the great American offensive of 1918 if the enemy was prepared for it? Or, if the defenses were not considered strong enough now to meet the offensive, was the enemy, warned by our messages, withdrawing?

The latter was the case. Our young officer had shown the General Staff the leak in the offensive, but it was too late to swoop down upon the Germans in a surprise attack. The messages were already in their possession and a retreat had begun. The American offensive of September 12, 1918, was considered a triumph, but it represents only a small part of what might have been a tremendous story in the annals of warfare, had the Germans not been forewarned. The stubborn trust placed in inadequate code and cipher systems had taken its toll at the Front. The enemy had actually been taken into American confidence, through the non-secrecy of communications. It was not a surprise attack which was achieved. Pershing pursued an already retreating horde and entered St. Mihiel on September thirteenth. The salient was broken, but the surprise attack never came to pass. Too many staff officers in France had, like our authorities in Washington, placed a childish unfounded trust in any encipherment which could not be read at sight.

Seldom are the curtains drawn back so that the intricate secret plots, dangers and discoveries may be known. In a history of the World War, one reads the story of this amazed young officer, in some short uninformative generalization. He knew that the code and cipher systems were inadequate; but all he could do was reveal his findings and give warning to the General Staff. The story of his revelation is one which, like many others enacted behind a curtain of warfare, is seldom told. It was too late to undo the damage after the young officer had revealed the inadequacy of the codes and ciphers. Of this whole episode we read but one sentence in a history of the World War:

Despite all Pershing's precautions for secrecy in the St. Mihiel sector, the Germans expected attack and began to withdraw.

By reading contemporary history of the World War we are led to believe that inefficiency was found on this side of the Atlantic only. Such is not the case. In fact, the foregoing incident is but one of the tragedies of the American Expeditionary Forces, led by General Pershing. The Signal Corps in France was using inexpert and ineffective codes and ciphers to carry over the wireless the secret orders of the General Staff in France.

We have now seen the ridiculous spectacle of President Wilson, Colonel House, the Department of State, George Creel, the War Department, and General Pershing in France attempting to conduct successful diplomacy and warfare with schoolboy codes and ciphers. Later on, as late as 1929, we shall hear something of a novice on whose shoulders rests the responsibility of maintaining inviolate the diplomatic secrets of the United States Government.

The Code and Cipher Compilation Subsection in America won a great deal of praise from the War Department in the form of letters of congratulation. One letter directed me to inform all the officers and clerks who had contributed to the preparation of the new codes that the ingenuity, skill and painstaking labor involved in their conception and execution were thoroughly appreciated and that the attention of the Secretary of War and the Chief of Staff had been called to the work being done in MI-8.

Such letters were addressed to me as Chief, MI-8, an abbreviation for Military Intelligence Division, Section No. 8. It became the official designation for the Cryptographic Bureau. It grew into an enormous organization, containing five subsections:

1. Code and Cipher Compilation
2. Communications
3. Shorthand (solution of intercepted shorthand documents)
4. Secret-Ink Laboratory
5. Code and Cipher Solution

The Code and Cipher Compilation Subsection had scarcely been organized when we began to realize that Military Intelligence must have its own Communications. Van Deman was covering the globe with his agents, some with definite missions, others free agents. Bits of information about our enemies were being collected by these agents and were trickling through the hands of Van Deman and on to his assistants to be evaluated and disseminated. Some of this information was of a sensational character, for it often touched the activities of so-called neutrals and of our Allies. General orders prescribed that the Adjutant-General of the Army encode and decode all staff telegrams, but it seemed obvious that a Military Intelligence should control its own communications if it were to be held responsible for its vital secrets.

Therefore I commissioned another man from the Department of State Code Room, drew up a plan of organization, cut in direct wires to the cable points, employed a corps of code clerks and telegraph operators and within a few weeks we had a subsection which rivaled, in speed, accuracy and economy of transmission of cables, that of the Associated Press. It was also the duty of this subsection to train clerks for our agencies abroad and to instruct the numerous Military Intelligence agents who passed through MI-8, in the use of codes and ciphers.

Although I had already surrounded myself with men and women who were interested in codes and ciphers, and had drawn up a course of instruction, it began to look as if the war had converted me into an executive instead of a cryptographer.

As I turned my attention once more to the organization of the Code and Cipher Solution Subsection, I was seriously interrupted by a curious document which came from the Department of Justice. (See second photo in insert.)

Colonel Van Deman called me to his office and handed me this strange letter. There were several pages.

"What's this, Yardley? Cipher?"

I looked the letter over very carefully.

"Looks like shorthand to me."

"I've already showed it to my secretary. She says it isn't Gregg or Pitman."

"Where did you get it?" I asked him.

"The letter is addressed to Mrs. Tismer. Her husband, Werner Tismer, probably wrote it. He is an interned prisoner at Fort Oglethorpe. He evidently gave the letter to a fellow-prisoner who was being transferred to another camp. This prisoner threw it out the window, hoping that it would be picked up and mailed. The person who found it sent it to the Department of Justice instead of putting it in a mail-box. The Department of Justice has a large file on Tismer and wants this letter deciphered at once."

Spies were hiding behind every bush in those days. Every document which could not be read was rushed to MI-8 for decipherment. We had solved any number of codes and ciphers, and translated seized documents in every known language—but shorthand was a new field.

21

"Do you think you can read it?" Van Deman asked.

It certainly was shorthand. But what system? What language?

"I think I can."

He dismissed me with, "I'd like to have it to-morrow."

That was Van Deman's way. He did not shout at you, still he spoke positively. If he said to-morrow he didn't mean day after to-morrow or next week.

Werner Tismer was a German, and I rightly reasoned that the letter was written in a German shorthand system. I knew nothing about the subject, and although the problem seems a simple one now, at the time I was puzzled.

I quickly got a car to the Congressional Library and with a little research found that the most widely used German shorthand system is Gabelsberger. I also found that in 1898 there was a magazine published which devoted much of its space to the study of this system. I called for the complete file of this magazine and began to turn the pages. There were many examples of Gabelsberger shorthand and it was not difficult to identify some of these outlines as identical with those in the Tismer letter.

Although this search can be recounted in a moment, it took me practically a whole day to make my discovery. But where would I find some one who could transcribe Gabelsberger?

The magazine before me was full of testimonials. "I have been studying Gabelsberger for six weeks and can already write fifty words a minute," etc.

I went through every publication of the magazine, copied down all the names and addresses of persons who had lived in Washington, D. C. There were only five. They had lived in Washington nineteen years ago and the chances of locating any one of them were small.

I hurriedly looked up all of these names in the 1917 Washington Directory. I found but one name. It was also in the telephone book. Quickly I called the number and asked for him. To my great surprise I was told that he worked in the Congressional Library. This was almost too good to be true.

After I had located the Secretary of the Library and told him my story he said, "Yes, your man works here, but if there is reason to believe this letter contains important information about German espionage I don't believe that I would show it to him."

"Why not?" I asked.

"He is a German-American," was the reply, "and there was a Department of Justice agent here the other day who told me he was under suspicion."

"I'd like to talk to him," I insisted.

When the man saw me in uniform he began to tremble. I talked with him a while and called up the Department of Justice to learn something of him before producing the letter. His greatest offense, as far as I was ever able to learn, was that he had belonged to a German society before the United States entered the World War. I could not see that this offense was a serious one and inasmuch as I had to have the letter interpreted, I decided to take the chance. I asked the Secretary to give us a room together.

It was long into the night before the letter was transcribed and in the meantime I had learned of a man in New York who wrote Gabelsberger. In order to have a confirmation I sent a photostat of the document to him and by noon the next day I had the two transcriptions checked by telephone.

Extracts from the letter follow:

My dear Darling,

The soldiers are leaving here and I am taking this opportunity to send you a few confidential lines. I would like to enter into secret correspondence with you whereby you write to me and I write to you on the reverse of the envelopes of our letters with lemon juice in invisible writing. This writing can be made visible by heating with a flat-iron and I do not believe that the censor will take the trouble to examine the envelopes for secret writing. It seems that the mail is now again forwarded quicker, as I received one of your letters in four days and in that case you could perhaps send me some old woolen underwear and a bottle of preserved fruit, perhaps apples or pears in transparent glass and into these fruits you could hide money by taking ten or twenty dollar bills, which you would roll with the yellow side outward and insert them into a long thin testing tube, and this will not be noticed from the outside. Whole fruit will be less suspicious in transparent glass, so that I believe they will not take the top off and see if money is hidden in the jar. It would also be well to use an original jar with a label, if possible, because then it will appear as though coming direct from the factory. In case peace does not come soon, I shall try to get us together by telling you where to go. At present in Chattanooga, the nearest large city here, there is strike and disturbance. It would therefore not be worth while to come here; the people are too excited.

Now after the military goes away about 1500 I.W.W.'s and other undesirables will come into camp. Then life will be still worse. Therefore I want to get out. I shall write you much more when we can secretly correspond. . . .

Write me also the name of a hotel in St. Louis where upon your arrival you can say you are awaiting your husband from the South where he is traveling. Upon receipt of my telegram telling you to depart, leave secretly for the place which we shall agree upon in writing entirely irrespective of what may be the contents of my telegram.

Harry and Ally can then say upon inquiry by the police that you have gone to Chattanooga in order to visit me; that you had received a letter from me which had been put into the letter-box by one of the seamen when they moved and further they know nothing. I just want you to prepare all this so that I may perhaps use it, because upon conclusion of peace it is possible that the authorities will be mean enough to send me out of the country without letting me come back to New York, and if they want to be very mean they can send me back to Honduras whence I last emigrated and then I shall have no money and I can not see you first and that surely would not do, my darling.

This was the first shorthand letter which had come to me. It contained, aside from the instructions for secret writing in lemon juice on the envelope and arrangements for the sending of money, a description of Tismer's plan of escape from prison through a tunnel that he was digging.

Shortly after this document reached the Department of Justice office we were swamped with shorthand note-books which had been seized in raids. Then, a little later the postal censorship, when it heard of our skill, sent hundreds of shorthand letters to us, which had been found in the mails. It became necessary to form a special subsection for the examination of these documents and to discover a scientific means of determining the shorthand system in which each document was written. We could read over thirty shorthand systems written in any language. The most common systems encountered were Gabelsberger, Schrey, Stolze-Schrey, Marti, Brockaway, Duploye, Sloan-Duployan and Orillana.

CHAPTER III

Secret Inks

THE Code and Cipher Compilation Subsection, the Communications Subsection and the Shorthand Subsection were all necessary. But the really exciting activities came through actual contact with German-spy cipher and secret-ink documents. If I had never dreamed that the organization of the three foregoing subsections would fall to my lot, as a cryptographer, the final surprise came when Van Deman called me to his office and handed me a folded sheet of ordinary blank writing-paper.

I unfolded it and held it up to the light. There was not a trace of writing. I wondered what the next mystery would be, for a Department of Justice agent had just brought me a dead carrier-pigeon and wanted me to determine whether or not its perforated feathers carried a hidden message. There seemed no limit to the variety of problems which I was called on to solve. I wondered if this sheet of blank paper, like the dead pigeon, was but a mistake, a false alarm, and whether or not I could determine its meaning so readily. For I had, after examining the pigeon carefully, plucked several of the unperforated feathers and placed them in my desk drawer for examination the following day. But upon taking them out again, to make this inquiry, I found that they had become perforated overnight. The deceased carrier-pigeon had been innocent of hidden messages. Its only offense was that it had lice!

And now—a sheet of blank paper.

Van Deman was dismissing another officer and finally he turned to me.

"What do you make of it?" he asked.

"Nothing," I said candidly.

"It has to be something," he replied in a serious tone. "We have had a woman suspect in Mexico under surveillance for some time. She is suspected of being in close touch with German espionage in Mexico, operating across the Rio Grande. When she attempted to cross the border, she was arrested and searched. This sheet of blank paper was found in the heel of her shoe."

"Secret ink?" I asked.

"Probably. See what you can do with it," he ordered, and then dismissed me.

Van Deman's success was due largely to the confidence he placed in his subordinates. We were so fond of him that I do not believe any one ever thought of telling him that something he suggested could not be done.

I knew nothing about secret ink except the little I had read in British reports of spy activities in England and the general fact, of course, that heat would make visible elementary forms of secret-ink writing. But I had little confidence in heat, for the British report had stated that Germany's most skilful chemists had discovered secret inks for the use of their spies which could not be developed by heat or any other known chemical reagent. But perhaps these new major inks had not yet reached German agents operating in Mexico and the United States.

I immediately telephoned the National Research Council which kept a list of scientists, and asked them for the name of the most skilful chemist in Washington. Within an hour he was in my office.

After I had handed him the sheet of blank paper and told him my story, he said, "I am a chemist but I know nothing of secret writing. Why don't you send this to the British laboratory in England?"

"That would take three weeks. Van Deman wants quick action. Why not subject a small portion of the paper to heat? I'm afraid to try it myself; afraid I'll scorch or seriously burn the paper. You can do this, can't you?"

"Yes, I can apply heat without injuring the paper."

"Suppose we go down in the basement and try it," I suggested. "Would a lighted candle do? Or a hot iron?"

He told me he had what he wanted in his laboratory, and I suggested he write a note for delivery to his assistant.

Immediately I sent a messenger to get the equipment he needed, and within a half-hour we were buried in the base-

27

ment. There, in our improvised secret-ink laboratory, the experiments began.

I watched him carefully as he took the paper in his skilful fingers and passed a small portion of it back and forth over the heat. Again and again he did this, but the endeavor seemed to be useless. The page remained blank.

I had given up all hope of developing the writing, if it contained writing, with heat. Suddenly I heard him exclaim:

"Here are traces of writing!"

He lowered the paper closer to the lamp, then held it under the light while we both studied the curious characters which had appeared as though by magic. But despite our encouragement only small portions of writing were visible and these were too faint to be made out. It had been impossible to anticipate in what language the message might be written although we had expected German, Spanish or English. We continued to study the faint traces of what was revealed to us thus far. Perhaps it was cipher. Then suddenly, as I bent over, studying the characters, my heart stood still.

"The writing is fading away!" I cried.

But the chemist, sure of his ground now, laughed at my distress.

"Heat will bring it back again," he assured me. "Have you a photostat-room here?"

"Yes."

"Have them get a camera ready. We will have to photostat this writing after I apply more heat."

I hurried back to him after arranging for the photostats, wondering hopefully and fearfully, what new developments had taken place. Had the writing, contrary to his assertion, faded away entirely and permanently? Or had the continued application of heat brought out the message clearly?

As I bent over the page again, I found that the latter was true. Distinctly visible on the strange document which had been, just a short while before, a piece of blank paper, were the clear but wholly unfamiliar figures of the message.

We rushed it to the photostat-room.

"It's written in Greek letters," he told me. "Is the camera ready?"

"Yes," I said excitedly. "But what does it say?"

"I don't know," he replied. "You'll have to find a Greek scholar."

A few moments later the photostat operator, his face the color of death under the dim green lights of the photostat-room, handed me several copies of this mysterious message. (See third photo in insert.)

After the seemingly impossible, or at least improbable, feat of producing visible writing upon a sheet of blank paper had been accomplished, the task of locating a Greek scholar was negligible. I found a man, obtained a translation of the message which was in modern Greek and within a few hours after Van Deman had handed me the mysterious paper, I was again before him with the solution of the problem. The translation read:

Mr. _____,
San Antonio, Texas.

I beg you to betake yourself quickly to Galveston, in order that the representative of _____ may deliver to you the $119,000 which you ask for in your letter of 5-8.

There is no need of your having trouble (disputes) with the I.W.W.

Your friend,
L. de R.

In the excitement which followed, I returned to my office and drafted a cable, for Van Deman's signature, to our Military Attaché in London, requesting that the British Government cable full instructions regarding necessary equipment and personnel for a secret-ink laboratory. The message also urged that they send at once one of their best chemists to the United States to act as an instructor.

We received an immediate reply, stating that Dr. S. W. Collins, England's foremost secret-ink chemist, would sail as soon as possible. The answer also gave us specific instruction for the organization of a secret-ink laboratory. I therefore immediately ordered commissioned several of our most brilliant chemists and instructed them to set up a laboratory according to the plan outlined in the cable from England.

While awaiting the arrival of Doctor Collins these chemists scoured the country for scientific information on the subject of secret ink. But as all had suspected, almost nothing was known in America on this subject. With the exception of a few scattered references in the classics, in the writings of alchemists and brief reports in encyclopedias, there was nothing to be learned.

What our chemists gleaned from their research was no more than a schoolboy knows of elemental forms of secret writing. These forms included the use of fruit juices, milk, saliva and urine, all of which may be developed by means of heat. It was obvious, then, that if our chemists were to compete with German scientists, who had already had four years' experience in this battle of tubes and chemicals, they would need, as an instructor, a man not only schooled in secret inks but one familiar with the ramifications of German espionage. We were all, therefore, awaiting the arrival of Doctor Collins with much impatience, for he was splendidly fitted to carry out our program. As an analytical chemist, employed by His Majesty's Postal Censorship in England, he had for several years dealt directly with the secret-ink letters of the most daring enemy spies.

As soon as Doctor Collins arrived, the work of training began. Unlike the Code and Cipher Solution Subsection of MI-8, this task was not so precarious, for Doctor Collins had, as his secret-ink students, men already trained in chemistry. The Code and Cipher Solution Subsection, however, had been unable to select students whom it knew in advance would be fitted for the particular type of work. Doctor Collins immediately began his exciting lectures, outlining clearly the use of secret inks by enemy spies, and the American requirements for a successful secret-ink laboratory.

"Germany, as you well know," he began, "at the outbreak of the war led the world in chemistry. And, as thorough in espionage as in warfare, she immediately summoned her scientists to concentrate upon the problem of developing secret inks which would defy the analysis of Allied chemists.

"For several years Germany was successful. So successful, indeed, that England and France scarcely made a move that was not promptly reported to headquarters in Germany by enemy spies. Secret inks were the spies' most powerful weapons. Although we, as well as France, set up a rigid censorship of all mail crossing the borders, the information which Germany desired still continued to pass.

"The German system of communication is elaborate and involves thousands of cover-addresses whereby letters in secret ink are mailed to persons in neutral and Allied countries who are *not* already under suspicion. Mail to enemy countries is, of course, held up. German spies are instructed to memorize long lists of cover-addresses of persons who would never be suspected by our Intelligence System of being in any way connected with German agents. The spy then writes letters to several of these in secret ink. After the ink dries, he writes an unsuspicious social or business message in ordinary ink, crosswise to the invisible writing. All three or four letters are mailed to the various cover-addresses, this multiplication assuring the arrival of at least one message. Upon receipt, either the letter or the secret information that is developed is delivered to the proper German authority.

"Further to complicate the system, these cover-addresses are carefully watched and compared. Thus, if a triplicate letter, for instance, sent to three different cover-addresses, reaches two correct destinations but fails to reach the third, the Germans know immediately that the third address is under suspicion and therefore no longer useful. In such cases, a new cover-address is procured and the old one abandoned. This of course is only one phase of secret writing, but it serves as an example of the intricacy of the whole system.

"Shortly after the declaration of war," the English chemist continued, "we were stunned when we discovered, through our own under-cover agents in Germany who had meanwhile cleverly entered the German Secret Service, that thousands of secret-ink letters were passing the censorship. The situation was critical, for we were unprepared for secret-ink espionage. We quickly gathered together many of our chemists and began the task of matching brains with German scientists. We slowly and painfully discovered reagents for developing the German inks, but no sooner had we done this than the Germans devised more difficult and subtle ones and put them immediately into operation."

Doctor Collins paused for questions, but there were none. Our chemists, judging by their long faces, were a bit awed by the grave responsibilities they had assumed, and were too anxious for him to continue to question him, convinced now that he was well fitted to instruct them in the intricacies of this scientific battle of wits.

"There are many ingenious ways of carrying secret inks," he continued, "so as not to arouse suspicion. In one case, because of the discovery of forged passports, we care-

31

fully examined the belongings of two suspects who had just arrived in England and finally concluded that they had no secret ink in their possession, although our authorities were certain of their respective missions. But at the last moment, we discovered the ingenuity of the agents. Had they carried cobalt salts, potassium ferrocyanide or other secret-ink materials with them openly, we would have seized them without delay. But the spies had brought them in concentrated form. One spy had cleverly concealed potassium ferrocyanide in a tube of toothpaste. The other German agent carried his supply in a cake of soap.

"This discovery of ingenious concealment led immediately to the institution of more thorough search of suspected persons, and this, in turn, led to amazing discoveries. The German system of secret writing was based on carefully considered chemical reactions, but it was also based on practicability. In every possible case German chemists labored to devise an ink which could pass as something else if discovered. Some of their inks reach a concentration so low that only a spectroscopic analysis can detect the presence of silver in them. Among the seized possessions of one agent the ink was in a scent bottle. The container concealed fifteen cubic centimeters of colorless liquid which had the appearance of many types of perfumes, and moreover it had an authentic though faint aroma. On examination the liquid revealed one one-hundredth per cent. solid matter.

"As the Germans progressed surely and not very slowly with their secret-ink discoveries, it became less and less common for the agent to carry ink in a bottle of any kind. The German chemists' technique had now developed to a point where they could conceal secret inks impregnated, without discoloring, in clothes, such as silk lingerie, handkerchiefs, soft collars, cotton gloves, silk scarfs, neckties and the like. The spy had only to soak the garment in distilled water or some other prescribed solution, in order to bring out the chemicals. He then wrote his letter, using this solution as his secret ink, threw away the immediate supply of ink in solution, dried the garment and put it away for further use in the same manner. Oftentimes the spy carried or wore the impregnated garment.

"There was one case of a suspect who, after a thorough search, seemed to have no ink in his possession. However, we noticed certain small iridescent stains on his black necktie. On this we focused our attention and soaked in distilled water a portion of the tie on which one of the stains appeared. Soon the liquid turned yellowish. Microchemical and spectroscopic analysis proved the presence of silver. The ink carried by this particular spy was of a kind which no ordinary ionic reactions for silver would develop. We found the same ink impregnated in the socks of other agents as well as in a black shoe-lace and in the cloth-covered buttons of an evening dress waistcoat.

"Each of these cases called for extremely careful chemical research before the nature of the ink could be determined. And without this analysis, its appropriate developer could not be discovered."

Here Doctor Collins was interrupted by a question as to the instructions received by German spies, type of pen and paper used, and other means of hiding secret writing.

"German agents are carefully instructed in the use of their inks," he informed us, "although they are seldom told what chemicals they contain. Many agents who send secret-ink letters do not receive any and have no idea how the ink they carry can be developed. They are instructed to use a ball-pointed pen; glazed paper is always avoided —there must be a rough surface. Oftentimes the secret writing is placed on the flap of the envelope or under the stamp. A few attempts have been made to write secret-ink messages on the tissue-paper lining of an envelope, but it became the policy of the postal censorship to remove all paper linings before resealing letters. Efforts are sometimes made to conceal the secret-ink writing even further by putting it between split post-cards, under photographs, labels, newspaper cuttings and articles pasted or gummed on paper.

"To return to the secret inks: not long ago Germany produced a new ink which the German chemists considered very secret indeed, but we surprised them by devising a developer. As a result, Germany lost a number of spies in England in one debacle.

"Let me explain the aims of the enemy scientists in this instance. Theretofore all their inks could be developed by more than one reagent. They now strove for the lowest possible concentration to produce an ink which could be developed by only one known chemical. In other words there was to be a total absence of development except by one specific reagent. This would greatly lessen the chances of our chemists who experimented on the letters.

"As a result of the experiments of the German scientists

33

they produced 'F' and 'P' inks—these are merely our arbitrary designations of these two famous inks. 'F' ink is very low in concentration. 'P' ink is similarly low, consisting of silver proteinate and complicated by the fact that a very similar substance is sold as an antiseptic under the name of collargol or argyrol.

"One of the most famous German-spy cases in England is that of George Vaux Bacon, operating between England, the United States and Holland, who possessed and used the 'P' ink. My testimony at the court martial was directly responsible for the sentence of death which was imposed. Bacon had been a suspect for some time and communicated with Schultz in Holland. He did not know how to develop the ink he carried and knew nothing of its chemical composition. All his instructions for writing with it came from Schultz, in a very simple code, from Holland.

"When Bacon, in his travels, again left Holland for England, Schultz, who knew he was under suspicion, warned him that under no circumstances was he to take a pair of impregnated socks with him into England. He was to use only the cloth-covered buttons of his evening dress waistcoat, which were similarly impregnated with the 'P' ink. But Bacon took his socks with him. He had received them in New York and had been given instructions to squeeze out the tops in water and use the liquid when it turned a pale whisky color. Some of his letters he wrote in the solution of socks, some in the extract of dinner-jacket buttons.

"When our authorities arrested Bacon, it was a bottle marked 'Argyrol,' found in his medicine-chest, which was responsible for his bad luck. Analysis of the contents revealed a small silver content, but Bacon protested. He said that he carried the argyrol as a medicinal remedy and antiseptic. But when the 'P' ink was discovered in his socks, he confessed.

"As a matter of fact Bacon was entirely sincere in protesting the argyrol. Having been given no information as to the chemical constitution of 'P' ink, he did not know its similarity to collargol or argyrol and to him the bottle so labeled was, in truth, nothing more than an antiseptic.

"I made an examination of all Bacon's possessions and found that the concentration was so low in the solution of the socks that it defied chemical analysis. I made a final test by spectroscopic analysis. The test revealed the presence of silver.

"George Vaux Bacon, who was condemned to death in January, 1917, told in his confession that he had never developed secret ink and that he did not know its composition. He stated that while in Sander's office in New York he saw some of the secret writing from Denmark developed. The letters were placed in a photographic dish and the colorless contents of two brown bottles were poured over them. In ten seconds, he said, the writing appeared, clear and very black. When the solutions were mixed heavy white fumes appeared. Bacon did not confess to the presence of 'P' ink in the dinner-jacket buttons. These were not discovered until after the trial."

This was our first authentic story of George Bacon, the American, who though condemned to death by the British Crown a few months before we entered the war, had been released and sent to the United States after strong representations by the United States Government, and sentenced to Atlanta Penitentiary for one year.

The story of George Vaux Bacon was used by me in an article for *The Saturday Evening Post* which was published April 4, 1931. A few days later I received a most interesting letter from Bacon which reveals another side of the story. The letter reads:

Dear Yardley:

Your article on Secret Inks in *The Saturday Evening Post* for April fourth was very interesting, although there are one or two very slight inaccuracies in Collins' report regarding me.

By the way, I still have the coat of that evening ensemble and my wife recently made a pair of knickerbockers for my eldest son from the trousers. If it is at all possible, I'd like to be informed whether or not my letters from England to Holland were ever brought out and read. In writing them, it had been my desire to make them "hot" enough to keep the Heinies thinking I was sincere, while at the same time not giving them any real information. What the British did not know was that I knew a great deal which I never sent. I am an American, but, after all, am of English descent and had no intention of allowing any act of mine to endanger any of my own blood, except possibly myself—and my own foolishness certainly almost cost me my life and has haunted me like a spectre for years.

It was nothing but a crazy adventure designed to produce an exclusive story on espionage, if I had gotten away with it. However, I had to swear to keep what I knew to myself, so the story was never written.

After leaving Atlanta in January, 1918, I tried to enlist in the Army at Chicago under the name of George Brown, but was rejected on account of severe myopic-astigmatism.

At the time I got mixed up with Sir Basil Thompson et al in London, I was 29 and an impractical and rather dissolute little fool. When the crash to my plans for a big scoop came, due to my own foolishness and carelessness, I was so overwhelmed by a feeling of disgrace that I was utterly unable to defend myself properly. I feel that only my mother's plea to Theodore Roosevelt and that grand old lion's insistence on clemency, together with the good heartedness of the British, made the continuance of life on this planet possible for me.

I thought you might be interested in hearing from one of the leading characters in your story. It has created great interest here and I find myself a sort of local historical character, for the time being—a somewhat sinister historical character, however.

Cordially,
(Signed) GEORGE VAUX BACON

Doctor Collins suggested that we now take up the problems already before MI-8, but we begged him first to tell us about other secret-ink spy cases. He smiled good-humoredly and continued:

"There is an earlier case of Pickard, a German spy. This man carried the first example of a really clever secret ink. Before his time the enemy had relied on simple processes such as lemon juice, potassium ferrocyanide and alum, as in the case told me by Captain Yardley in which he developed by heat secret writing in a sheet of blank paper which a woman had concealed in the heel of her shoe. Pickard was convicted of espionage and condemned to death by court martial in September, 1916. He carried his ink in a bottle which also contained a small quantity of alcohol and perfume, hoping that the scent would be a protection.

"Alfred Hagn, like Pickard, carried the same ink. He possessed two bottles of this, one bearing the label 'Gargle' and the other marked 'Toothwash.' We later found in his possession a sponge, three canvas collars and a scarf all impregnated with the same ink. Hagn's mission as a German agent was to report the movements of hospital ships and three of his letters got by our censor. But on May 12, 1917, a detective slipped into his hotel while he was out and stole a bottle marked 'Edinol Dentifrice' into which Hagn had poured a part of his ink. This I analyzed, and upon my report he was promptly arrested.

"In another case we read a letter of instruction from one German agent to another and caught the spy red-handed. The letter instructed the colleague to 'boil nearly enough water to cover the impregnated handkerchief and let it boil fifteen to twenty minutes. Then add four or five spoonsful of water and boil ten minutes more. Then the invisible ink is ready for use.' The agent was also instructed to use unglazed paper, and to write 'stop' at the end of the invisible portion of the message if it did not go beyond one page. This, obviously, would save extra effort on the part of the person who received and developed it. The agent was further instructed, after the secret ink had dried, to mix an ammonia solution, 'strong enough to bring tears to the eyes,' and wipe the paper with this on both sides. The reason for applying the solution to both sides was that the ammonia solution slightly discolored the paper, and in order to make both sides the same, the application must be made with great care. For this reason, envelopes of an entirely different color were always used. 'When done,' wrote the agent's instructor, 'fold up the paper, put it between leaves of a heavy book and sit on it a couple of hours to get it flat.' Afterward, of course, an ordinary social message was to be written in ordinary ink crosswise to the invisible message."

Here I interrupted Doctor Collins, for I was anxious to know just how the British Censorship chemist went about discovering secret writing.

"As far as I can see, your Intelligence Service, through your secret agents, first obtains information that leads them to suspect that a certain person is engaged in German espionage. Then you either examine his belongings in order to see if they are impregnated with secret inks, or you examine the letters he mails for traces of secret writing. If you are successful in either case you have sufficient evidence for court martial."

"That is true."

"If you actually find ink impregnated in the belongings of a suspect you analyze the solution and by this means discover a reagent for developing his secret writing. But this is the only method by which you can discover a specific reagent."

"Yes. Having in this manner discovered a reagent for a particular ink, we attempt to prevent word of the agent's arrest from leaking back to the enemy so that other German spies will continue to use the same ink. The science of invisible writing is still in its infancy; so far all we can do is to use the reagents we have already discovered."

"Can you illustrate this?" I asked.

He opened his brief case and extracted a sheet of paper which he held up for us to see. (See sixth photo in insert.)

"These different colored strips were made with a brush, each strip with a different formula. Now if this particular letter is written with an ink for which we have not discovered a reagent our treatment will not reveal invisible writing.

"This brings me to the point that I wish to emphasize. At the present time we can not develop secret writing unless we have the specific reagent. Because of this we are always several steps behind our enemy, for by the time we discover a specific reagent for his new ink, he launches forth another. Until a general reagent is discovered, a reagent that will develop all secret inks, we can not hope to compete with German espionage. The scientists of France and England are engaged in this task. I want you to join us in the search for this great discovery, a discovery that will in one stroke reveal every spy letter written in invisible writing."

There was a great deal of shaking of heads among our chemists. Their task was becoming more difficult every moment.

"There is just one other point," I again interrupted, "and I will get back to my work and leave these chemical mysteries to chemists. While I was with the Department of State I remember decoding a cablegram from Berne, Switzerland, which stated that when our Embassy Staff passed through Switzerland on its way from Berlin to the United States directly after war was declared, German agents approached one American and offered him a large sum of money if he would report the insignia of French soldiers he saw on leave on his way through France—from these the German General Staff would be able to locate certain French divisions. The agent instructed this American first to dip a clean pen in cold water and write his secret message, dry the letter in the manner you have already described, write a social letter with ink crosswise to the secret writing, and mail in triplicate to cover-addresses in The Netherlands and Switzerland.

"Now it occurs to me that if the German chemists can develop a letter written with a clear water, they themselves must have already made this great discovery for which the Allied chemists are searching. I am not a chemist, but it appears to me that if the Germans can develop water they can develop anything."

"Yes, unfortunately this is true. This case was reported to us. From other sources too your opinion is confirmed. I am frank to admit that the German chemists have so far outwitted us. They have without question discovered this general reagent for which we are all searching.

"This is more serious than it seems. The responsibility of developing secret inks for our own spies rests on our chemists. And since our enemy has discovered this secret formula for developing all kinds of inks, the life of every one of our spies who uses secret writing hangs by a thread. In this respect we are helpless. It is useless for us to develop new inks. But once we discover this general reagent, we doubtless will discover a defense against its successful use.

"The last words of my superiors, just before I sailed, were: 'For God's sake, find this general reagent. Beg America to join us in our researches.'"

CHAPTER IV

Patricia

I LEFT these chemists with their strange tubes and chemicals and returned to my office to draw up plans for a direct liaison between our laboratory and those of the French and British.

Our group of scientists was now divided into two sections: one, for research for the great discovery; the other, for technical study under Doctor Collins, which included the restoration of secret ink after development, opening and resealing of letters, forging of letters and diplomatic seals, photography, duplication of paper and envelopes in cases where they were injured, duplication of post-marks, replacing or duplicating seals, etc. Some of these duties required the employment of America's most adept criminals, skilled in forgery and counterfeiting.

The problem of discovering a general reagent for which the United Allied scientists struggled was finally limited to one field: if the Germans could develop a letter written in clear water, their reagent obviously was not based upon chemical reactions. Was water used merely to keep the pen from scratching the paper? Or was there another purpose? Would not any fluid which touched paper disturb the fibers of the surface? These premises seemed sound enough. Elaborate apparatus were therefore installed for photographing and enlarging letters written with distilled water. Though it seemed obvious to all that the fiber had been disturbed by the water, photography brought no results.

For months chemists and photographers worked over this problem, for they were convinced that whatever form a general reagent might take, it would inevitably be one which revealed these disturbed fibers of the paper.

And then overnight the discovery! Credit for this discovery which revolutionized the technique of secret-ink laboratories is hard to place. There was such a close liaison between the scientists of all Allied laboratories, as each idea was flashed back and forth by cable, that I hesitate to mention one man or one nation. Suffice it to say that the long-dreamed-of general reagent was discovered. And like all great discoveries, it was so obvious, so simple that it left all the chemists dazed, wondering why they had not thought of it before.

A glass case: an iodine vapor! Nothing more!

Insert a secret-ink letter in a glass case and shoot in a thin vapor of iodine. This vapor gradually settles into all the tiny crevices of the paper, all the tissues that had been disturbed by pen and water. Even to the naked eye there forms a clear outline of writing.

No longer did it matter at all what secret inks enemy spies used. An iodine-vapor bath—and, like magic, appeared secret writing!

There was rejoicing throughout the American and Allied espionage circles. Our chemists had now caught up with those of our enemies. But we must surpass them. Germany too knew of the iodine vapor or some similar treatment and, as Doctor Collins had pointed out, could develop the secret letters of the Allied spies. Many of these spies had been captured and condemned to death. The lives of others were in the hands of Providence. Our chemists must discover a formula of invisible writing that defied iodine vapor or any similar process.

While engaged in this worthy cause our scientists received a most disconcerting blow. It seemed incredible, but we were faced with the facts. Our examiners reported that iodine vapor no longer revealed secret writing even in cases where invisible writing was absolutely known to exist —known to exist from unimpeachable sources of information! What did this mean? It meant but one thing. Our great discovery had reached the ears of enemy spy headquarters in Germany. And with true genius in chemistry German scientists had quickly discovered a method of secret writing in which the iodine-vapor treatment was not effective—a method for which Allied chemists had been feverishly searching. German chemists were still one step ahead of us!

It may seem incredible that the iodine-vapor discovery was so quickly known by the enemies and a preventive method devised. To understand this rapid transmission of secret discovery to German headquarters, it is necessary to keep in mind constantly the intricacy and subtlety of the espionage system.

In this regard I recall the case of a French liaison officer who delivered a secret lecture before our Military Intelligence Division. Every precaution was taken to keep the meeting secret from any persons save those who were admitted by virtue of their respective positions of responsibility. Only a small group heard the lecture and they were Intelligence officers. The doors of the room were locked and bolted; guards were stationed outside so that no one could listen or come near the room. In his talk the liaison officer gave in great detail, for the instruction of our Intelligence Section, an account of the French positive espionage in Germany, recounting activities of French spies in enemy territory. These activities were of such a daring and sensational nature that the lecturer's words produced a tremor throughout the small audience. It was a necessary lecture, for the American positive espionage system had been pronounced inadequate by our officials and steps were being taken to increase its effectiveness.

Forty-eight hours after delivering his secret lecture, the French liaison officer received a cable from his government ordering him to return to France to explain his indiscretion! This meant that even in that audience which heard him, that audience composed of selected officers of the Intelligence only who listened to his words behind closed and bolted doors with guards stationed outside, there was a Frenchman to report the man's speech to French headquarters. And those to whom he reported deemed this man's lecture an indiscretion. How were the French to know that there was not, even in the uniform of an American Intelligence officer, a German spy to send back to enemy headquarters the sensational outline of French espionage which had been given? This story of the indiscreet liaison officer serves to illustrate the secret and rapid transmission of news, and by keeping it in mind we can better grasp the whole problem of secrecy. No wonder the triumph of our Secret-Ink Laboratory was discovered!

Now our scientists had to begin all over again. What had the Germans done to prevent the success of iodine tests? What made iodine-vapor tests possible? Disturbed tissues of the paper—disturbed by the pen or fluid. How could this disturbance be prevented?

After over one hundred experiments American chemists discovered that if a letter is written in secret ink, dried, dampened lightly by a brush dipped in distilled water, then dried again and pressed with an iron—the secret ink can not be developed by an iodine-vapor bath. Why? Because the dampening process disturbs *all* the fibers of the paper. Since the original crevices formed by pen and water were now destroyed, the iodine vapor settled on the entire surface of the letter but revealed no outline of secret writing.

This was a long-sought-for discovery. Germany could no longer develop the secret-ink letters of our own spies. Nor could we develop those of our enemy!

The development of secret writing was now at a standstill on both sides. We had at last caught up with the Germans. Would we surpass them? There was now no known process of developing ink without knowing the reagent, provided the letter had first been dampened. In other words we were right back where we had been when Doctor Collins arrived.

We were engaged in a deadlock with the Germans except for one thing. We suddenly made another important discovery. We found a method of streaking suspected letters with two different chemicals—*and if these two streaks ran together it proved that the letter had been dampened.* And who would ever think of dampening a letter except a spy? Whether we could develop the ink or not, a dampened letter was sufficient proof that we were dealing with a spy message.

But this was not enough. Our scientists must discover a reagent to develop *all secret-ink letters even though the letters were dampened.*

Inevitably in the battle of wits came this startling and greatest of all triumphs, a triumph that marked a new and final epoch in the achievements of secret-ink chemistry—the infallible reagent that revealed secret-ink writing under any and all conditions.

This secret was of such vital importance to successful espionage and was so jealousy guarded—I doubt if a dozen men know of its existence—that it did not find its way to enemy ears. Even here it would be unethical to reveal the nature of this scientific formula, which came only after repeated discouragements and after long months of experiments by all the Allied chemists.

Shortly after our chemists made this discovery our censor on the Mexican border intercepted a letter (see "Patricia" letter in insert) which aroused his suspicions because of certain hieroglyphics on its second and fourth pages.

The character of the secret ink and the importance of the plan revealed by the secret-ink writing indicate that this letter is from an important spy.

The secret ink as developed reads:

I wrote you about the incarceration of the trio, etc.

This must refer to three suspects that have been arrested—spies are often vague in their secret-ink letters.

Let me know as soon as you can about the boys going to France. If of no use in France they are preparing to flee.

Our department had already uncovered information that German agents planned to have at least one spy in each regiment. Patricia, who signs the letter, obviously is asking her superior how these boys are to operate when they reach France. There is more on this subject.

I'm wondering if this ink is good. Let me know if those boys would be of any use to you in France.

Preparations are being made for training and drilling in use of big guns in U.S. Officers returning from France for that purpose.

I regret to say that "Patricia" was never captured. This was due to over-zealousness on the part of our agents on the west coast. I also regret that we were never able to decipher the hieroglyphics. They certainly contain a hidden meaning, for, as any one knows, the scansion of the two lines of poetry is ridiculous. The first line, "A thing of beauty is a joy forever," is the opening line of Keats' *Endymion;* and the second, "Of man's first disobedience and fruit," is the opening line of Milton's *Paradise Lost.* In scanning poetry, each syllable, or each word of one syllable, takes but one mark, either accented or unaccented. The words *first* and *and* each have two marks, and rather curious ones at that. Perhaps the reader can decipher these cryptic signs. Or perhaps Patricia, if she sees this, will tell us all about them!

Patricia also writes that she is sending fashion sheets and face creams. Fashion sheets suggest nothing; however, secret ink was often sent in face creams by spies. "Cephalic index" is clear enough, but the diagrams below these words are a complete mystery.

There is one thing about the "open" letter that is reminiscent—the name Hopkinson-Smith. A red-haired young lady, obviously a German agent, once made the statement to one of my cryptographers, "You and I must work for the same cause." She gave her name as Smith-Hopkinson and her address in care of a certain bank in Los Angeles, which is not so very far from San Francisco where this letter was mailed.

Is Patricia, who writes of Hopkinson-Smith, the red-haired Miss Smith-Hopkinson? They both disappeared very mysteriously.

A successful secret-ink laboratory is by no means entirely devoted to research. There are every-day problems to solve. Unless he is thoroughly trained for this particular type of work, even a skilled chemist is of small value. When our own postal censorship was established our Secret-Ink Bureau was confronted with the task of examining thousands of suspicious letters. At one time over two thousand letters a week were tested for secret writing. Many of these were not outwardly suspicious, but to insure some measure of security a percentage of mail leaving or arriving at each port of entry was carefully examined by our chemists.

There were two types of suspected mail, that addressed to persons under suspicion, and that which referred to business or social affairs in a mysterious or veiled fashion. Letters of this type were submitted to "major" tests—that is they were treated by chemicals which at that particular moment were known to be in use by German spies.

Our laboratory developed a very delicate technique in the restoration of secret ink after it had been developed and photographed. For it was often important that these secret-ink letters, after they had been read by our Bureau, be sent on to the addressee in order to avert suspicion. Sometimes it was better to wait a while and intercept more letters than to make a hasty arrest.

In cases where it was suspected that the embassy, legation or consular officials of certain supposedly neutral countries were aiding the enemy, it was necessary for us clandestinely to intercept and open the diplomatic pouch and the letters it contained, photograph the contents, and then restore the communication to its original intact state before sending it on to its proper destination. This was more than difficult, for diplomatic mail is always sealed with diplomatic seals. The problem often called for proficiency in forgery. Moreover, in some cases where the envelopes became injured during opening, the paper had to be duplicated and all signs of damage removed. This necessitated the manufacture of new identical envelopes, the forging of diplomatic seals and handwriting, and in similar cases the duplication of the postmarks on the original intercepted letter.

There were, of course, cases in which some of the American diplomatic or consular representatives or their families were under suspicion of dealing with the enemy. Their correspondence, not being subject to censorship, was of necessity opened surreptitiously and the contents photographed before resealing.

Such activities upon our part, as it may be suspected, were painstaking and were executed with the utmost care and skill. In opening letters, we held the letter for a few seconds in the steam from the spout of a kettle filled with rapidly boiling water. We then inserted a desk knife with clean narrow blade and long handle under the flap of the envelope while the letter was still being held in the jet of steam, and by running the knife blade carefully between the flap and cover, we raised the flap without much difficulty.

After photographing the contents, we resoftened the remaining gum on the envelope flap by the steam method and if sufficient gum did not remain, rubbed the edge against the moistened gummed edge of an unused envelope. This was better than application of glue for it assured the adherence of just the right quantity. Otherwise, an oversupply might ruin the job by making it sticky and splotched. In case any gum marks showed after the letter was resealed, we brushed the cover lightly with moistened blotting paper, followed by blotting with similar dry material. In cases where the seams were obviously affected by this steam process, we pressed them out with a hot iron and removed all traces of our work.

Replacing or duplicating seals was a much more difficult task than that of opening and resealing envelopes.

The operation required more skill, and the process sometimes depended upon the nature of the seal. For a rough small seal, we used a thin sheet of lead with a backing of india-rubber placed on it and screwed down under a writing press. This took only a few seconds and any impressions which were made on the envelope during the process could be ironed out satisfactorily. For a perfect large seal, the operation was much more complicated.

We first dusted it with French chalk. Then we placed a piece of gutta-percha, slightly mixed with oil and heated with hot water, over the seal. This we put under pressure until the gutta-percha became firm and cold. Then, with another piece of gutta-percha, similarly heated, we made a second impression from the cold material after it had been covered with graphite and put under pressure as in the first operation. After taking the second impression, and after again thoroughly graphitizing, we put it in a copper-plating bath and started an electric current. Depending on the amount of current we could force, the process of obtaining our copper deposit took from twenty minutes to an hour or more. When we broke away the copper deposit from the gutta-percha we had a perfect seal. The back we then filled in with ordinary solder and supplied a handle.

Even more difficult than constructing a mold, was the process of getting the original seal off the diplomatic letter. We heated the wax to a certain temperature by a small electric hot-plate. Our success depended on applying just the correct amount of heat to the seal. At the proper stage we scraped the wax from the envelope with a small scraper. With this old wax, in case the seal was broken, we made a duplicate with the mold already described.

Such tasks as these scarcely came within the duties of the chemists. It was obvious that specialists in this particular science must be added to the American Secret-Ink Laboratory. Thus two of the most adept criminals who had been convicted for forgery and counterfeiting were sought out and their particular skill incorporated with that of the Secret-Ink Subsection of MI-8.

There was one case in particular that always amused me. We were asked to open and photograph the contents of a letter addressed to General Carranza, President of Mexico. Before opening this letter, our counterfeiter made a copy of the seal, but after opening the letter, photographing the contents, and resealing the envelope, we discovered that the duplicate seal which had been made was too defective to be used. We were at a loss to know what to do. Finally the counterfeiter told us that he could perhaps approximate the original by engraving a seal. While this move was under discussion, he made a closer examination of a portion of the original seal and discovered, happily enough, that it had been made with an old and rare Spanish coin. This simplified a distressing problem in engraving, for it was only necessary to obtain one of these coins from an obliging collector to make a perfect seal.

Note: The official history of this bureau will be found on page 99 in *Report of the Chief of Staff U. S. Army to the Secretary of War, 1919*:

Code and Cipher Section (MI-8)—Codes and Ciphers.—The work of this section concerned an important field of endeavor which before the war with Germany was almost entirely unknown to the War Department or to the Government of the United States as a whole. . . . As finally developed this section comprised five bureaus, as follows:

• • •

Secret-Ink Bureau.—By direct liaison with the French and British Intelligence Services, this bureau built up a useful fund of knowledge covering this hitherto little-known science which is at once so useful and so dangerous. Over 50 important secret-ink spy letters were discovered which led to many arrests and prevented much enemy activity. Prior to the lifting of the postal censorship an average of over 2,000 letters per week were tested for secret inks.

CHAPTER V

Madame Maria de Victorica

A GREAT deal of romance has been written about the famous German spy, Madame Maria de Victorica, alias Marie de Vussière, the "beautiful blonde woman of Antwerp," but the authentic story of her activities, detection and arrest has never been told. Though she had been sought by the British Secret Service since 1914, it was the Secret-Ink Bureau of MI-8 that finally proved her nemesis.

Madame de Victorica was the most daring and dangerous spy encountered in American history. Her activities in this country between her arrival and arrest comprise a story of ruthless espionage and wholesale destruction that surpasses the wildest fantasies of our most imaginative fictionists. But like many other German spies, Madame Victorica did not reckon with our skilled chemists, whose glass test-tubes and varicolored liquids at last undid her.

On November 5, 1917, the British authorities gave us information, which, though it had no direct bearing on Madame Victorica, finally led indirectly to her identity. We were informed that a German agent of unknown name and nationality had recently left Spain for the United States with instructions to pay ten thousand dollars to A. C. Fellows,* 21 Sinclair Avenue, Hoboken, New Jersey, and, if not feasible, to K. Lamb,* 43 East Avenue, Woodside, Long Island.

Investigation at these addresses led to the information that both persons had disappeared, whereabouts unknown. The addresses were then placed under continuous and careful observation.

* Names and addresses have been changed.

Two months later, January 6, 1918, we intercepted a letter addressed to Fellows, which, though mailed in New York, bore the legend "Madrid, Nov. 3rd, 1917." This was two days before the date of the British warning.

The letter itself was vague, and though our chemists worked over it feverishly, they failed to develop secret writing. This was very discouraging for as yet our Secret-Ink Laboratory had not distinguished itself. Four days afterward, late in the afternoon, one of our agents, breathless with excitement, rushed into the laboratory.

"Another letter addressed to Fellows!" he exclaimed.

Both sides of the letter were quickly photographed, and the envelope was then held over a jet of steam and carefully opened. This is what we found inside, written in English. (See "Maud" letter in insert.)

Dear Mrs. Gerhardt:*

When I met you last I quite forgot to tell you that I had received a message from our mutual friend Frank. You will remember that he has been very ill and could not look after his business for months. He now writes to me that he has entirely recovered and is feeling strong enough to take up his former life. His recovery seems to have come at the right moment for there can be no doubt according to what Frank says in his letter that his long absence from the office has been a serious drawback for his business. He is now keeping this direction again firm in hand showing full confidence in the future. Knowing that you are taking so much interest in everything connected with Frank I would not fail to pass this good news on to you. I am going to write a nice letter to Frank both in your name and mine which I hope will be a further encouragement for him.

Give my love to all the friends and a lot for yourself.

Your affectionate

Maud

To the reader this letter may mean little or nothing, but spy letters even when they carried no secret writing were usually written in this tenor. Illness of any kind means that the spy is under observation and can not successfully carry on his activities. A recovery from illness means that he is no longer under suspicion or has escaped observation.

* Name has been changed.

The last few lines of the letter mean that another letter is on its way to "our mutual friend Frank"—no doubt another spy. To the reader this may sound a bit far-fetched, but let him withhold his judgment for a while.

Several other things about the letter need explaining. The envelope is addressed to Fellows; the return address on the envelope is D. Crain, 932 E. 108th Street, New York;* and the letter itself begins, "Dear Mrs. Gerhardt." Here are enough discrepancies to awaken the suspicions of any novice.

"Have you investigated Crain at 932 E. 108th Street?" our chemist inquired. "That is the return address on the envelope."

"The report that came with this letter said that he was being investigated and promised to telephone in any information that was picked up."

"Be sure to tell me the moment it comes in. It might help us with our secret-ink tests."

As the iodine-vapor test had not yet been discovered, there was nothing to do but to test the letter with the reagents already known to be in use by German agents. Our chief chemist unfolded the letter and with deft fingers rapidly drew a line with a brush dipped in chemicals crosswise on the paper. When no visible writing appeared, he took up another brush dipped in another bottle and drew another line. At the third attempt faint traces of invisible writing appeared.

"It's written in 'F' ink—here's secret writing," he exclaimed; "in German script!"

"How long will it take to develop all the letter?"

"It may take all night. This is an important spy letter and we will have to work carefully in order not to injure the paper. We may wish to restore the secret writing." The secret agent turned to go, but was called back. "And by the way, you had better inform your gum-shoe men that the letter itself begins with 'Dear Mrs. Gerhardt.' This may mean more than is apparent at this time."

While our chemists carefully developed the secret writing and prepared a translation, our agents in New York were discovering some very curious things.

The return address on the envelope, 932 E. 108th Street, was a rooming-house, but no one by the name of D. Crain lived here. However, quiet investination of the roomers

---

* Name and address have been changed.

revealed one Allison,* a steward on the S. S. *Christian-iafjord* which was now docked in New York. Under severe grueling he gave the following story.

Just before he sailed from Christiana (Oslo), Norway, a porter in the Metropole Hotel gave him two letters to smuggle into the United States and mail in New York: one to A. C. Fellows, and the other to Mrs. Hugo Gerhardt, 830 W. 96th Street.† After arrival he obtained new envelopes, the present ones being badly damaged as at times he carried them in his shoes, and readdressed the letters, using the alias Crain but the correct number of his rooming-house as a return address.

And now occurred one of those fatal coincidences which, though not permitted in fiction, nevertheless shape the lives and destinies of all of us. But for this coincidence Madame Victorica would doubtless never have been captured.

Allison, after readdressing the letters, inadvertently placed them in the wrong envelopes! The one intended for A. C. Fellows was addressed to Mrs. Gerhardt—this was never recovered. The one intended for Mrs. Gerhardt was addressed to Fellows—and intercepted!

Attention now turned to Mrs. Gerhardt.

By the time this report came in, the secret ink in the Gerhardt letter had been developed and translated. This document, termed the "Maud" letter because of the signature, is one of the most amazing spy communications ever uncovered. It is often phrased in vague language, the usual practise of German spies, the reason no doubt being that it is more difficult to convict a person before a jury when the language in intercepted documents is not specific. However, the true meaning will be clear to the reader.

Translation of Secret Writing in "Maud" Letter

Please examine both sides of the sheet of paper for secret writing. I confirm my letter No. 7 of October sent in several copies.

Spies always send their letters in duplicate, triplicate or quadruplicate.

You now are free to take up your business affairs [spy

---

* Name has been changed.
† Name and address have been changed.

activities] in South America entirely, and to invest capital in the [plan to blow up] great war industries, docks, and navigation as you judge best.

The works for obtaining quicksilver in the West were particularly recommended to me by well-informed persons.

This refers to the destruction of quicksilver mines.

In view of the enormous ship-building program of the United States, capital should preferably be invested in the docks over there, but the firm must not become known to the banks as a stockholder in ship-building companies.

Germany is concerned with our "enormous ship-building program," for our plans call for the construction of as many tons of shipping as Germany destroys by her campaign of unrestricted submarine warfare, and instructs her spies to destroy our docks, taking care however not to jeopardize their identity. The next sentence explains this better.

Your Irish friends will surely not lose the opportunity of speculating in such a good thing. It will therefore be all the easier for these friends to play dummy in this affair.

This suggests the feasibility of employing anti-English Irish patriots to carry out the actual blowing up of the great war industries, docks, mines, navigation, etc.

Remittances are on the way. Furthermore, sufficient credit has been opened for you in South American Branch companies. Therefore get into communication with South America.

In Argentina business is to stop until further notice.

The German Government at this time was trying to placate Argentina. "Business" is to stop there, but only "until further notice."

On the other hand, Brazil is now a very good place to invest capital in, to which I call the special attention of the Branch offices in Brazil.

On the other hand, Brazil declared war against Germany on October 26, 1917; so it is a suitable place to "invest capital."

Mexico naturally does not interest me on account of the absolutely confused political conditions now prevalent there.

Nothing must be done to embroil Mexico with Germany. Germany is already trying to bribe Mexico to remain neutral—see the Nauen wireless code messages, Chapter VI—for Mexico is an ideal point from which to direct espionage in the United States.

You must leave no stone unturned to get a good neutral, or better still, American, not German-American, cover-address, and let me know it at the first opportunity.

Here follow several cover-addresses in Holland, Denmark, and Switzerland.

The use of such unsuspect cover-address should facilitate cable communications. Cable communication is to be provided in the following cases:

All cables are censored and are never delivered until the address has been thoroughly investigated; therefore "leave no stone unturned to get a good neutral, or better still, American, not German-American, cover-address," which will not be suspected of being connected with German espionage.

(1) If business [espionage] with the United States is to be stopped, I will cable over
CANCEL ORDER
to be followed by close description of the business to be cancelled.
(2) If business with the United States is to be taken up again, I will cable
BUY
to be followed by a description of the wares, papers, etc., to be bought.
(3) If the firm over there, owing to losses for instance [owing to capture], should no longer be able to take care of my interests as heretofore, you cable

here to follow name of shares, etc., of a well-known American enterprise dealt in in Europe.

This clever means of evading censorship needs no comment. There is no way of preventing it so long as the names of the sender and receiver are not under suspicion, because from all appearances this type of cablegram is nothing more than a business communication between persons in the United States and a neutral country.

The following sentences are especially interesting for they prove conclusively that the person for whom the "Maud" letter is intended is the guiding genius of German espionage, in so far as it deals in explosions, both in the United States and South America.

It must under all circumstances be avoided that possible losses or unlucky speculations should lead to the breakdown of my whole enterprise over there.

Therefore a second firm must be established entirely independent of the present one, which, pursuant to the commercial law there, can not in any way be made responsible for the operations of the present firm, and which will have no internal or external connection with the present firm, but which will be in a position to deal with me directly.

German spy headquarters in Germany, realizing that their whole plan for destruction by explosives in the United States and South America is directed by only one group, orders the recipient of this letter to form an entirely independent "firm" so that in case of "losses" or "unlucky speculations" that would lead to the "breakdown" of their "whole enterprise," there will still remain another "firm," having "no internal or external connection with the present firm" to carry on "operations."

The reader may well imagine the consternation that the development of this secret writing caused within American espionage circles. Though our prisons were full of suspects and interned German subjects, though millions had been spent for counter-espionage, it was obvious to all after reading this letter that the master spy who directed explosions in the United States and South America was still at large.

The questions on every one's lips were: Who is he? Where is he? How find him?

All the names connected with the "Maud" letter had been thoroughly investigated except that of Mrs. Hugo Gerhardt, 830 W. 96th Street. Careful inquiry here revealed the fact that she had moved; also that the letter intended for Fellows but inadvertently addressed to her had been returned by the postman to Allison's rooming-house and destroyed by the landlady.

Careful investigation finally not only revealed Mrs. Gerhardt's present address but also the fact that she had received a number of mysterious letters not for her. It seemed too much to expect that this woman, a widow and in apparently destitute circumstances, could be the master spy for whom we were seeking. Often German spies used perfectly innocent Americans as cover-addresses for their spy letters, having some unknown person closely connected with the addressee who could obtain the letters after they arrived.

We discovered that though Mrs. Gerhardt had not received any of these mysterious letters for several months, she had seen the name Victorica in some of the earlier ones. This was something definite to work on and we immediately cabled this information to the British authorities.

The British Censorship had a difficult task in the censorship of cables and their methods were necessarily very thorough. All cables that passed through their hands, all messages intercepted by their wireless stations, were not only carefully analyzed but the addresses and signatures as well as any names mentioned in them were accurately indexed by name, subject-matter and source.

Now when we cabled the contents of the "Maud" letter and the name Victorica to the British, they immediately cabled us the following message, dug up from their old files, which mentioned the name Victorica:

From Germany
To Schmidt & Holtz,* New York.

February 4, 1917

Give Victorica following message from her lawyers lower terms impossible will give further instructions earliest and leave nothing untried very poor market will

* Name has been changed.

56

quote however soonest our terms want meanwhile bond have already obtained license.

Disconto

We did not know this at the time, but after developing the secret writing in some of Victorica's letters which revealed her secret code, we deciphered this telegram (see Chapter VIII) as instructing Madame Victorica to draw thirty-five thousand dollars from her bankers and place the money in a secure place because of threatened war with the United States. Diplomatic relations had been severed between Germany and the United States the day before the date of this cable.

The firm of Schmidt & Holtz, New York, told us that after an exchange of several telegrams with the Discontoge Gesellschaft they had paid Madame Victorica thirty-five thousand dollars in cash on February 20, 1917. Since this date Victorica had never communicated with them, but at the time had given the Foreign Mission, 46 High Street,* as her address and had showed them letters of introduction and her passport as identification.

Through the records at Kirkwall, England, where all passengers are closely scrutinized, and those of our own immigration authorities, we learned a great deal more about Madame Victorica.

She had left Berlin January 5, 1917, traveling via Sweden, Christiania and Bergen, and sailed from the latter port on the *S. S. Bergensfjord* for New York where she arrived January 21, 1917. She traveled on an Argentine passport which had been issued by the Argentine Consul in Christiania.

Her bankers had described her as a "stunning blonde, about thirty-five years of age." The British cabled:

Believe Victorica to be beautiful blonde woman of Antwerp for whom we have searched since 1914.

The French cabled that a few days before her arrival in the United States they had arrested at Pontarlier one Manuel Gustave Victorica, an Argentine citizen. He was being held for espionage and was awaiting sentence by the Council of War. As Madame Victorica traveled on an Argentine passport there might be some connection between the two. This man later proved to be her husband.

---

* Name and address have been changed.

At the Foreign Mission, 46 High Street, the address given by Madame Victorica's bankers, where it was customary for foreigners to receive their mail, we carried on a quiet investigation, it being important, if we hoped to make an arrest, that no word reach her regarding our activities. Here we surreptitiously obtained several letters addressed to her. But here also ended her trail.

While these letters were being examined for secret writing by our chemists, our secret agents of course continued their search for her; but the threatened war between the United States and Germany had obviously frightened her, for she seems to have severed all connection with those who knew her name and address. The dates of the letters also confirmed this, as they had been at the Foreign Mission for over a year. She no doubt was afraid to call for them.

It is interesting to note that the letters bear no postmarks. They doubtless had been smuggled into the United States and delivered by messenger.

When we opened the first letter this is what we found:

Christiania, February 13, 1917.

My dear Friend:

I hope that you received in the meantime my last letters from 8/1 and 3 inst. and also my remittance by wire, although I was informed today by the bank, that you asked for further money, but I hope that everything is settled now. I cabled also on the 4th inst. to your bank asking to give you the message from your lawyers and no doubt the message must have reached you.

This refers to the code cable to Victorica, instructing her to withdraw thirty-five thousand dollars from her bank.

How are you going on? How is the market there?

This of course is an inquiry as to the progress of her activities.

Now, goodbye, with the kindest regards I am

Yours truly,

Fels

This letter contained secret ink written in German but not enough of it could be developed to make a straightforward translation. The secret ink that was used contained a chemical that decomposes quickly and these letters were now over a year old. The reagent cited in the third open letter, "kalium iodatum," would not bring out all the writing and it was necessary for our chemists to discover a more refined reagent. They used this letter to experiment on and by the time they had discovered a refinement the letter was badly mutilated. Fortunately, however, there were several other letters. The following is the next in order of dates:

March 7, 1917.

My dear Mrs. Victorica:

I was very pleased to hear from you that you had such a good passage under such circumstances, your message delighted my manager very much, of course I informed all your other friends, including Rev. Father.

This letter shows that Victoria had reported her safe arrival in the United States by letter, and that since "my manager" is delighted with her letter she must have reported some success in her negotiations.

Did you meet my friend there? I am very busy and plenty work has still to be done, but the principle thing is, to have good success, but so far, I have not any; but I hope very much, that with the assistance of all my friends, the result will be very soon a good one. Every day other difficulties, but so far, we were very lucky to get clear always.

It seems obvious that Madam Victorica's immediate superiors are having trouble evading detection.

How is your health?

Are you under observation?

I hope you enjoyed your trip after all. Have you heard from your husband? Since I saw him last, I have no further news from him. . . .

The French authorities captured her husband at Pontarlier, January 10, 1917, two months before this letter was written. He had been commissioned by the German Secret

Service to go to Buenos Aires, Argentina, to communicate departures of steamers to France and England. He was sentenced, April 25, 1918, by Council of War at Besançon to life imprisonment. Madame Victorica's superiors are obviously worried about his disappearance!

Please write as soon as you can, as I am waiting for your report, if possible by wire, the time is too long.

Now, goodbye and hoping this letter will reach you in best health I am with the kindest regards.

Yours truly,
A. Fels

The secret writing in the letter which follows reveals a most amazing series of plots.

. . . Telegraphed through same intermediary to immediately put money in a safe place for fear the intermediary be closed.

This is another reference to her withdrawal of thirty-five thousand dollars from her bank.

Telegram of arrival promptly received. Cover-addresses are. . . .

Here follow several names and addresses in Holland, Sweden and Denmark.

Code numbers to be reversed:

Here follows Victorica's new code keys for use in cabling messages as explained in Chapter VIII.

Advise immediately where U-boat or sailing boat material sacks can be sunk on American coast—perhaps between New York and Cape Hatteras. Position must be free of currents. . . . Water depth not more than twenty meters. Can a messenger be landed there? The marking of sinking positions with buoys is successfully carried out in Spain. Wire agreement and where material is to be sunk. Take as few persons as possible into confidence. Indicate in writing at once how plan is to be carried out.

This paragraph is especially significant for it shows that the German Secret Service had planned to establish submarine bases along the Atlantic coast as early as February 13, 1917, the date of the first letter where traces of these plans could be deciphered from the secret writing, only a few days after Germany officially announced her policy of unrestricted submarine warfare. That the plan was quickly carried out there is no doubt, for it was not long afterward that Atlantic seaboard shipping was thrown into a panic by the appearance of German submarines. Also, incidentally, it is proof that Germany successfully maintained submarine bases off the Spanish coast. These bases account for the unbelievably long cruising radius of German submarines.

The next paragraph in the secret writing revealed a plot too fantastic to believe until it was confirmed by investigation. Among Victorica's letters found at the Foreign Mission was one containing introductions to many Catholic priests. (See photo of Madame Victorica's credentials in insert.) Since all letters were sent either in triplicate or quadruplicate she must have received other copies of these documents. Whether these priests were duped or taken into her confidence there is no way of knowing, but it is certain that through them Victorica planned to import the new German high explosive tetra for the destruction of mines, wharves, docks, shipyards, merchantmen, war-ships, etc. From other letters we discovered that there were plans for the importation of this chemical concealed in children's toys.

In this connection the secret ink of still another letter, though so badly decomposed that only phrases can be read, is of tremendous interest:

work and try to get on English war-ships as . . . workers. The munitions come on the war-ships would be very susceptible for such lead pencil sticks. Large rewards may be promised. If . . . can blow up dreadnaughts. A million is at . . . service. . . .

Concealing lead pencil sticks containing tetra is one method used by the Germans for producing explosions.

But let us return to the secret-ink writing in this letter and read the exact words of Victorica's fantastic instructions for the importation of explosives.

Order as soon as possible through a trustworthy priest by wire from Atlantic export, Arnold—Zurich, St. Anne-hof, by the following telegram:

> Altar containing 3 holy figures, 4 columns about 2 meters in height . . . to match 6 meters wide and 3 meters high. Style Renaissance—baroque, painting in rural style.

Also cable receivers addresses.

These columns and holy figures of saints, manufactured from imitation marble, were to contain the new German high explosive tetra!

The reader may well ask why is it necessary for Madame Victorica to have a priest cable this order, or why cable at all? To answer this I must remind the reader that during the war England established both a cablegram and a merchandise blockade. No cablegram, no merchandise could slip through this blockade without first passing a rigid inquiry. The question in the minds of the English were: Is this an authentic business or social cablegram? Is this merchandise intended for the person who ordered it? Is there a German plot hidden in this cable or concealed in this merchandise?

Now a cablegram from a priest ordering holy figures for a chapel would scarcely arouse the suspicion even of the most hardened censor. And when the actual shipment of holy figures of saints, columns and balustrades came for examination, who among the most suspicious would ever dream that they contained high explosives for destruction?

Earlier, when I made the statement that German espionage was subtle—this was what I meant. But that this was feminine and not masculine subtlety I have not the faintest doubt. It is too much to believe that Madame Victorica's masculine master was so clever. Does not the open letter which contained this secret writing state that her superior, "my manager," is "delighted very much" with her letters? Being a Roman Catholic by faith and having introductions to many prominent priests, she was well fitted for this plot. Did she not outline the whole scheme in her first letter, and request her superior to arrange for the manufacture of these holy figures?

The next letter is quite long and I shall therefore quote only a few lines of it, before taking up the secret ink portion.

March 22, 1917.

My dear friend,

Have many thanks for your kind letters, dated 2 and 3 ult. which I received at the same time with a letter from your uncle. Everything was very interesting for me. . . . In the meantime I received your first letter, dated 25th of January, and I found that your writing was far better than in those dated 2 and 3 ult.

The "writing" of course refers to the secret ink. It was easier to develop in the first letter than it was in the following two.

How do you like my specialty "kalium iodatum?" Are you satisfied?

Here is a blunder, a reference to the reagent which will develop these letters. Her superior wants to know if she can develop his letters.

. . . You will be pleased to hear that my cousin Oscar will call upon you on his trip to the South. Give him every assistance you can.

With kindest regards, I am yours truly,

Fels

Oscar refers to an important German spy who is on his way to Brazil. He had many aliases and we later intercepted many of his messages.

The secret ink developed in this letter gave a long list of cover-addresses both in America and in European neutral countries. There was further reference to the importation of holy figures. The secret ink was very difficult to develop and the sentences are not all complete. I shall therefore quote only the part that is clearly developed:

. . . establish agents on American war-ships. Where and how can a sailing vessel of a hundred tons get secret material on land over there? What can be undertaken against the Panama Canal?

These three sentences are especially significant for they positively prove that Germany planned to establish agents on American war-ships and destroy the Panama Canal even before the declaration of war!

Although there are several letters that I have not quoted, there is none between the date of this letter, March 22, 1917, and the "Maud" letter, the one that led to the name "Victorica."

These letters give us a vivid picture of Madame Victorica's instructions: destruction of mines, munition factories, docks, shipyards, merchantmen, men of war—"a million is at . . . service," "if . . . can blow up dreadnaughts"; plans for espionage in Brazil; establishment of submarine bases along the Atlantic coast and points on land where supplies can be picked up; plans for placing Irish and Americans on war-ships for which large rewards are offered; plans for destruction of the Panama Canal; and finally, an elaborate scheme for the importation of explosives in holy figures of saints.

The "Maud" letter gives us the most accurate view of Victorica's importance and shows conclusively, since it orders her to establish an independent "firm" to carry on these activities in case of her arrest, that as late as the date of this letter she still remains the dominating leader. Aside from all this, here is a woman who receives as much as thirty-five thousand dollars in one payment alone. Such sums are not advanced to unimportant spies.

It is clear enough that Madame Victorica is the directing genius of German espionage in the United States, and that her arrest will seriously cripple the activities of the group she controls. But where is she? How find her?

To trace all the steps taken to discover her whereabouts would take a book in itself; there were many false leads, and much floundering about in the efforts to locate her. I shall therefore take the reader through only the successful steps, leaving to some one else the story of repeated failures.

Of course while these letters were being developed and analyzed by the Secret-Ink Laboratory, our secret service agents were not inactive. It was impossible to send out a general alarm for we wished above all to capture rather than frighten her off. Each step therefore was taken with the utmost secrecy. Instead of direct inquiries, our investigations were of necessity slow and cautious.

One of these steps was the quiet and careful investigation of all the hotels and expensive apartment-houses in New York City. This at last led to the discovery that Madame Victorica had registered at the Hotel Knickerbocker on January 21, 1917, the day of her arrival in the United States. But she had suddenly checked out on February third.

Now what caused her sudden departure? Was it because diplomatic relations were severed between Germany and the United States on this date, when Secretary of State Lansing handed Ambassador von Bernstorff his passports? Had she become frightened and fled?

We picked her up again at the Waldorf Astoria where she had registered on February third. But again she had suddenly disappeared on February twenty-first. Was it the arrest two days earlier of Charles Nicholas Wunnenberg, known in Germany as "Dynamite Charley," that precipitated her departure? Wunnenberg was suspected of being mixed up in sabotage. Did she fear that he would talk?

Again we found her at the Spencer Arms where on February twenty-first she had taken an expensive apartment. But she had suddenly left on March second, only nine days later, though her rent had been paid until June twentieth! Here her trail ended.

In February she had severed all connection with her bankers, and had obviously kept away from the Foreign Mission where we found several of her letters. Had she withdrawn from all those who knew her as Madame Victorica? Had she assumed a new name? Obviously a woman clever enough to devise the holy-figure plot would not be easy to find.

But like all hunted persons she had overlooked one thing. In her case, the Secret-Ink Laboratory. The development of the secret writing in her letters had revealed too much information for her to remain very long at large and at the same time continue her activities.

These letters, it will be recalled, gave many cover-addresses in Holland, Sweden, Switzerland, and even in the United States. I did not quote these names because I did not wish to link any one with this famous spy.

Two of these cover-addresses, however, were of persons in New York City. Not only these two people but also every one connected with them were kept under careful and close surveillance.

On several occasions our agents reported that a young girl, a cousin of one of these two suspects, was observed at exactly the same moment, on the same day each week, entering the imposing Cathedral of St. Patrick that occupies the entire block along Fifth Avenue from Fiftieth to Fifty-first Street.

There was nothing odd about her entering the Cathedral for worship once a week. But why at the same moment—

just at dusk, just as the Cathedral chimed the quarter-hour? And although she had been shadowed repeatedly and every move she made watched, it was not until the evening of April 16, 1918, that our secret agents were able to discover any connection between her and Madame Victorica.

On this April evening, just as the street lights were switched on along Fifth Avenue and the Cathedral chimed the quarter-hour, this slender schoolgirl, barely sixteen, a folded newspaper held tightly under her left arm, carefully picked her way through the jammed busses and squawking automobiles, and without so much as turning her head, squeezed a path through the late shoppers, and quickly disappeared into the grim Cathedral.

Inside, the Cathedral was dim and almost deserted. Only here and there knelt a person in prayer.

The slender figure stopped at pew thirty and for a few moments knelt in silent worship, then suddenly arose, leaving the newspaper behind her, and quickly disappeared through the doors.

But as she hurried up the aisle she passed a stooped well-dressed man who also carried a folded newspaper under his left arm. For a few moments he too knelt in pew thirty, and had you carefully observed you would have seen him exchange newspapers, his gray head still bowed in worship. At last he crossed himself, arose and disappeared into the crowded throngs, the newspaper squeezed tightly beneath his arm.

And had you followed you would have seen him hail a taxi that discharged him at the Pennsylvania Station, where he caught a train for Long Beach, Long Island. Here again he took a taxi to the Nassau Hotel that overlooks the sea. And had you followed him inside you would have seen him seated alone on a lounge in the lobby quietly smoking.

After nearly a half-hour, he did a most curious thing. Without a sign of recognition, his face a perfect blank, with not even a glance in either direction, he suddenly arose and disappeared, but he, like the girl, left his newspaper behind.

No sooner had he risen than a beautiful blonde woman, strikingly gowned, appeared and took his place. In her arms she carried several newspapers which she placed beside her and picked up a magazine. For nearly a quarter of an hour she remained seated, reading and slowly turning the pages.

Then, apparently oblivious to her surroundings, she at

last gathered up not only her own papers but also the one left by the stooped man; and, slowly and gracefully strolling across the lobby, disappeared into the elevator.

What was in the newspaper?

Twenty one-thousand-dollar bank-notes that had been smuggled across the Mexican border from the German Minister von Eckhardt.

And the woman?

Madame Maria de Victorica! The beautiful blonde woman of Antwerp, for whom the British had searched in vain since the stirring days of 1914. She was now registered as Marie de Vussière at the fashionable Hotel Nassau, which overlooks the sea where every American transport, loaded with munitions and American troops, must pass in close review.

Eleven days later, on April 27, 1918, Madame Victorica was arrested on presidential warrant. Among her belongings were found several ball-pointed pens and two beautiful white silk scarfs which were impregnated with the now famous German "F" secret ink.

This famous spy was of royal birth. Her father was Baron Hans von Kretschman, a General in the German Army in the Franco-Prussian War, an author of treatises on military science. Her mother was Countess Jennie von Gustedt, daughter of a Prussian diplomat. Madame Victorica spoke many European languages fluently and had many university degrees. As early as 1910 she was received by the German Minister for Foreign Affairs and Prince von Bülow, and invited to enter the Secret Service.

When arraigned before the American authorities, Madame Victorica fenced cleverly for many long grueling hours.

"Why did you, a German, come to the United States in 1917 when it was plainly evident that the United States was going to declare war against your native country?"

"I really can not say, unless it was because I wanted to marry again."

"Was that really the reason? Then there were no eligible young men in Germany in 1917? How much money have you spent in this country?"

"About fifteen thousand dollars."

"How did you spend it?"

"Paying hotel and living expenses, and my maid whom I paid one hundred dollars per month."

Poor Victorica! She came to the United States to marry

again, and her inquisitors had seen her secret-ink instructions! Fifteen thousand dollars! And her inquisitors had seen her receipt for thirty-five thousand dollars in one payment alone! How many other payments no one knew. And the secret-ink phrase, "A million is at . . . service!"

Her inquisitors had been merely playing with her, giving her false hopes. She would now need more than her proud Prussian courage and tradition, for they suddenly and without warning confronted her with documentary evidence of her activities as a spy. At this she completely collapsed and was taken to the prison ward in Bellevue Hospital for treatment.

Years of constantly facing the danger of detection had taken its toll even of this handsome and clever woman. Like so many other successful spies, Madame Victorica was of necessity a drug addict.

On June 7, 1918, the Federal Grand Jury found an indictment against her for conspiracy to commit espionage in time of war. She was never brought to trial, and though treated with every consideration, for the American authorities held her in the highest esteem, she aged rapidly behind prison bars.

Finally, a pitiable, broken creature, her beauty and charm gone, her spirit crushed, she died on August 12, 1920, and was buried at Kensico, New York, in the Gates of Heaven Cemetery.

Madame Maria de Victorica, who had cleverly escaped detection since 1914, was but the victim of coincidence and the Secret-Ink Section of MI-8. Though a pathetic figure in death, may she remain immortal in the annals of espionage.

CHAPTER VI

Two German
Wireless Intercepts

By January, 1918, the Code and Cipher Solution Subsection of MI-8 had grown to ambitious proportions. We not only had to train students for our own use, but were also required to teach recruits for General Pershing's Cryptographic Bureau in France. This double function severely handicapped us, for we felt that in justice to the American Expeditionary Forces we should send abroad the students who showed the greatest promise for successful code and cipher attack. I regret to say that not more than two of all those we sent to France distinguished themselves, but this was not the fault of MI-8.

The successful cryptographer requires a type of mind difficult to describe. The work is absolutely foreign to anything he has ever done. To excel, he not only needs years of experience but great originality and imagination of a particular type. We call it "cipher brains." I know of no better description. We were never able to formulate an intelligence test that would indicate the future of a student. The most successful students, when put on their own responsibility, were, more often than not, utterly worthless, except for clerical work. I was later to have the unusual opportunity of studying under the British, French and Italians. I learned that they too had the same experience. In the combined Cipher Bureaus of England, France, Italy and America there were thousands of men and women devoting their lives to this science, but among these thousands there were no more than a dozen who had "cipher brains."

By tracing the actual decipherment of a code message, the reader may be better able to appreciate the type of mind required for successful code attack. The following two code messages, destined to make history, are especially adapted for this purpose. The column of letters at the left are not a part of the telegrams. They are added for reference purposes.

Code Message No. 1 "G"

(A)	49138	27141	51636	02062	49140	41345
(B)	42635	02306	12201	15726	27918	30348
(C)	53825	46020	40429	37112	48001	38219
(D)	50015	43827	50015	04628	01315	55331
(E)	20514	37803	19707	33104	33951	29240
(F)	02062	42749	33951	40252	38608	14913
(G)	33446	16329	55936	24909	27143	01158
(H)	42635	04306	09501	49713	55927	50112
(I)	13747	24255	27143	02803	24909	15742
(J)	49513	22810	16733	41362	24909	17256
(K)	19707	49419	39408	19801	34011	06336
(L)	15726	47239	29901	37013	42635	19707
(M)	42022	30334	06733	04156	39501	03237
(N)	14521	37320	13503	42635	33951	29901
(O)	49117	46633	02062	16636	19707	01426
(P)	11511	42635	11239	04156	02914	12201
(Q)	23145	55331	49423	03455	12201	30205
(R)	33951	38219	50015	04156	43827	06420
(S)	23309	19707	33104	42635	00308	29240
(T)	05732	54628	01355	39338	02914	12201
(U)	06420	11511	24909	27142	33951	49223
(V)	49618	42022	42635	17212	55320	15726
(W)	12201	06420	38219	21060	46633	37406
(X)	43644	33558	22527			

Code Message No. 42 "D"

(A)	19707	21206	31511	31259	37320	05101
(B)	33045	28223	28709	24211	06738	28223
(C)	51336	28709	42635	42235	13301	33045
(D)	28223	51336	28709	42635	02408	49853
(E)	40324	19707	29240	33104	42635	47239
(F)	03237	38203	41137	20344	21209	24735
(G)	47239	30809	19003	36932	42635	49223
(H)	31416	46027	35749	33045	28223	28709

(I)	44049	02957	03237	55934	14521	21206
(J)	34842	03846	29913	37320	55927	02803
(K)	03455	12201	50015	34004	49542	38055
(L)	01936	50015	31258	21737	24909	32831
(M)	33951	05101	06738	28223	28709	24211
(N)	33045	28223	51336	28709	42635	42235
(O)	13301	06738	28223	51336	28709	42635
(P)	19707	49633	55841	42635	26424	45023
(Q)	09415	22436	36050	06738	28223	49633
(R)	28709	42635	34128	48234	49419	31259
(S)	55142	41111	33158	15636	54403	47239
(T)	01602	21630	02915	42635	28539	50015
(U)	55934	14210	37320	37112	41345	47239
(V)	19801	34011	06336	15726	47239	21060
(W)	46633	37406	43644	04628	33558	23934

These two wireless messages were sent out by the powerful German wireless station POZ, located near Berlin, on an arc of sixteen thousand two hundred meters. The messages were transmitted without address or signature, and repeated over and over again nearly every day. One of them was intercepted by our intercepting stations more than sixty times.

It seemed very significant to us that the messages were sent without address or signature and were transmitted on a high arc. They were undoubtedly intended for German secret agents in some hostile or neutral country a great distance from Berlin, possibly in the United States or another country in the Western Hemisphere where the establishment of a high power transmitting station was not permitted, but where the small equipment required for interception could be readily concealed from the authorities.

We had some reason at least to believe that they were intended for Mexico; that they were in answer to some curious messages that were being sent each day from an unknown station in Mexico by a transmitting set of high power. The following is a typical example of these messages; note the repetition of each group:

HSI HSI HSI
DE DE DE
HSI HSI HSI
ATTENTION ATTENTION ATTENTION
WNCSL PYQHN CPDBQ TGCK I?
WNCSL PYQHN CPDBQ TGCK I?

WNCSL PYQHN CPDBQ TGCK I?
PERIOD PERIOD PERIOD
BREAK BREAK BREAK

The station call, HSI, which begins the message, was not officially assigned to any radio station. Listening for this operator each night we observed that he always gave a different call and never signed any call of his own. This led to a closer observation, and we discovered that he sent the code message every night at the same hours: ten-thirty, eleven, eleven-thirty and twelve. Later, however, he operated only three times during the evening, sending longer messages at different times from about ten-thirty-five to twelve-fifty. At first the messages were exactly the same with the exception of the number of times each code word was repeated. A few days later there were slight varations in the code words.

This operator was using a transmitting set of high power. The signals were just as strong at Dallas, Texas, as at San Antonio. At times the back-kick of his sending condensers could be heard at San Antonio, indicating high power and overloading of his condensers.

He sent very slowly and carefully, and repeated every word five or six times. He usually called the call-letter at least five minutes before starting his message, and sometimes as long as twenty minutes.

The fact that he used a transmitting set of high power convinced us that he was endeavoring to send the messages a great distance. His slow and careful sending, his repetitions of signals were to make sure that every word was correctly received.

He received no answer, never allowed for the possibility of an answer, for at the end of each message, unless it was the last one of the night, he sent the character "wait," and on the last message the character "finish." All these facts made it evident that he operated on some agreed schedule.

By the use of a radio goniometer at different points along the Mexican border we determined the exact position of this strange station. A radio goniometer is an instrument that shows the direction from which the wave emanates. Thus, if you take a reading at Laredo and draw a line on the map, then take a reading at Del Rio and draw another line, the point on the map at which these two lines converge is the correct position of the sending station.

Much to our amazement the lines converged at Chapultepec, the most powerful Mexican wireless station! Was Mexico in league with the Germans? Were they permitting the Germans to use the official Mexican Government wireless station for the transmission to Berlin of information that German spies were running across the Rio Grande? Was Chapultepec receiving messages from Berlin and delivering them to the German Minister at Mexico City? There could be no other conclusion.

The two code messages sent in five-figure groups (pages 70 and 71) must be destined for Mexico and must be secret indeed if Germany dared not send either address or signature. Let us try to solve them.

A casual glance at these two messages convinces us that they are encoded in the same code. Note the high frequency of occurrence in each message of such groups as 42635, 19707, 47239, etc. To facilitate further analysis let us make a frequency of each figure group found in both messages. (See Fig 1, p. 74)

Figure 1 not only shows us how often each five-figure group occurs, but also shows us that the smallest number in the messages is 00308 and the largest 55936. This would indicate that the code in use had approximately 60,000 words and phrases. Such a code is not unusually large; many codes contain 100,000 or more words and phrases.

We know from experience that a code of only 10,000 words will express any language, except for unusual words, cities, names of people, etc., which may be spelled out either letter by letter in the code, or if the code so provides, by syllables.

The code we are dealing with, then, can contain only about 10,000 of the more common words and the remaining 50,000 will be devoted to proper names, tables and common phrases and sentences. It should also have several different code groups for the first thousand most common words. These we call variants. In English some of them would be *telegram, you, your,* etc. The variants for the word *you* might look something like the following in this code book:

> you..49138
> you..06439
> you..13542
> you..57754
> you..19327
> you..20648

FIGURE 1

Frequency of Five-Figure Code Words in Nauen Messages

1 00308	1 16329	1 30809	2 42235
1 01158	1 16636	1 31258	16 42635
1 01315	1 16733	2 31259	1 42749
1 01355	1 17212	1 31416	2 43644
1 01426	1 17256	1 31511	2 43827
1 01602	1 19003	1 32831	1 44049
1 01936	8 19707	4 33045	1 45023
3 02062	2 19801	3 33104	1 46020
1 02306	1 20344	1 33158	1 46027
1 02408	1 20514	1 33446	3 46633
2 02803	2 21060	2 33558	6 47239
2 02914	2 21206	6 33951	1 48001
1 02915	1 21209	1 34004	1 48234
1 02957	1 21630	2 34011	1 49117
3 03237	1 21737	1 34128	1 49138
2 03455	1 22436	1 34842	1 49140
1 03846	1 22527	1 35749	2 49223
3 04156	1 22810	1 36050	2 49419
1 04306	1 23145	1 36932	1 49423
2 04628	1 23309	1 37013	1 49513
2 05101	1 23934	2 37112	1 49542
1 05732	2 24211	4 37320	1 49618
2 06336	1 24255	2 37406	2 49633
3 06420	1 24735	1 37803	1 49713
1 06733	5 24909	1 38055	1 49853
4 06738	1 26424	1 38203	6 50015
1 09415	1 27141	3 38219	1 50112
1 09501	1 27142	1 38608	4 51336
1 11239	2 27143	1 39338	1 51636
2 11511	1 27918	1 39408	1 53825
6 12201	8 28223	1 39501	1 54403
2 13301	1 28539	1 40252	1 54628
1 13503	8 28709	1 40324	1 55142
1 13747	3 29240	1 40429	1 55320
1 14210	2 29901	1 41111	2 55331
2 14521	1 29913	1 41137	1 55841
1 14913	1 30205	2 41345	2 55927
1 15636	1 30334	1 41362	2 55934
4 15726	1 30348	2 42022	1 55936
1 15742			

Variants are used to confuse the cryptographer. In this case he must identify six different code words for *you* instead of one. This would also be true for several hundred other common words. The code may also have several hundred "nulls," code words with no meanings which are scattered at random throughout the code messages in order further to confuse the analyst.

Now then, if this code has approximately 50,000 code groups dealing with nulls, phrases and variants, and entire sentences, there should be very few repetitions. If, however, the code consists of single words only, and has no nulls, variants, phrases or sentences, all words and phrases will always be sent in the same manner. This will pile up high frequencies and many repetitions.

Let us refer to Figure 1 again and compile a small table of the more frequent groups:

FIGURE 2

42635	occurs	16	times
28709	"	8	"
28223	"	8	"
19707	"	8	"
50015	"	6	"
47239	"	6	"
33951	"	6	"
12201	"	6	"
24909	"	5	"
06738	"	4	"
37320	"	4	"
33045	"	4	"
15726	"	4	"
51336	"	4	"

The two messages contain a total of only 279 groups. Does it not seem unusual that in two messages of only 279 groups one of them occurs 16 times? Is it possible to write 279 words of text and repeat one of the words that often? Pick up a newspaper and at random select an article and count off 279 words. What word occurs most often, and how many times does it occur? Omit the words *a, of* and *the* for in telegraphic correspondence they are seldom required.

The highest frequency I find by such an experiment is 4. The word *be* occurred 4 times. I also noted other common words and compared their frequencies with those in Figure 2. Let us match them and note the differences.

FIGURE 3

High frequencies in 279 code words in two Nauen messages			High frequencies in 279 words newspaper text		
42635	occurs 16 times		*be*	occurs 4 times	
28709	" 8 "		*in*	" 4 "	
28223	" 8 "		*to*	" 3 "	
19707	" 8 "		*with*	" 2 "	
50015	" 6 "		*will*	" 2 "	
47239	" 6 "		*by*	" 2 "	
33951	" 6 "		*is*	" 2 "	
12201	" 6 "		*has*	" 2 "	
24909	" 5 "		*at*	" 2 "	
06738	" 4 "		*this*	" 1 "	
37320	" 4 "		*for*	" 1 "	
33045	" 4 "		*which*	" 1 "	
15726	" 4 "		*that*	" 1 "	
51336	" 4 "		*they*	" 1 "	

The highest frequency of the newspaper text is the word *be* and occurs only 4 times, as against 42635 in the code messages which is repeated 16 times. This is 4 to 1.

What is the reason for this? What sort of code are we dealing with that produces such high frequencies?

Let us keep in mind the fact that these two messages are from the powerful German station in Nauen, Germany, and probably intended for Mexico. The reader will recall the sensational Zimmermann-Carranza note which the President read before Congress just before we entered the war, the note in which Zimmermann, German Minister for Foreign Affairs, promised Mexico financial aid and the states of New Mexico, Texas and Arizona if she declared war against the United States. This telegram was deciphered by the British Cryptographic Bureau early in 1917, just before we entered the war. The Germans are aware that their latest code between Germany and Mexico has been solved. They must establish secret communication. But how? It would be almost impossible for Berlin to deliver another code book to her Minister in Mexico, for a code book is too bulky to escape the censor. Yet in spite of this we know that we are dealing with a *new code!* What kind?

Before we go any further we must identify the language. The natural supposition is that the message is either in German or Spanish. We must try these two languages and, failing, next try English. To make this piece of exposition shorter we shall not go through the analysis of German and Spanish, for as a matter of fact such analysis leads to a blank wall. We shall, therefore, assume the message is in English. This will not be difficult to prove.

New codes that are scientifically constructed do not give such enormous repetitions as we have discovered; so it is fair to assume that this is an alphabetical code; that is, the text words or meanings in the code are arranged in alphabetical order, and their figure equivalents arranged in numerical sequence.

Turning back to Figure 1 we find several pairs of figure groups that are very close to each other:

Figure 4

| 02914 | 21206 | 31258 | 49138 | 55934 |
| 02915 | 21209 | 31259 | 49140 | 55936 |

This is not a coincidence. Each pair must mean words that are close together in the English language; such as,

| 02914 arrive | 21206 go | 31258 mail |
| 02915 arrived | 21209 gone | 31259 mailed |

If the book is alphabetically arranged, and it must be, we should be able to place with reasonable accuracy in the alphabetical arrangement of the English language the approximate position of each figure group. Any unabridged English dictionary will help us.

We will begin with the assumption that 00308, the smallest figure group occurring in the two messages, equals a word beginning with the letter *a;* and that 55936, the largest figure group, equals a word beginning with *y* or *z.*

Note the last three groups in Figure 1: 55927, 55934, 55936. Here we have three groups all beginning with 559; they must equal words occurring near the end of the alphabet, words that are close together. Words beginning with *z,* being infrequent, can be discarded. They must therefore begin with y. Keep in mind that 55927 and 55934 each occur twice. These must be common words and they begin with y.

The only dictionary I have before me is Appleton's *New Spanish Dictionary*. I have opened to the y's in the English-Spanish section and have searched the four columns of y's. The word *you* seems to be the outstanding word. Let us copy down the words that immediately follow *you* in the dictionary.

you	younker
young	your
younger	yours
youngish	yourself
youngling	youth
youngster	youthful

Let us now assume that 55927 equals *you* and see how the figure groups 55934 and 55936 fall.

55927 *you*	55932 youngster
55928 young	55933 younker
55929 younger	55934 *your*
55930 youngish	55935 yours
55931 youngling	55936 *yourself*

The figure groups match this particular dictionary perfectly, for we now have,

55927 you
55934 your
55936 yourself

all of them very common words.

We have without question correctly identified three words, *you, your* and *yourself*.

Is it possible that these messages are encoded in an English dictionary, the first three figures indicating the page, the last two the line? This seems impossible, yet our discovery can hardly be a coincidence.

Let us examine the code words in the two messages again; see Figure 1. We already have the range of the first three figures which is 003 to 559. Suppose we tabulate the last two figures and see whether this suggests any new ideas?

FIGURE 5

Last Two Figures of Groups

01	09	17	25	33	41	49	56
02	10	18	26	34	42	50	57
03	11	19	27	35	43	51	58
04	12	20	28	36	44	52	59
05	13	21	29	37	45	53	60
06	14	22	30	38	46	55	62
07	15	23	31	39	47		
08	16	24	32	40	48		

The numbers range from 01 to 62. Why is it that though we have a total of 279 code words, the last two figures of none of them are above 62? What has happened to the endings from 63 to 99?

This can be due to but one reason. If the first three figures indicate the page of a dictionary, and the last two the word or line number, we would not expect the last two figures to run very high, for there are seldom more than sixty words on a dictionary page. This accounts for the absence of the figure 63 to 99.

Then, too, why is there no occurrence of 00? This should occur before 01 in a code book. The reason is, of course, that the first word on each page of a dictionary must be indicated by 01. There would be no manner of using 00.

The use of a dictionary would also account for high frequencies and repetitions, for the same word would always be expressed in the same manner.

We are, then, most certainly dealing with a dictionary. Through their spies the Germans have slipped word through the censor to the German Minister in Mexico to use an English dictionary for encoding dispatches.

We have already identified *you* and *yourself* without very much effort. The complete solution of these famous messages is not quite so simple. But we have made an important discovery. We have outwitted the German cipher experts, after a few hours' labor. But shall we really be able to solve the entire message?

Let us make a more careful analysis of the most frequent group, 42635. Examine Figure 6 which shows the prefix and suffix and the position of each occurrence of

42635. The first line means that 42635 is preceded by
01158 and followed by 04306 in message 1, line H.

FIGURE 6

Prefix	Suffix	Reference
	42635	
01158	04306	1..H
02915	28539	42.T
11511	11239	1..P
13503	33951	1..N
28709	02408	42.D
28709	19707	42.O
28709	34128	42.R
28709	42235	42.C
28709	42235	42.N
33104	00308	1..S
33104	47239	42.E
36932	49223	42.G
37013	19707	1..L
42022	17212	1..V
55841	26424	42.P
41345	02306	1..B

From this table we see that 42635, although frequently
having the same prefix, nearly always has a different suffix.
42635 obviously must be a termination or ending of some
sort. It would do very nicely for *stop* but it doesn't seem
impossible that in 279 words there can be as many as 16
stops.

It must begin a word starting with *r* or *s* if we take Appleton's Dictionary as a guide. We know that it equals
some sort of termination. What?

How are the plural forms of words expressed in a code
message encoded with a dictionary? By adding *s*, of course.
S is a termination, the end of a word. Does 42635 mean *s?*
It fits perfectly into its alphabetical position and answers
the requirements of high frequency and termination. We
shall therefore assume that *s* is correct.

Let us now see if we can not read some of the message.
The beginning of message No. 42 "D" offers possibilities.

This telegram begins 19707 21206 31511 31259. Now
19707 occurs 8 times (see Figure 2), and of course must
be a common word. If we had the correct dictionary before us we would find the word it means on page 197,
line or word 7. Let us search for this word in any English

dictionary having approximately six hundred pages by turning to page 197 and looking in both directions, backward and forward, at least 10 pages.

The most common word I can find is *for,* which occurs on page 203, line 11, or 20311. This is 6 pages farther advanced; that is, 6 pages from 19707 to 20311.

Let us, then, add 6 pages to the next group, 21206, which gives 21806, and turn to page 218 and search for a common word. On page 217, line 20, I find the word *German.* We now have two words, *For German.* This begins to look interesting.

We should almost guess the next word, 31511, but let us stick to the dictionary. Adding 6 to 31511 we have 32111. My dictionary tells me that this word must begin with the letter *m.* What is it?

For German M—that's right! *For German Minister.*

The next word, 31259, occurs just 3 pages earlier in the dictionary than 31511. It must be some word between *let* and *mic: For German Minister Let—Mic.*

This message must be to Mexico. What is the word? *Mexico* of course.

For German Minister Mexico!

Then the Germans have established communication by wireless to Mexico. Chapultepec, the official Mexican station, is operating illegally. As already suspected, Mexico is in league with the Germans!

What do the telegrams say? They must be extremely important if the facts that they bear neither address nor signature mean anything. And if not extremely important to the German Government why are they sent by wireless every day?

There are two methods of completing the solution of these two telegrams. Several days of painstaking work will unravel their secret, or we may go to the Congressional Library and search through every English dictionary in print. If we are lucky we shall find the right dictionary.

If the reader searches thoroughly enough he will discover that these two historic documents were encoded by the German Foreign Office in the English-French half of Clifton's *Nouveau Dictionnaire Français.* Message No. 42 "D" reads as follows:

Decode of Message No. 42 "D"

For German Minister Mexico. Bleichroeder any time

ready for loan negotiations. At present remittance from Germany impossible. Meantime firm places ten million Spanish pesetas at your disposal German Oversea Bank Madrid. You are authorized to offer this preliminary amount to Mexican government in name of Bleichroeder for three years, interest six, commission half per cent, *on supposition that Mexico will remain neutral during war.* All good arrangements left to your discretion. Please reply. Foreign Office Busshe. General Staff Political Section Berlin number hundred.

Mexico is offered a bribe to remain neutral. America and her Allies have been straining every effort to force Central and South American countries to declare war against a common enemy.

Let us read the other message which has more to say about German and Mexican machinations.

Decode of Message No. 1 "G"

Telegram January two and telegraphic report S. Anthony Delmar via Spain received. Please suggest president [Mexico] to send to Berlin, agent with fuller power for negotiation of loan and sale of raw product. Do not embroil yourself in Japanese affair because communication through you too difficult. If Japanese are in earnest, they have enough representatives in Europe for that purpose. Foreign Office Busshe. Machinery plans for rifle manufactory can be put at disposal. Details of machinery, technical staff, and engineer for aircraft could be arranged here with the authorized man of president [Mexico] to be sent by him for negotiations about loan. We agree purchase arranged by Craft (Kraft) in Japan of ten thousand rifles, etc., wished by president. General Staff Political Section number (?)

There was general excitement in Washington when these two messages were deciphered, for this would obviously open a new avenue to the United States for information of not only the intrigues of Germany, but also of the true aims and intentions of Mexico and, perhaps, Japan. What would the decipherment of further messages reveal? A hundred instruments tuned in on the powerful Nauen wireless station in order to intercept the next message that would surely follow.

But Nauen was now suddenly silent. Why? Because news of our success had been flashed back to Berlin? There can be no other reason, for when Nauen finally again begins to send out messages their system of encoding has changed. MI-8, with all its care in the selection of its personnel, has a German spy within its doors. A finger of suspicion now points at every cryptographer.

CHAPTER VII

Pablo Waberski

EARLY in February, 1918, Colonel Van Deman buzzed for me on the inter-office dictograph and asked that I come to his office at once.

He motioned to me to sit down beside him and without comment handed me a sheet of ordinary writing paper on which was typed the following series of letters:

15-1-18

seofnatupk	asiheihbbn	uersdausnn
lrseggiesn	nkleznsimn	ehneshmppb
asueasriht	hteurmvnsm	eaincouasi
insnrnvegd	esnbtnnrcn	dtdrzbemuk
kolselzdnn	auebfkbpsa	tasecisdgt
ihuktnaeie	tiebaeuera	thnoieaeen
hsdaeaiakn	ethnnneecd	ckdkonesdu
eszadehpea	bbilsesooe	etnouzkdml
neuiiurmrn	zwhneegvcr	eodhicsiac
niusnrdnso	drgsurriec	egrcsuassp
eatgrsheho	etruseelca	umtpaatlee
cicxrnprga	awsutemair	nasnutedea
errreoheim	eahktmuhdt	cokdtgceio
eefighihre	litfiueunl	eelserunma
znai		

There was no address or signature—nothing but a jumble of letters, bearing the date January 15, 1918.

I had been with the War Department now for nearly eight months, and though thousands of code and cipher documents as well as secret-ink letters had passed through

my hands, I still felt a thrill at the mystery of the unknown when a jumble of letters met my eye. And aside
from this I well knew that Colonel Van Deman did not
ask me to see him personally unless he had something out
of the ordinary to discuss.

I took it for granted that this was an important cipher,
but I could not know that I was holding in my hand a
document that would lead to one of the most extraordinary
cases in American history—a document that would be responsible for the death sentence of a daring German spy.

"What do you make of it?" Van Deman asked.

"It looks like cipher and not code to me," I replied.
"There are long sequences of consonants such as *shmppb*
in the second line, and *snbtnnrcndtdrzb* in the fourth line.
Usually, code groups are formed by combinations of vowels
and consonants. Yes, I'm quite sure this is cipher. Would
you mind telling me its source—where it came from?"

"Have you ever heard of Lather Witcke, alias Pablo
Waberski?" he asked.

"Not a great deal—nothing except that he is suspected
of being one of the most dangerous and unscrupulous German spies operating across the Mexican border."

"Well, we arrested him on the border a few days ago.
Nothing was found on his person but this slip of paper.
And since he is traveling on a Russian passport, we shall
be unable to hold him even though we know that he is
a German spy unless this cipher contains incriminating
evidence." He paused and looked me squarely in the eyes.
"Yardley, I want this message deciphered," he said in his
incisive voice. "I want to know what it says. I am depending upon the cleverness and ingenuity of MI-8. Don't come
back until you can bring me the decipherment." And he
curtly dismissed me.

On only one other occasion had I seen Van Deman,
usually even-tempered, so exercised over a cipher message.
Several months earlier he had given me a spy message and
almost demanded a decipherment by the next morning. I
had worked on it all night and, basing my opinion on scientific analysis, had told him the document was not a
cipher but a fraud, or, as we called it, a fake cipher. Van
Deman was very impatient at my report, but in the face of
criticism I maintained that the message was a pure fraud
and had been constructed by some one who simply sat before a typewriter and pecked out a jumble of letters.

Van Deman's secret operator was plainly disgusted with both me and my report, but at my insistence consented to give the two principals in the case a severe cross-examination. As a result they confessed that they had made up the cipher out of pure malice in order to implicate a third person. The suspect was released from jail, and from that day no report from MI-8 was ever questioned.

Experiences of this type, however, led to one very grave difficulty—it soon became a tradition that MI-8 could decipher anything, and this often placed us in an undesirable light. As I left the room I wondered how successful we should be in deciphering the Waberski cipher.

I hurried through the corridors to the photostat-room and had six copies of the document made; then rushed up-stairs to my office with the negatives, still damp from their chemical bath. Since I was already convinced I knew the type of cipher we had to deal with, I distributed the six copies to different clerks with instructions to prepare the preliminary work.

To the experienced cryptographer, this message would appear to be a transposition cipher written in German. A student of cryptography would arrive at this conclusion by the following analysis.

The first step is to discover how often each letter occurs in the cipher; that is, to discover the number of *a*'s, *b*'s, *c*'s, etc. This is done by placing a mark after each letter of the alphabet for each occurrence of the same letter in the cipher. This produces the frequency table shown in Figure 1.

Now since this cipher was found on a German coming from Mexico to the United States, it is fair to assume that is to be expected in Spanish, English and German.
quency appears to be a normal language frequency; that is, the letters *a, e, i, n, r, s, t* occur very frequently which it to be expected in Spanish, English and German.

The cipher then appears to be a transposition cipher:

FIGURE 1
Frequency Table of Pablo Waberski Cipher

A	︴︴ ︴︴ ︴︴ ︴︴ ︴︴ ︴︴ ︴︴ III
B	︴︴ ︴︴
C	︴︴ ︴︴ ︴︴
D	︴︴ ︴︴ ︴︴ III
E	︴︴ ︴︴ ︴︴ ︴︴ ︴︴ ︴︴ ︴︴ ︴︴ ︴︴ ︴︴ ︴︴ ︴︴ ︴︴ IIII
F	IIII
G	︴︴ ︴︴ I
H	︴︴ ︴︴ ︴︴ ︴︴
I	︴︴ ︴︴ ︴︴ ︴︴ ︴︴ ︴︴
J	
K	︴︴ ︴︴ II
L	︴︴ ︴︴ I
M	︴︴ ︴︴ II
N	︴︴ ︴︴ ︴︴ ︴︴ ︴︴ ︴︴ ︴︴ ︴︴ I
O	︴︴ ︴︴ IIII
P	︴︴ III
Q	
R	︴︴ ︴︴ ︴︴ ︴︴ ︴︴ I
S	︴︴ ︴︴ ︴︴ ︴︴ ︴︴ ︴︴ ︴︴
T	︴︴ ︴︴ ︴︴ ︴︴ II
U	︴︴ ︴︴ ︴︴ ︴︴ ︴︴
V	III
W	II
X	I
Y	
Z	︴︴ II

The message was first written in Spanish, English or German and the letters of the message then disarranged by some prearranged formula.

But what language is it in?

We can discard Spanish because this message contains 12 *k*'s and *k* does not occur in the Spanish language. Aside from this, *q* is a frequent Spanish letter and there are no *q*'s in this message.

Is it in English? Now *z* and *k* in the English language occur very seldom and in this message *z* occurs 7 times, and *k* 12 times. We can therefore disregard English.

There now remains German to consider. In order to make a scientific comparison of the Waberski document with a normal frequency table of the German language, let us reduce the Waberski frequency table to a basis of 200 letters and compare it with a normal German language frequency table which has been reduced from a count of 10,000 letters to a basis of 200 letters.

By superimposing the two tables, we can easily determine their relation.

FIGURE 2

* represents Waberski cipher frequency.
. represents normal German frequency.

A************ ********
....

B*****
.....

C*****
...

D*********
....

E******************** *************** ****
....

F**
...

G****
....

H********
....

I************ *****
....

J

K*****
..

L******
......

M******
.....

88

N^{•••••••• •••••••••}
......................."

O^{•••••••}
....

P^{••••}
.

Q

R^{•••••••• ••••••}
....

S^{••••••••• ••••• ••••••}
....

T^{••••••••••}
....

U^{••••••••••}
....

V^{••}
..

W[•]
...

X

Y

Z^{•••}
...

Note how closely these two tables resemble each other. Such a close resemblance would indicate that there is no doubt about this being a German transposition cipher.

How does one go about deciphering a transposition cipher? If in the spring of 1918 you had searched the libraries of the world you would not have discovered so much as one word that would give you the least idea how to attack such a problem. Even the pamphlet used by the United States Army for instruction in codes and ciphers would have given you no clues. This is what I meant earlier when I made the statement that the cryptographer in order to be successful must make his own discoveries; there is no beaten path to follow.

Now in German the letter *c* is always followed by the letter *h* or *k*, except in a few rare words and proper names. If you first write a message in German and then disarrange the letters by a formula, it follows that the letters of all the digraphs *ch* or *ck* are disturbed or disarranged in the same manner. And if you can discover a method for matching up correctly all the *c*'s with their affinity *h* or *k*, you have made long strides in the solution of the message.

The scientific method as developed by MI-8 for such a problem is first the tabulating of the number of letters in the cipher message that separate each *c* and each *h* or *k*. The message therefore was turned over to clerks to compile these statistics.

Was it possible, I wondered, that German cryptographers had not made this discovery? Evidently not, for the Waberski cipher was without question a transposition cipher. Perhaps it was a double transposition! Oh, well, the charts being prepared would tell the story.

While this preliminary work was being done, I went down to see the officer who had charge of the Southern Department, for I wished to learn more about Waberski. The solution of a problem is often possible only when one knows all the circumstances under which the cipher message was intercepted.

The officer in charge of the Southern Department handed me a large file to read, and was extremely excited when I told him that we were working on the Waberski cipher, and that there was a fair chance of our being able to read it even though the message was not very long.

To understand the importance that officials attached to the Waberski case, one must keep in mind the ancient and private feud between President Wilson and President Carranza of Mexico, the punitive expedition into Mexico of American troops in 1916, the publication of the Zimmermann-Carranza note in which the German Minister for Foreign Affairs promised Mexico the states of New Mexico, Texas and Arizona if she declared war against the United States, and the resultant and very natural hatred of most Mexicans for the "gringo" Americans, which had made Mexico a haven for German spies.

Mexico was openly pro-German. Our own spies who had been sent into Mexico reported that hundreds of German reservists who fled across the border at the declaration of war were recruiting and drilling Mexican troops; that high German officials, such as Jahnke (Chief of German Secret Service), Von Eckhardt (the German Minister), and the German Consul-General to Mexico were extremely friendly and operated openly with President Carranza.

Our agents reported that German spy plans were of a most ambitious nature: destruction at the opportune moment of the Tampico oil fields; establishment of a wireless station for direct communication with Berlin with the knowledge and cooperation of General Carranza (a most flagrant violation of neutrality—see Chapter VI); stirring up strikes in the United States through the I. W. W.; fomenting discontent among the Negroes in the South, who, at the proper moment, were to start a series of massacres; destruction of war industries in the United States; and every other conceivable phase of war-time espionage.

We were of course deciphering all of the Mexican Government's diplomatic cipher telegrams which gave us a fair picture of the attitude of General Carranza toward the United States.

That our own spies were not exaggerating matters may be gleaned from the Nauen messages. (See Chapter VI.)

That Von Eckhardt, the Consul-General, and Jahnke were not only ambitious but ruthless in their activities may be surmised from the following which is a translation of a German cipher message, deciphered by M1-8, sent by the German Consul-General in Mexico to all German Consuls a few weeks after the Armistice. A copy of the cipher message was sent to M1-8 by a spy I placed in the Mexico Telegraph Office in Mexico City shortly after I arrived at the War College, for the purpose of stealing copies of German diplomatic and consular code and cipher messages from the Mexican Telegraph Company files.

The cipher message follows:

DEUTSCHE GESANDTSCHAFT.
    Tgb. Nr. 143/19

                                   Mexico, den 10. Jan., 1919

nogaaaimue	saeesntraa	seienewwei
heuamaoeid	zcdkeftedt	edgeigunri
eceutnninb	mhbebanais	iteaarukss
tdscmoorob	aeuoermotd	hzzzdibgtt
fceumlreri	eeoemffcea	iqeirenuef
drisrrbnle	enznuhbtpf	kgtineenel
anvescalrr	adngdceoeu	tiailuiorl
bkrnnoeeqe	hhananvsdf	niemineiee
eetreegdmp	eilsbihlnu	hodciageef

sttheetdbe	ugmuaudnuu	dnsfnenenn
umtralgtnu	rehnemenbe	mntngefsae
kltzedrkii	rhficnvaks	onbtguhewn
thitzmsrmd	lghireicsc	enpneiette
nhvdnvhbvn	nrsnecnemn	ngepniceuh
eortsgesie	eneonfiend	wnpkcevemd
isrhwlften	amucnosazr	ahelnehiln
crseamilnb	eutceszrth	rsaeoszclx
mneouhslcu	nmenenefae	eckerglnra
bgfireubli	roznnsseuz	csthpusica
ufohunndbn	betfmmcirt	unfrnsrbna
dsukouiust	bmgdreninu	lusneadash
scecfaonen	ehsmnrgoot	erzruierne
incneinfee	etkstnbika	zeugdednkr
ibhideeree	aeuneinzet	dendaoerea
ighueuoanu	uzasruoddi	eeemcutiee
teanchchdd	igrrrrrnso	esiereerde
emiehdeade	nhdthmnosm	elolmeennd
rhktendend	uockehaete	eresfjhouk
fhbmkttemn	ledsetuehl	enimliaern
ehzeuesesg	snmeuhaimd	rrensshikh
rahdhennjh	osesedfhin	meerneaseh
udzsgifmri	uoisoehsna	dietfeebsa
ekamhceant	eaoabeunou	flrnneizua
nfpbhmnfon	gusdiporth	fhrsmdndrl
tmaurrwini	ulnezsknts	hdrsdbbnip
osedlsuctb	ctidafsaue	ttunwirhbr
ngnedumiis	veurakklne	enrcmtdtea
nsinleimgr	iehnlemnlg	gkhegdatee
eaaeegtero	arusrelari	graenuinbi
eeikdnspni	ribhhpkuze	tkfseshdne
haravntsee	ipreicseuu	emozusmudh
ipitnndark	nalccssgle	ursttrlecp
irbdnsaend	recoeteian	mdtnnheamt
ntzeomtier	nukwmttcke	ucebdihtnf
eswgowgeen	notzreasnu	caahnbgeil
ceernsnrta	lgghcue*	

---

* After reading the decipherment of the Waberski document, the reader may wish to attempt to decipher this. The translation of the German decipherment follows.

Translation of Decipherment

[Addressed to all German Consuls in Mexico]

Please carefully and immediately burn without remainder, and destroy the ashes of, all papers connected
with the war, the preservation of which is not absolutely
necessary, especially papers now in your hands or reaching you hereafter which have to do with the Secret Service and the service of the representatives of our General
Staff and Admiralty Staff (strictest silence concerning
the existence and activity of these representatives is to
be observed now and for all future time, even after the
conclusion of peace) which might be compromising or
even unpleasant for us if they came to the knowledge of
our enemies, who are still endeavoring to obtain possession of such papers.

Lists, registers, accounts, receipts, account-books, etc.,
are especially included in these papers, as well as correspondence with this Embassy by letter and telegraph
on the subjects mentioned.

Cipher books, codes and cipher keys and directions
that are still in use are excepted for the present, and
most particular attention must be paid to keeping them
in absolute safety.

Please report in writing *en clair* the execution of this
order so far as it relates to papers now on hand and
then burn this so-called order for burning, which, for
further reference, I herewith designate as PQR, and the
contents of which together with this designation you will
please retain in memory.

[Signed by the German Consul-General]

General Churchill, who was Director of Military Intelligence at the time this message was received, was especially pleased with our successful decipherment of this important document. He wrote MI-8 a highly complimentary
letter, stating that the decipherment was an achievement
worthy of the high standard which MI-8 had always
maintained. He instructed me to give a copy of the letter
to each officer and clerk who had contributed to the
decipherment.

This German cipher message, officially designated PQR,
is without question the frankest and most open document
treating on the subject of espionage, excepting the Soviet

spy document in Chapter XIII, that I have ever seen. I am always amused at the frankness with which diplomats express themselves in secret code telegrams, and their childlike faith that a cipher or a code can keep their utmost secrets from prying eyes. Diplomats, as we read more of them later on, are almost as naïve as children.

In retrospect, it is no wonder that my superiors were concerned about the cipher document found on Pablo Waberski, for Mexico was full of spies operating across the border and, so the reports read, Pablo Waberski was the most dangerous of them all. There were even reports from the British who suspected him of being responsible for the Black Tom explosion in New York Harbor in July, 1916.

Pablo Waberski, so the reports stated, entered the United States at Nogales, Arizona, on February 1, 1918, traveling on a Russian passport. He was not aware that our secret agents in Mexico had reported his activities and was surprised when arrested as he crossed the border.

He was rushed to the Military Intelligence Officer at the camp of the 35th Infantry and searched. Nothing but a sheet of writing-paper containing a series of ten-letter groups was found on his person. However, since our authorities already had reports of his activities, he was kept under close guard.

I returned to MI-8 with no small concern, for I understood better the importance of the Waberski document. Van Deman had placed the issue squarely in the hands of MI-8. Would we be able to outwit the German cryptographers? Was our skill greater than theirs?

When I returned a great deal of progress had already been made. All the necessary statistics had been prepared and several cryptographers, under the direction of Captain Manly, were busily engaged in piecing the message together.

The Waberski cipher had been retyped and each letter given a number; thus,

s e o f n a t u p k etc., etc.
1 2 3 4 5 6 7 8 9 10

Our frequency table already tells us that there are 15 c's and 20 h's. All the c's were underlined in red and all the h's in blue, so that the eye could readily find them. They

94

were then typed on another sheet of paper together with their letter-numbers; thus,

H	H	H	H	H	H	H	H	H	H
14	17	52	56	69	71	152	172	181	193

H	H	H	H	H	H	H	H	H	H
217	253	264	307	309	367	373	378	396	398

C	C	C	C	C	C	C	C	C
85	109	145	199	201	259	266	270	290

C	C	C	C	C	C
294	319	331	333	381	387

Now, as already explained, our problem is to find the mathematical formula that the Germans used in disarranging the original text. And since in pure German the letter c is nearly always followed by h or k (only the digraph ch will be considered in this problem, as the analysis of ck will not be necessary), if we subtract the letter-numbers of all the c's from the letter-numbers of all the h's, we should find a common factor, unless the cipher is a grille or double transposition.

Let us, therefore, take this first step and see whether the resultant figures indicate the type of cipher we are dealing with. The distances between the c's and h's can be graphically shown by writing the h's and their letter-numbers in a horizontal column, and the c's with their letter-numbers in a vertical column, on cross-section paper. By subtracting each figure in the vertical column from each figure in the horizontal column we arrive at the distance, or number of letters, between each c and each h. In cases where the h number is smaller than the c number it will first be necessary to add 424, the number of letters in the message, to the h number before subtracting; thus, in the first case H-14 plus 424 equals H-438 minus C-85 equals 353.

Figure 3 on the following page shows the result of this process.

By carefully examining all these figures we find that the figure 108 is common to all the lines except five. This can scarcely be a coincidence. But what does it mean? If not a coincidence, it means that the formula used by the Germans in disarranging the original message has separated each c from its h by 108 letters.

Let us condense Figure 3 to a smaller one, so that we

FIGURE 3

	H 14	H 17	H 52	H 56	H 69	H 71	H 152	H 172	H 181	H 193	H 217	H 253	H 264	H 307	H 309	H 367	H 373	H 378	H 396	H 398
C 85	353	356	391	395	408	410	67	87	96	108	132	168	179	222	224	282	288	293	311	313
C 109	329	332	367	371	384	386	43	63	72	84	108	144	155	198	200	258	264	269	287	289
C 145	293	296	331	335	348	350	7	27	36	48	72	108	119	162	164	222	228	233	251	253
C 199	239	242	277	281	294	296	377	397	406	418	18	54	65	108	110	168	174	179	197	199
C 201															108					
C 259																108				
C 266																	108			
C 270																		108		
C 290																				108
C 294																				
C 319																				
C 331																				
C 333		108																		
C 381																				
C 387							108													

can more easily determine the letter numbers of each *c* and each *h* that belong together.

FIGURE 4

C-85	belongs	to	H-193—distance		108 letters	
109	"	"	217	"	108	"
145	"	"	253	"	108	"
199	"	"	307	"	108	"
201	"	"	309	"	108	"
259	"	"	367	"	108	"
266	"	"	?	"	?	"
270	"	"	378	"	108	"
290	"	"	398	"	108	"
294	"	"	?	"	?	"
319	"	"	?	"	?	"
331	"	"	?	"	?	"
333	"	"	17	"	108	"
381	"	"	?	"	?	"
387	"	"	71	"	108	"

Figure 4 shows in more graphic form that with the exception of five cases there is a common distance of 108 letters between each *c* and one of the 20 *h*'s.

Let us therefore retype the original cipher message in vertical columns of 108 letters (Figure 5), and see whether such an arrangement throws any of these *c*'s and *h*'s together. Since there are 424 letters in the cipher message the first three vertical columns will contain 108 letters but the fourth column will contain only 100 letters. The lines are numbered consecutively for convenience of reference.

This arrangement has thrown together the digraph *ch* in the following lines.

Line	1	scha
"	37	iche
"	43	lich
"	54	eich
"	74	usch
"	85	chen
"	91	iche
"	93	schu

FIGURE 5

	1st column	2nd column	3rd column	4th column
1	s	c	h	a
2	e	n	p	a
3	o	d	e	t
4	f	t	a	l
5	n	d	b	e
6	a	r	b	e
7	t	z	i	c
8	u	b	l	i
9	p	e	s	c
10	k	m	e	x
11	a	u	s	r
12	s	k	o	n
13	i	k	o	p
14	h	o	e	r
15	e	l	e	g
16	i	s	t	a
17	h	e	n	a
18	b	l	o	w
19	b	z	u	s
20	n	d	z	u
21	u	n	k	t
22	e	n	d	e
23	r	a	m	m
24	s	u	l	a
25	d	e	n	i
26	a	b	e	r
27	u	f	u	n
28	s	k	i	a
29	n	b	i	s
30	n	p	u	n
31	l	s	r	u
32	r	a	m	t
33	s	t	r	e
34	e	a	n	d
35	g	s	z	e
36	g	e	w	a

	1st column	2nd column	3rd column	4th column
37	i	c	h	e
38	e	i	n	r
39	s	s	e	r
40	n	d	e	r
41	n	g	g	e
42	k	t	v	o
43	l	i	c	h
44	e	h	r	e
45	z	u	e	i
46	n	k	o	m
47	s	t	d	e
48	i	n	h	a
49	m	a	i	h
50	n	e	c	k
51	e	i	s	t
52	h	e	i	m
53	n	t	a	u
54	e	i	c	h
55	s	e	n	d
56	h	b	i	t
57	m	a	u	c
58	p	e	s	o
59	p	u	n	k
60	b	e	r	d
61	a	r	d	t
62	s	a	n	g
63	u	t	s	c
64	e	h	o	e
65	a	n	d	i
66	s	o	r	o
67	r	i	g	e
68	i	e	s	e
69	h	a	u	f
70	t	e	r	i
71	h	e	r	g
72	t	e	i	h

	1st column	2nd column	3rd column	4th column
73	e	h	e	i
74	u	s	c	h
75	r	d	e	r
76	m	a	g	e
77	v	e	r	l
78	n	a	c	i
79	s	i	s	t
80	m	a	u	f
81	e	k	a	i
82	a	n	s	u
83	i	e	s	e
84	n	t	p	u
85	c	h	e	n
86	o	n	a	l
87	u	n	t	e
88	a	n	g	e
89	s	e	r	l
90	i	e	s	s
91	i	c	h	e
92	n	d	e	r
93	s	c	h	u
94	n	k	o	n
95	r	d	e	m
96	n	k	t	a
97	v	o	r	z
98	e	n	u	n
99	g	e	s	a
100	d	s	e	i
101	e	d	e	
102	s	u	l	
103	n	e	c	
104	b	s	a	
105	t	z	u	
106	n	a	m	
107	n	d	t	
108	r	e	p	

Our first rearrangement of the original cipher has accounted for 8 of the 15 *c*'s. This is much better than we could have hoped for. Aside from this, we see in Figure 5 many common German syllables, and here and there either words or parts of words.

Note especially *peso*, line 58. As this message was brought across the border from Mexico it would not be too much to expect to find the Spanish word *peso*. Whether the reader is familiar with German or not, he must recognize many combinations of letters in Figure 5 which are common to any language. This will be more evident if he will again examine the original cipher which is obviously nothing more than a mixture of vowels and consonants that has no resemblance to any language.

It seems certain that we are on the right track, though it is difficult to believe that MI-8 is cleverer than the German cryptographers who obviously have not discovered a method for solving transposition ciphers or they would never have recommended such a system. Let us be fair to the German cryptographers. Perhaps German officials are like our own and do not take the recommendation of cryptographers as serious as they should.

We have already noted that 8 of our 15 *c*'s are properly placed, or at least they are followed by *h*. Let us see if we can place the remaining 7 *c*'s.

C, line 50, is followed by *k; ck* is a very common German digraph.

C, line 78, is followed by *i* in the four-letter group *n a c i*. This is most unusual because in pure German the letter *i* never follows *c*. Have we made an error? Perhaps the copyist has made an error, or the German who enciphered the message. If not, and we are on the right track, *n a c i* must be a group of letters from a foreign word. We have already noted the Spanish word *peso*. Perhaps *naci* is the beginning of the Spanish word *nacional—national*. This seems reasonable for in line 86 we find *onal*.

C-319, line 103, is the final letter of the trigraph *nec*. This *c* is apparently also not followed by *h*, for a reference to Figure 4 shows a question mark. As *nec* suggests no word, let us pass to the next *c*.

C-331, line 7, and *c*-381, line 57, have question marks after them in Figure 4. They either are not followed by *h* or the technical construction of the table used by the

Germans to encipher this document has separated them from their affinities.

The remaining digraphs *ch* are *c*-333 *h*-17 and *c*-387 *h*-71. If the lines in which these digraphs occur are brought together we have *peschena* and *utscherg*.

We have now accounted for all the digraphs *ch* and are well along in the solution of this document. Here and there we see words and parts of words and are tempted to try to join up the lines, but we must proceed cautiously. For if the cipher reveals any important information about Pablo Waberski, the suspected spy, we may need mathematical proof that we have arrived at the correct solution. Aside from this, it is always safer and often quicker to attempt to discover the underlying system. Once this is discovered all the letters of the cipher will fall into their proper places.

Let us examine again the eight-letter group *utscherg* that we have just placed together. Do these letters suggest a German word? By prefacing the letters *de* we have the German word for *German—Deutscher. g.* Let us therefore return to Figure 5 and search for a group ending in *de.* The first one we find is in line 47, *s t d e.*

By placing these letters before our eight-letter group we have *st. Deutscher. g.* Do these letters suggest another word; either one ending with *st,* or another beginning with *g*? It looks as if we have gone as far as we can. Suppose we start at another place.

Turn back to Figure 5 and search for a familiar word. Do you find a line that suggests a word? How about line 10, *k m e x.* The letter *x* is very uncommon in any language. For this reason we should be able to guess a word from the combination *k m e x.* Pablo Waberski had been arrested as he crossed the border from Mexico. *Mex* certainly suggests the German word for *Mexico—Mexiko.* Let us see if we can find a line beginning with *i k o,* the last three letters of *Mexiko.* This we find in line 13, *i k o p.* Placing these two groups together we now have *k. Mexiko. p.*

Does *k. Mexiko p.* suggest another word? Can you think of a word ending in *k* that might precede *Mexiko*? How about *Republik Mexiko*? Let us try this.

In line 8 we find *u b l i* and in line 108 we find *r e p.* By placing these in their proper order we now have *Re-*

publik Mexiko. p. Does the letter *p* suggest a word? If not we shall have to begin all over again.

Before doing this, however, let us summarize the words and groups we have brought together and see if we can discover a system, showing at the same time the lines in which the groups of letters have been discovered and the intervals or number of lines between the combination of groups.

FIGURE 6

Lines		Intervals
78–86	*nacional*	8
9–17	*peschena*	8
63–71	*utscherg*	8
47–63–71	*st. Deutscher. g*	16–8
10–13	*k. Mexiko. p*	3
108–8–10–13	*Republik Mexiko. p*	8–2–3

In order to follow the next analysis it will be necessary to understand what is meant by the word "intervals." Take the first case, for example. We found *naci* in line 78 and *onal* in line 86. The "interval" between line 78 and 86 is 8. In the last case we found *rep* in line 108, *ubli* in line 8, *kmex* in line 10, *ikop* in line 13. From line 108 to line 8, the interval is 8; from line 8 to line 10, the interval is 2; from line 10 to 13, the interval is 3. The intervals, then, are 8-2-3.

Figure 6 doesn't give a great deal to work with, but note the intervals 16-8 between the lines in which we discovered *st. Deutscher. g.* Note also the intervals between the lines of *Republik Mexiko. p*—8-2-3. These two groups give us the sequences 16-8 and 8-2-3.

Since the figure 8 is repeated in both sequences, let us drop 8 in one of them and join them together. We now have the sequence 16-8-2-3.

Let us therefore take *st. Deutscher. g*, interval 16-8, and join to it the lines in intervals 2-3.

The last four letters of *st. Deutscher. g* we find in line 71. Now beginning with line 71 and counting forward 2 lines, the next interval, we find *e h e i*, line 73. The next interval is 3; so the next line should be 76. Here we find *m a g e.* Let us now join *e h e i   m a g e* to *st. Deutscher. g.* This gives us *st. Deutscher. geheim. age.*

Geheim! Secret! *Deutscher geheim!* German secret! German secret what!

The last three letters are *a g e.* Is it possible this stands for *agent? German secret agent!*

Yes. We find it in line 84.

> ### st. Deutscher. Geheim. agent. pu.
> ### German   secret   agent

Without question we are dealing with a spy document. Some one is mentioned as a German secret agent. Who?

Can it be Pablo Waberski?

It will take MI-8 all night to answer this question, for every step must be carefully recorded. There must be no mistakes. Guesses, yes. But guesses that are later confirmed by a mathematical formula.

The word *agent* gives us the next sequence 8; and this in turn reveals other sequences. At last we piece together the entire sequence, 16-8-2-3-8-12-8-11; then the sequence began to repeat itself.

Now a sequence of 8 represents 9 groups or lines as we have termed them in Figure 5. The figure 9 is significant for it factors into 108, the number of lines that we are dealing with. Nine times 12 equals 108.

To expedite the solution we now arranged the 108 lines into a rectangle 9 by 12 (Figure 7). This without question was the manner in which the original text was enciphered.

By tracing the sequences 16-8-2-3-8-12-8-11 backward and forward we find that we can read the entire message by shifting or transporting the horizontal lines, writing line 2 first, line 9 second, line 8 third, line 1 fourth, line 4 fifth, line 3 sixth, line 6 seventh, line 5 eighth, and line 7 ninth. This gives us Figure 8, page 104.

Keeping in mind the sequences 16-8-2-3-8-12-8-11 we can now read the message by beginning at column 1 and following the diagonal lines. Then with column 2; column 3, etc.

Let us type this message in horizontal lines so that we can more easily check up the sequences (Fig. 9). Note that in every column the sequence remains the same. This is ample proof that we have arrived at the correct solution.

FIGURE 7

1 scha	10 kmex	19 bzus	28 skia	37 iche	46 nkom	55 send	64 ehoe	73 ehei	82 ansu	91 iche	100 dsei
2 enpa	11 ausr	20 ndzu	29 nbis	38 einr	47 stde	56 hbit	65 andi	74 usch	83 iese	92 nder	101 ede
3 odet	12 skon	21 unkt	30 npun	39 sser	48 inha	57 mauc	66 soro	75 rder	84 ntpu	93 schu	102 sul
4 ftal	13 ikop	22 ende	31 lsru	40 nder	49 maih	58 peso	67 rige	76 mage	85 chen	94 nkon	103 nec
5 ndbe	14 hoer	23 ramm	32 ramt	41 ngge	50 neck	59 punk	68 iese	77 verl	86 onal	95 rdem	104 bsa
6 arbe	15 eleg	24 sula	33 stre	42 ktvo	51 eist	60 berd	69 hauf	78 naci	87 unte	96 nkta	105 tzu
7 tzic	16 ista	25 deni	34 eand	43 lich	52 heim	61 ardt	70 teri	79 sist	88 ange	97 vorz	106 nam
8 ubli	17 hena	26 aber	35 gsze	44 ehre	53 ntau	62 sang	71 herg	80 mauf	89 serl	98 enun	107 ndt
9 pesc	18 blow	27 ufun	36 gewa	45 zuei	54 eich	63 utsc	72 teih	81 ekai	90 iess	99 gesa	108 rep

FIGURE 8

Column:	5	3	8	9	4	6	7	1	10	11	2	12
Line 2	2 enpa	11 ausr	20 ndsu	29 nkis	38 erhr	47 stle	56 hibt	65 ahdi	74 usbb	83 icse	92 ndcr	101 ede
Line 9	9 peuc	18 blew	27 ufkn	36 gewa	45 zulu	54 eilb	63 utse	72 trhb	81 ekli	90 ieb	99 gese	108 rep
Line 8	8 ubli	17 hcsa	26 alter	35 gsse	44 elhe	53 ntau	62 sahg	71 hesg	80 mauf	89 scel	98 ento	107 ndt
Line 1	7 scha	16 kmer	25 bzus	34 skna	43 iche	52 nkbm	61 send	70 ehoe	79 eilei	88 arsu	97 iche	106 diei
Line 4	3 ftbl	12 ikop	21 erde	30 lssu	39 noer	48 mash	57 pcso	66 rige	75 mage	84 chen	93 nkbn	102 nsc
Line 3	6 odet	15 skon	24 urkt	33 npan	42 sser	51 inhe	60 msuc	69 sovo	78 rdor	87 ntpu	96 schu	105 sll
Line 6	5 arbe	14 eleg	23 suba	32 stke	41 ktvo	50 eik	59 besd	68 hauf	77 mei	86 utte	95 nkte	104 tzu
Line 5	4 ndbe	13 hoer	22 ramn	31 rawt	40 ngse	49 neek	58 punk	67 iese	76 vesl	85 onel	94 rdben	103 bsa
Line 7	1 tzic	10 isla	19 deni	28 eand	37 lich	46 helm	55 srdt	64 teri	73 sist	82 ange	91 vorz	100 nalm

FIGURE 9

	65	81	89	91	94	102	6	14	25
1	andi	ekai	serl	iche	nkon	sul	arbe	hoer	deni
	92	108	8	10	13	21	33	41	52
2	nder	rep	ubli	kmex	ikop	unkt	stre	ngge	heim
	11	27	35	37	40	48	60	68	79
3	ausr	ufun	gsze	iche	nder	inha	berd	iese	sist
	38	54	62	64	67	75	87	95	106
4	einr	eich	sang	ehoe	rige	rder	unte	rdem	nam
	2	18	26	28	31	39	51	59	70
5	enpa	blow	aber	akia	lsru	sser	eist	punk	teri
	47	63	71	73	76	84	96	104	7
6	stde	utsc	herg	ehei	mage	ntpu	nkta	bsa	tzic
	56	72	80	82	85	93	105	5	16
7	hbit	teih	mauf	ansu	chen	schu	tzu	ndbe	ista
	20	36	44	46	49	57	69	77	88
8	ndzu	gewa	ehre	nkom	maih	mauc	hauf	verl	ange
	29	45	53	55	58	66	78	86	97
9	nbis	zuei	ntau	send	peso	soro	naci	onal	vorz
	74	90	98	100	103	3	15	23	34
10	usch	iess	enun	dsei	nec	odet	eleg	ramm	eand
	83	99	107	1	4	12	24	32	43
11	iese	gesa	ndt	scha	ftal	skon	sula	ramt	lich
	101	9	17	19	22	30	42	50	61
12	ede	pesc	hena	bzus	ende	npun	ktvo	neck	ardt

Sequence in each of the above lines is 16-8-2-3-8-12-8-11:

After dividing Figure 9 into German words, it reads:

Decipherment

An die Kaiserlichen Konsular-Behoerden in der Republik Mexiko Punkt.

Strenggeheim Ausrufungszeichen!

Der Inhaber dieses ist ein Reichsangehœriger der unter dem namen Pablo Waberski als Russe reist punkt Er ist deutscher geheim-agent punkt Absatz ich bittn ihm auf ansuchen schutz und Beistand zu gewæhren komma ihm auch auf, Verlangen bis zu ein tausend pesos oro nacional vorzuschiessen und seine Code-telegramme an diese Gesandtschaft als konsularamtliche Depeschen abzusenden punkt

VON ECK(H)ARDT

It was daylight before the message was completely deciphered and translated. It was too late to telephone Van Deman. Aside from this I hesitated to telephone the fact that the Waberski document had been deciphered. Since it was Sunday, he would not be at the office before ten o'clock. The message had produced too much excitement for sleep; so there seemed nothing to do but wait for him.

I tried to appear calm when Colonel Van Deman entered his office. He seemed a bit surprised when he found me waiting.

"What's on your mind, Yardley?" he asked as he sat down at his desk.

"I have a very important document for you," I began, and I think my voice trembled a bit; "but I hesitated to telephone you—the message seemed too important to telephone."

He made no comment and I handed him a translation of the Waberski cipher.

Translation

To The Imperial Consular Authorities in the Republic of Mexico.

Strictly Secret!

The bearer of this is a subject of the Empire who travels as a Russian under the name of Pablo Waberski. He is a German secret agent.

Please furnish him on request protection and assistance, also advance him on demand up to one thousand pesos of Mexican gold and send his code telegrams to this embassy as official consular dispatches.

Von Eckhardt.

Van Deman read the translation over and over again.

"It is a translation of the Waberski cipher," I explained. "It is addressed to all German Consuls in Mexico and signed by the German Minister von Eckhardt."

Van Deman leaned back in his chair.

"A most amazing document," he said. "It ought to hang Waberski." Then, "What kind of a cipher was it?"

"Here is the German from which we made a translation," I began, handing him the German text. "It is a German transposition cipher. The address, signature and the message itself were first written in German and then by a prearranged diagram the letters were mixed up. Our problem was to discover the formula by which the letters were disarranged."

"Have you discovered the diagram?"

"Yes."

"Please offer my sincere congratulations to the personnel of MI-8," he said. "If for no other reason, the decipherment of this document justifies your bureau."

For an hour or more we discussed the decipherment of

the Waberski document, and the feasibility, now that we had discovered the German espionage method of identifying their secret agents, of drafting identification ciphers along the line of the Waberski cipher for use by our own agents in Mexico, so that they could pose as German spies.

On February sixteenth Pablo Waberski, manacled and under heavy guard, was taken by train to San Antonio, and from there to the military prison at Fort Sam Houston. Though carefully guarded while incarcerated there and awaiting trial, Waberski composed a cipher message and attempted to have it smuggled out of prison. It was intercepted and sent to MI-8 for decipherment.

It was addressed to Señor K. Tanusch, Calle Tacuba 81, Mexico, D. F. The translation reads:

> Need my note-book which I left in Mr. Paglasch's safe. Very necessary. The address, Señor Jesus Andrada, Box 681, San Antonio, is absolutely safe and it will be delivered to me in secret. I have forgotten certain names and addresses which I need in order to show the people here that I am innocent. Need money.

Waberski obviously recognized that he was in a desperate position.

In the hope of intercepting the reply, our authorities mailed the cipher message. But no answer ever came.

Finally in August, 1918, Pablo Waberski, whose real name was Lather Witcke, was tried before a military court. He was charged with being a German spy. The trial lasted two days. He was found guilty, and the court sentenced him to be hanged by the neck until dead.

The failure of Pablo Waberski, like that of many other spies, was due to the skill of MI-8. As our skill increased, our power as an organization was not only to affect the life of a single person but was also to shape the decisions of governments.

CHAPTER VIII

A Stolen Code

ONE morning my correspondent at the Department of State called me on the telephone and asked me to come over as soon as possible. The whole Department of State is controlled by a small clique in the diplomatic corps, and this man was considered one of its most brilliant leaders. He was a staunch supporter of MI-8 and dealt directly with the Secretary of State.

He was positively the most mysterious and secretive man I have ever known in my sixteen years of experience with the United States Government. Although I dealt personally with him for several years, I know less about the man now than I did the first day I saw him. He was almost a human sphinx and when he did talk his voice was so low that I had to strain my ears to catch the words.

He offered me a cigarette without any greeting and lighted one himself. A good minute passed before he spoke. Being accustomed to this procedure I always forced him to open the conversation. Sometimes several minutes passed.

"The Spanish code?" he almost whispered.

By this he meant when were we going to be able to read Spanish diplomatic messages. Our powerful wireless station on the coast of Maine was intercepting hundreds of Spanish diplomatic code telegrams passing between the Spanish Ambassador at Berlin and the Spanish Foreign office at Madrid. These telegrams were handled by the Nauen wireless station "POZ" in Germany and station "EGC" in Spain. Besides these messages we received of course those sent and received by the Spanish Ambassador in Washington.

"Ten people are working on the Spanish code," I replied. "We are progressing slowly. We have identified the meanings of a few code words, not many, but enough to convince us that in time we will be able to read the messages as quickly as the Spanish Embassy. How long it will take, I can not say. Spain uses several codes, but they are all of the same type. When one is solved, the others will fall apart rapidly."

Neither of us spoke a word for several minutes, but he looked me squarely in the eyes. I turned away and put out my cigarette. What goes on in the man's brain, I mused.

"Can't *you* do something about it?"

"I'm doing all I can."

Another long pause.

"Are you sure?"

I wasn't sure what he meant, but I imagined that I knew.

"I'll do my best," I replied, and that ended the conference.

From other sources I knew that Spain was suspected of assisting German espionage. This was why MI-8 was so often asked the question, "Have you solved the Spanish code?" Only the day before, my chief had made inquiries. It began to look as if I had better take drastic measures.

If every one was in such a stew for quick action it was obvious that I must assist my cryptographers with some information; perhaps a scrap of paper, a single decoded message. Why not try to steal a Spanish code and photograph it?

Before leaving the State Department I copied the histories of each member of the diplomatic staff of the Spanish Embassy. I must see a certain Captain on my return.

A great Intelligence organization must necessarily contain many strange characters, but the strangest of all was a certain Captain whom I shall refer to as Captain Brown. He had been commissioned for no other reason, as far as I was ever able to determine, than that when a woman agent was required for espionage to tear a secret from some poor devil, he could, on a moment's notice, find a woman to fit any requirement. Old or young, fat or thin, beautiful or homely, blonde or brunette—it made no difference to Captain Brown.

His duties were not very arduous and I found him smoking alone when I returned from the State Department. Perhaps the Captain could manage a little gum-shoe work.

"Sit down," he greeted me.

"How's business, Captain?" I asked.

"Not bad," he smiled.

"What's become of that beautiful blonde you sent to Miami to lie in the warm sand with the —— Consul?"

He pulled his feet off the desk and jerked out a drawer. "Rest your eyes on this," and he handed me a snapshot. "Just came in this morning. That's the Consul beside her. He's sure a handsome brute in a bathing suit. Look like young lovers, don't they?"

They were sitting on the beach, protected by a large sunshade. Her right hand was in his and with the other she poured fine sand on her slender legs. Her head was tilted back and her smile showed magnificent flashing teeth.

"She's beautiful," I said, returning the picture.

"Beautiful! She's my masterpiece!" he exclaimed. "The Consul won't hold out long. We get reports from her every day now. Why, he flirted with her for two weeks before she would even look at him. That's what makes a man fall. He's in love with her now, crazy about her. In another week he'll spill his connections with the German Secret Service."

As a matter of fact, in another week she did become his mistress. This, of course, was all according to plan. The trouble, however, was that she also fell in love with the handsome Consul, and the reports stopped coming in. Women agents were of little value for this reason, but there was always a chance.

"I've got a job for you, Captain. I——"

"What for?"

"I'm not going to tell you what for. I want a Washington society girl who——"

"I don't deal in society girls."

"You ought to. This girl must speak Spanish like a native. She must have not only culture and charm, but also brains. She must be a conversationalist. She must have as her background the nationalistic traditions of the Navy, or the Army, or the diplomatic corps. Her age must be close to thirty. All these requirements she absolutely must have. As for beauty—I'll let you be the judge. But I want to see her here to-morrow afternoon."

He hesitated a moment before replying. Then, "If you would tell me what it is all about it would help."

"I can't tell you."

"All right. I'll go see Mrs. Blakeslee.* She rules the society roster in Washington. I'll give you a buzz when your lady friend shows up."

Van Deman had been ordered abroad. We had a new director of Military Intelligence now, General Churchill. As he was very close to the Chief of Staff, General March, he was to have a freer hand than Van Deman. Although I had had several conferences with the new Director, it was with some misgivings that I approached his office. He had seemed favorably impressed with MI-8, but how would he react to this venture?

Several officers were waiting to see him, but as chief of a section I had preference and did not have long to wait.

He was alone, talking to the Department of Justice over his private wire when I opened the door. Unlike Van Deman, he had a splendid figure and carried himself like a line officer. His eyes were gray and piercing. His chin was firm, his mouth straight, but he could smile on occasions. Although his air was that of a soldier, there were no formalities between him and his subordinates. All of us were holding our minds open to this new Chief, but it did not take us long to discover we were serving under one of the greatest executives developed during the war.

He finally hung up the receiver and asked me to sit down. "What is it, Yardley?"

"The State Department called me over this morning. They are restless about these Spanish messages."

"We all are."

He had spent several hours in MI-8 and knew in a superficial way the enormous task of solving an unknown code.

"General Churchill," I began, "the Spanish Codes will eventually be solved. When, I can not say, without any outside help. But a successful Cryptographic Bureau should have its secret agents to ferret out scraps of information about foreign codes. I shall not take your time with details. Generalizing, I can say this: the types of codes and ciphers are almost infinite. A cryptographer working behind closed doors must first determine the type. Even with unlimited material, unlimited clerical assistance, it may be months before he can determine the type, much less begin the ramifications of analysis that lead to solution. A cryptographer should not be required to work in the dark on such

* For obvious reasons the correct name can not be given.

problems. He should be furnished information of this sort by the Intelligence Department. His job, even then, will require all of his ingenuity."

"I can very well appreciate that. What do you recommend?"

I then told him of my conversation with Captain Brown and what I planned to have the woman do.

"Go ahead," he told me. "Is that all?"

Should I offer the rest of my plan? This seemed an opportune time.

"No," I said, "that is only the beginning. Briefly, I want to send an agent to South America to obtain a photographic copy of one of the Spanish Government's codes."

"Whom would you send?" he asked.

"You have of course been informed of Boyd."*

"Yes."

"I want to use him for this job."

"But he's our best South American agent!" protested Churchill.

"I know that," I answered.

The General looked at me and frowned for a moment. Then he said, "Talk the matter over with him. Make your plans, estimate the amount of money required, then both come to see me."

Boyd, I soon learned, was not in the city and would not return until the following day. I arranged, however, to see him in my office just as soon as he arrived.

Late in the afternoon of the next day, Captain Brown called me on the inter-office dictagraph and asked if I could come down. He seemed to be in good humor.

"Have you found her?" I asked eagerly.

"You come on down," he chuckled, "and see for yourself. And say, that was a good tip you gave me."

When I entered his room I had a most obvious reason for believing that the Captain was an excellent judge of beauty. Most of his types were blondes, but this girl was brunette. She was dressed in a dark elegant suit and small close-fitting hat. Her eyes were brown and large. As Captain Brown introduced us, her full red lips parted in an engaging smile. The Captain himself beamed happily, obviously proud of his discovery. The two seemed to be on very good terms, for when I entered the office they were

* For obvious reasons the correct name can not be given.

talking like old friends. After the introduction, Captain Brown handed me three or four typewritten pages and left us alone.

Slowly I read over the secret report of this girl's history, wondering how I should proceed. This business was scarcely in my line.

"What has the Captain told you, Miss Abbott?"* I began.

"Nothing, except a very amusing story," she said.

I felt a certain reluctance about taking her into my confidence, not because her report was by any means discouraging, but because I had heard so many stories of the failures of women agents. But there was always the chance of success; and even if she did tip off our hand, all that she could disclose would be the fact that the United States Government was making an effort to solve the Spanish Government's codes. Should Spain learn of this it would mean a change of codes. We had already made a great deal of progress and I knew I would have to impress this on Miss Abbott.

"You have no idea why you were asked to come here?" I began again.

"No. Mrs. Blakeslee telephoned me that I was wanted here. She gave no reason. She was very mysterious about the matter, but she always is."

"You know the Spanish Ambassador?" I asked her.

"Yes."

"Any of the Embassy staff?"

"Slightly."

Perhaps, I thought, the best plan would be to tell her as little as possible until I had an opportunity to judge her character and discretion.

"You could cultivate a better acquaintance with some of these men?"

"One might." She smiled. "One sees them here and there."

She must be burning up with curiosity, for she knew she was being questioned in the office of Military Intelligence. She asked no questions, and whether that was a good sign or a bad one, I was not sure. At least she was intelligent and possessed rare beauty.

"We wish to know which Spanish diplomatic secretary has direct charge of the diplomatic code books. Just his

---

* For obvious reasons the correct name can not be given.

name; no more. Do you think you could find this out for me—in a casual way, without attracting any attention?"

"I think so," was her confident reply. "That doesn't sound very difficult."

"Very well. Come to see me just as soon as you are successful. If you are interested in this sort of thing there may be opportunities for you later."

"I am more than interested, of course. But I must be sure of my instructions. You want the name of the man who has charge of the diplomatic codes, and you want his name without the Embassy suspecting that any one is interested in the matter."

"Exactly."

I think she rather pitied my inexperience, for at the door she smiled and said, "I'll be back to-morrow."

When I went up-stairs I found Boyd in my office. He was a well-built man with thick black hair and an alertness about him which attracted one. He was extremely intelligent and dependable. We immediately began a discussion of the probems before us, and he was tremendously interested.

Boyd had a fine reputation in successful espionage. He spoke Spanish like a native, having spent his whole life in South America as a representative of New York bankers. He had an intimate acquaintance with every one who was worth knowing in the southern Republics.

"Just how would you go about getting a copy of the code?" I asked.

"Now that isn't a fair question," he returned. "If I am allowed a reasonable appropriation I'll get you a copy of the code and make an accounting of the expense. But whether or not I have to bribe an official, employ a safecracker, or waylay a messenger, I should prefer to keep to myself."

I laughed. "That's fair enough. How much money should we ask for?"

He thought a while before answering.

"Suppose we say twenty thousand dollars."

"I think we can arrange for that sum," I said.

Boyd was pacing up and down, silently, and I did not interrupt him. Finally he said:

"There are going to be a great many difficulties. I shall first go to the Panama Canal Zone and see what I can do there. If unsuccessful, I will proceed to Colombia and then to Chile. My best connections are in these places. But I want nothing to do with the Intelligence officer at Panama; and nothing to do with American representatives in these other countries. I will have to work alone."

"That seems a good plan," I agreed with him.

"Should it be necessary to establish connections with our representatives, I must have some means of identification."

"We can follow the usual practise."

"Yes. But we shall need to establish cable communications with Washington. I may need instructions. I may want to report my progress. How?"

"Of course," I replied, "you could have your cables sent through our official representatives but that would disclose your identity. As you well know, cables, unless they are from our known representatives or those of neutral countries, can not be sent in a private code. All other cables must be sent in plain language, or, if in code, must be encoded in one of the standard commercial codes. If sent in a commercial code, the censor, before passing it, decodes the message and if he considers that the message might contain a hidden meaning, the cable is never forwarded."

"I can't have a censor reading these messages," he said.

"Of course not. We will have to assume that you are in the same position as a German agent. You are in Central America with information you wish to cable to Washington. This cable must be sent to the cover-address in Washington, to some one who can bear an investigation without uncovering any suspicion."

"The cover-addresses at both ends are simple enough in our case," Boyd replied, "but we will have to fool the censor. Send what appears to be an innocent message in code, but which is, in reality, something else."

"I'm coming to that," I said. "We will have to beat the censor. That's easy. I will write up instructions tonight. To-morrow you can go over them, memorize them. Then I'll turn you over to the Secret-Ink Laboratory. We may need to use the mail. You will be given a secret ink, will receive instructions in its use, how to prepare your letters, and how to develop the secret writing in our letters to you."

Boyd nodded. Then he asked, "What method will you use for defeating the censor by cable?"

"Well, we can use a modification of the German method. Madame Victorica, Germany's famous woman spy, was arrested in New York a few months ago. We have intercepted many letters intended for her and have developed secret writing in a great many of them. The secret writing in one of these communications gives detailed instructions for sending cables which will pass the British Censor. The method is ridiculously simple, but would escape the eyes of a skilled cryptographer. Suppose I show you her method now, while we are talking about it."

With this I opened the safe and pulled out a file of papers. Boyd's eyes followed me with interest.

"Just before we entered the war, she received the following, apparently an innocent cablegram from Germany," I said, and showed it to him:

From Germany
To Schmidt & Holtz, New York

February 4, 1917

Give Victorica following message from her lawyers lower terms impossible will give further instructions earliest and leave nothing untried very poor market will quote however soonest our terms want meanwhile bond have already obtained license.

Disconto

"This cablegram appears on its face to be harmless," I said, "and seems to concern a lawsuit or a sale. In any case, it readily escaped the British Censor for Victorica was unknown at that time."

I now pulled out another document. "Here," I said, "is a photograph of the letter containing instructions for decoding cables of this type. You can see the secret writing as developed in our laboratory.

"The first consonant of each word in a clear text message stands for a figure. In the case of this particular cable the equivalents are:

$$1 = d \ t$$
$$2 = y \ n \ z \ y$$
$$3 = m \ w$$
$$4 = q \ r$$
$$5 = s \ sh$$
$$6 = b \ p$$
$$7 = v \ f \ ph$$
$$8 = h \ ch \ j$$
$$9 = g \ k \ x$$
$$0 = l \ c$$

"If we apply to this table of values the first consonants of the cablegram already quoted we have:

0 = lower		3 = market	
1 = terms		3 = will	
* = impossible		4 = quote	
3 = will		8 = however	
9 = give		5 = soonest	
7 = further		* our	
* instructions		1 = terms	
* earliest		3 = want	
* and		3 = meanwhile	
0 = leave		6 = bond	
2 = nothing		8 = have	
* untried		* already	
7 = very		* obtained	
6 = poor		0 = license	

"Dividing these figures in groups of five, we have 01397 02763 34851 33680. The instructions were to read the 5-figure groups backward. We then have 33680 34851 02763 01397.

"The most widely used code is the ABC, which may be found in almost any cable office. Her instructions were to apply these five-figure groups to this code. The message then reads:

33680 = Remittance sent to-day
34851 = as safe as possible
02763 = you must arrange immediately or it is useless
01397 = on account of political affairs

"Ingenious, of course," answered Boyd, "and safe too."
"All right. I'll draw up a modification of this system and see you in the morning."

I was surprised to find Miss Abbott in the reception-room when I reached the office next morning. There was an air of excitement about her. Her eyes were flashing.
"What! Already?" I exclaimed.
"The name is Gomez,"† she smiled.
"How did you learn it so quickly?"

---

* Words beginning with vowels are to be disregarded.
† For obvious reasons the correct name can not be given.

117

"Quite by accident I ran into one of the Embassy Staff last night. During our conversation I mentioned that I was seriously thinking of doing something more interesting than promoting Liberty Bond sales. The United States was adding to its staffs both here and abroad. I couldn't type or take dictation, but perhaps I could be a file clerk, or perhaps decode telegrams. Was it so terribly difficult? And so on. Finally the name of Gomez came up, and mention of his connection with codes."

"You say 'quite by accident.' Or was it by design?"

She said nothing. Her eyes laughed at me.

"Do you know Gomez?" I asked.

"Not now, but——"

"Then you wish to continue?"

"Of course. I'd love to."

When we were alone in my office I showed her a series of Spanish diplomatic messages.

Example of Original Spanish Diplomatic
Code Telegram

                                                              W U
4-8-18   Govt Code
Dato Ministre Affaires Etrangeres G Madrid Ambassador Espagne Washn

30116	2379	1626	6350	0675	7747	4396	4327
2424	4338	0803	3883	1214	0571	1638	1215
1899	3369	1214	1703	5156	1214	5180	1703
1093	7276	7632	0414	7987	2413	8330	7096
6815	0733	1214	1126	8676	5686	6815	0673
3780	8373						

Dato Ministre Affaires Etrangeres (stop)

"One of our problems is the solving of Spain's diplomatic codes," I explained to her. "These groups of figures represent a letter, a syllable, a word, a phrase or, perhaps in some cases, an entire sentence. Analysis will finally determine the meanings of these code-groups. We have, already, scraps of information in our possession about the Spanish code system, but we need to know much more. Any information you obtain from Mr. Gomez may save us months of labor.

"For instance," I continued, "we want to know the size of the code, whether or not it is alphabetically arranged

118

Herbert O. Yardley
Outside of State Department Code Room

Page of Werner Tismer, prisoner-of-war letter. The translation is in Chapter II.

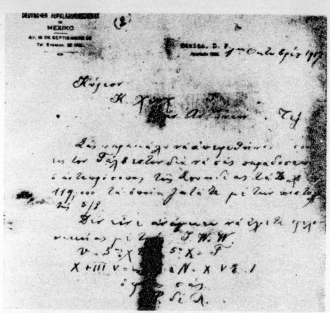

Secret-ink, modern Greek development of sheet of blank paper found in the shoe-heel of a woman suspect, who was arrested as she crossed the Mexican border. The translation is in Chapter III.

British Secret-Ink Laboratory, responsible for the capture of many famous German spies.

A message written with invisible ink on the inside of the flaps of an envelope by a German prisoner of war. The message contained information concerning conditions prevailing in the camp.

Opposite, above: Secret writing in German between the lines of a letter in French from Brazil to Germany. The message referred to the raid of the German submarine U-53 on American ports and the impression produced in South America by this event.

Opposite, below: This shows how a letter looks after it has been treated for secret ink. Each streak is made by a different reagent or chemical.

Pages one and four of the "Patricia" letter, addressed to a German cover-address in Mexico. An important spy message was written between the lines in invisible ink.

Pages two and three of the "Patricia" spy letter. The mysterious symbols have never been deciphered.

Portion of Madame Victorica's scarf impregnated with "F" secret ink.
This invisible ink was used for communicating with the enemy.

The famous "Maud" letter. Note the German secret-ink writing as
developed by our chemists, running crosswise to the "open" letter,
written in English.

Kölnische Volkszeitung

Morgen- Mittags- Abend-Ausgabe.

Köln, den 4. Februar 19..

S. H. Herrn

N e w - Y o r k , N.Y.

U. S. A.

Sehr geehrter hochwürdiger Herr!

Gestatten Sie uns, die Ueberbringerin dieses Briefes, Frau Maria v.K de Victorica, angelegentlichst zu empfehlen mit der Bitte, ihr nach Möglichkeit förderlich sein zu wollen.

Mit vorzüglicher Hochachtung ergebenst

One of Madame Victorica's credentials to the priesthood in America.

7/8/17

My dear Mrs Victorica,

I am very pleased to hear from you that you had such a good passage under such circumstances, your message delighted my manager very much, of course I informed all your other friends, including her Father.

Will you meet my friend there? I am very busy + plenty work has still to be done, but the most important thing is, to have good nurses, such

Page one of spy letter addressed to Madame Victorica. This letter contained invisible-ink instructions for the fantastic, holy-figure plot.

Lather Witcke, alias Pablo Waberski, the only German spy in America during the war who received the death sentence.
Photo by Brown Bros.

Opposite, above: Cipher notes made by Pablo Waberski while in prison awaiting trial. The message begged for assistance from German spy headquarters in Mexico City.

Opposite, below: Cover to Spanish Government's code book, photographed by secret agent.

Cifra 74

Para la correspondencia reservada

entre

El Consulado de España en Panamá

y

El Ministerio de Estado y la Legación en Washington

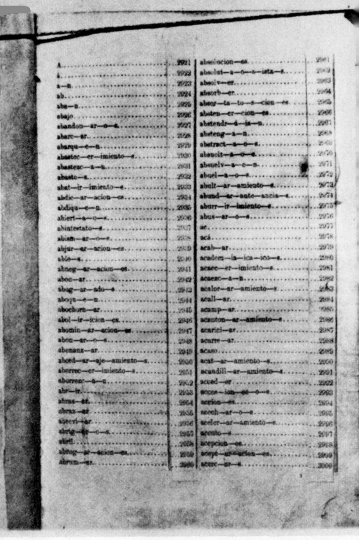

A	2921
á	2922
a—n	2923
ab	2924
aba—n	2925
abajo	2926
abandon—ar—o—s	2927
abarc—ar	2928
abarqu—e—n	2929
abastec—er—imiento—s	2930
abastezc—a—n	2931
abasto—s	2932
abat—ir—imiento—s	2933
abdic—ar—acion—es	2934
abdiqu—e—n	2935
abiert—a—o—s	2936
abintestato—s	2937
abism—ar—o—s	2938
abjur—ar—acion—es	2939
able—s	2940
abneg—ar—acion—es	2941
aboc—ar	2942
abog—ar—ado—s	2943
aboy—e—n	2944
abochorn—ar	2945
abol—ir—icion—es	2946
abomin—ar—acion—es	2947
abon—ar—o—s	2948
abonanz—ar	2949
abord—ar—aje—amiento—s	2950
aborrec—er—imiento—s	2951
aborrezc—a—n	2952
abr—ir	2953
abras—ar	2954
abraz—ar	2955
abrevi—ar	2956
abrig—ar—o—s	2957
abril	2958
abrog—ar—acion—es	2959
abrum—ar	2960
absolucion—es	2961
absolut—a—o—s—ista—s	2962
absolv—er	2963
absorb—er	2964
absorb—ta—to—s—cion—es	2965
absten—er—cion—es	2966
abstend—á—ia—n	2967
absteng—a—n	2968
abstract—a—o—s	2969
absuelt—a—o—s	2970
absuelv—a—e—n	2971
abuel—a—o—s	2972
abult—ar—amiento—s	2973
abund—ar—ante—ancia—s	2974
aburr—ir—imiento—s	2975
abus—ar—o—s	2976
ac	2977
acá	2978
acab—ar	2979
academ—ia—ica—ico—s	2980
acaec—er—imiento—s	2981
acaezc—a—n	2982
acalor—ar—amiento—s	2983
acall—ar	2984
acamp—ar	2985
acanton—ar—amiento—s	2986
acarici—ar	2987
acarre—ar	2988
acaso	2989
acat—ar—amiento—s	2990
acaudill—ar—amiento—s	2991
acaud—er	2992
acce—ion—ad—o—s	2993
accion—es	2994
acech—ar—o—s	2995
aceler—ar—amiento—s	2996
acento—s	2997
acepcion—es	2998
acept—ar—acion—es	2999
acerc—ar—s	3000

A page of photographed Spanish Government's code book. Note the string at top of page used by secret agent to hold the book open while photographing.

00 **Binseninudsen** (Japan)	50 **Blaavands** Huk
01 bino	51 black
02 **Bintang** L	52 **Black** Deep F.-Sch.
03 **Binz** (Rügen)	53 **Black Head**
04 bio	54 **Black Isle**
05 bioya	55 **Blackeney Overfalls** Untf.
06 bioye	56 **Blackpool**
07 bir	57 **Black River**
08 **Bird** Id.	58 **Black Rock**
09 **Bird Key**	59 **Blacksod** B.
10 biri	60 **Blackwater** B.
11 biria	61 **Blackwater** Bnk.
12 **Birkenhead**	62 **Blackwell** I.
13 **Birma**	63 **Blair**, Port —
14 **Birmingham**	64 **Blairhafen** (Malacca)
15 **Biscaya Golf**	65 blas
16 **Bisceglie** (Ital. O.-Küste)	66 blanc
17 bisch	67 **Blanc**, Port —
18 bise	68 blanca
19 **Bisé** (Frkr.)	69 **Blanca** I.
20 **Bishop** Id.	70 blanche
21 **Bishop Rock**	71 **Blanche**
22 **Bishop Auckland**	72 **Blanche** B. (Neu-Pommern)
23 **Bishop, North-**	73 **Blanc Nez** K. (Frkr.)
24 **Bishop, South-**	74 blanco
25 **Bishop u. Clerks** Bnk.	75 **Blanco** K.
26 **Bismarck** +	76 blank
27 **Bismarck** Archip.	77 **Blankenberghe**
28 **Bismarck-Berg** Ft. (Tsingtau)	78 **Blanquilla** I.
29 **Bismarckburg**	79 blas
30 **Bissagos** In.	80 **Blas, San-**
31 **Bissao**	81 **Blasket** I.
32 bit	82 blat
33 **Bittersee, Gr.** —	83 **Blauort** Sd.
34 **Bittersee, Kl.** —	84 **Blavet**
35 bitz	85 **Blaye**
36 biv	86 ble
37 biz	87 blee
38 **Bizerte**	88 blem
39 bj	89 blen
40 **Björkö** (Rußl.)	90 **Blenheim**
41 **Björkö Sund**	91 bler
42 **Björn** I.	92 bles
43 **Björneborg** (Finnland)	93 bless
44 **Björnnabben** (Storgrund)	94 blet
45 **Björnö**	95
46 **Björnsund**	96
47 **Bjaröklubb**	97
48 bl	98
49 bla	99

A page of the German High Fleet code, stolen by a secret agent
from within the German Admiralty.

TABLA N.º 3

AMERICAN COMMISSION to NEGOTIATE PEACE

PASS

No. 92

Permit Bearer YARDLEY, H.O., Capt.

To enter HOTEL CRILLON,

PLACE DE LA CONCORDE

R. H. VAN DEMAN
Colonel, General Staff
U.S.A.

CONFIDENCIAL N.º 2

Santiago, 17 de Abril de 1918.

				1	А, Б	1 4
ач, ная	баю	бес	бог (бож)			
аэроплан, ов	бе, г	би (бй)	бок, ов	бр, а	В, Г	0
аэродром	бед (бѣд)	бир, ск	бол, от	бре	Д, Е	2
аю, тся	беж (бѣж)	бит	боль, н	бригад, а	Ж, З, И, I, Й, К	5
ающ, ій	без	бл, а	болѣ, е	бро, н	Л, М, Н	7
ая (ах)	безъ перемѣнъ	близ, и	бох, б	брос (брош)	О	1
Б.	бех (бен)	блинд. ировав	бон	бря	П, Р	6
ба, я	бензин, у	бя, о	бор, а	бу, дут	С, Т	9
бат, аліон	бер, ег	бо, и	бот, у	буд, ьте	У, Ф	3
батаре, я	бере, ж	бой	бота, йте	буе (бую)	Х, Ь, Ц, Ч	8
	2	**0**	**3**			

Page one of Russian code book.

Opposite, above: Chilean table for enciphering their code messages, and official letter from the Foreign Office, obtained in mysterious manner by Miss Abbott.

Opposite, below: Pass issued to the author at the Peace Conference.

Original Japanese code message in groups of ten letters, and the first step in the decipherment of the Japanese text. This famous telegram contains Tokyo's secret instructions to the Japanese plenipotentiaries at the Armament Conference in Washington. See Chapter XVI for full English translation.

Page from "skeleton code" of ten thousand words showing British Foreign Office code book during process of decipherment by the American Black Chamber. This is an example of a thoroughly disarranged code.

or in two parts. Of course I can not explain by showing you the American system, but look at the captured German trench code as an example (below).

"This book contains only about twelve hundred groups. It was published in two volumes, one for encoding and one for decoding. It is what we call a disarranged code.

Wache	uwl	*weisse Leuchtkuglen	rbl
Waffe	rjw	weit	ksi
*Wagen	apl	*zu weit	sqr
während	sjk	weiter	rsq
wahrscheinlich	ktf	weitergeben	aov
Wald	apw	welcher	sfi
wann	rqv	*Welle	kvx
*war	upx	wenig	aex
*waren	rvp	*zu wenig	ung
warm	kkv	wenn	acd
warten	rej	werden	kdo
warum	uxw	*wird	uoz
was	rrd	werfen	rtw
Wasser	kud	*geworfen	uqk
*Wasser, destilliertes		Westen	rle
	rzl, sga	westlich	spd
Wechsel	aqs	Wetter	uke
*Wechselstrom-maschine	rlf	Wetterwarte	anj
weder	ubm	wichtig	umx
Weg	rkx	Widerstand	smj
*weg	aiv	*wie	rfe
Wegegabel	ryx	wieder	uvd
Wegekreuz	klj	wiederholen	sip
wegen	sse	wiederholt	kcr
weichen	uuh	wiedernehmen	adv
weiss	kvw	Wiese	ulf
		wieviel	ajf

Blinde Signale . . . . sxk, kio, urm, ayo, rbi

---

Note that the German words run in alphabetical order but that their code equivalents are disarranged. The first German word on this page is *Wache* and is represented by the code word *uwl*. The next German word in alphabetical order is *Waffe*, but instead of being represented by a code

119

word beginning with *uw,* its equivalent is *rjw.* The order of the code words, you see, has been arbitrarily disarranged.

"Note also," I told her, "the line at the bottom of the page: *Blinde Signale . . . . sxk, kio, urm, ayo, rbi.* These three-letter groups are *nulls;* they have no meaning. They are to be scattered here and there throughout a code message. These are very confusing to the cryptographer and are extremely difficult to identify as nulls.

"We suspect that the Spaniards use nulls in their messages. If you can obtain information such as this, it will help us a great deal."

I paused while she carefully examined the German trench code.

"I think that I have followed you," she finally said.

"If you have," I answered, "you can appreciate the enormous value which scraps of information are to the cryptographer."

I had no intention, of course, of telling her anything about Boyd's mission. Even if Boyd were successful in all he was about to undertake, this girl could be of tremendous value.

"Analysis of these messages indicates that the Spaniards use about ten different codes between different points," I said. "This is something I doubt. I am convinced that there are no more than one or two basic codes. The others are merely secondary codes based on the one or two original codes. We call them encipherments. Instead of publishing a new code they have merely rearranged the old ones in some manner. Now, I don't expect you to find out *how* they rearranged them. But if you can find out whether or not they do use an encipherment, this information will be of incalculable aid to us."

If Boyd could only get a copy of one of these codes, and if this girl could find out whether or not the others were secondary copies, we need only discover the system, or if there was no system, the mere fact that there were primary and secondary codes would aid us. Negative information is often as valuable as positive.

"I think I should like to study cryptography," she said.

"All right. I'll give you a copy of our short course of instruction. But don't clutter up your mind with this. After all, one cryptographer can't do very much. If you can pick up odd scraps of information for us you will be much more valuable. Suppose you cultivate Mr. Gomez. If you succeed in this task you will be our best cryptographer."

"I'll try," she said.

And one had only to look at her to know that she would succeed. I must confess that I felt rather sorry for Mr. Gomez.

The girl prepared to leave, and I turned to her.

"Communicate with me at once if you learn anything. Of course I should warn you to be discreet and all that sort of thing, but I don't think it is necessary."

"It isn't," she said simply. Then she flashed a reassuring smile at me and was gone.

Boyd left Washington for the Panama Canal Zone a few days later, and it was not long before I received an inquiry from him requesting me to cable him at once several copies of different Spanish diplomatic messages. In response to my inquiries about his success, I had only the laconic reply that he was progressing satisfactorily.

Then came a message requesting funds on the Royal Bank of Canada with the urgent demand for quick execution. And then he seemed doubtful about the code he was preparing to photograph. He did not seem sure that it was the code we desired.

Boyd had stolen into the Consulate at night, opened the steel safe which protected the diplomatic code, but had been unable to decipher the messages which we had cabled. For this reason he doubted that he had discovered the correct code. Boyd also explained that only a few pages of this book could be photographed each night and to make a photograph of each page, with the facilities he had available in his secret proceedings, would require time.

We were not surprised that the book Boyd found would not decode telegrams passing between Spain, America and Germany. Miss Abbott had already supplied us with detailed reports regarding all phases of the Spanish diplomatic codes. There was an amazing network of codes within codes.

According to Miss Abbott's reports, and of course confirmed by cryptographic analysis, the Spanish Government was using in all twenty-five codes. Each message was prefaced with an "indicator," a special number indicating the particular code which was used to encode the message. The complete list, so far as we were able to determine, of indicators and the cities to and from which they were in use, follows:

121

9	San Juan
32	Santo Domingo
74	Panama
101	Berlin, Bogota, Havana, Washington, Lima, London, Vienna
123	Mexico
129	Buenos Aires
131	Caracas, New York
132	Mexico
133	Mexico
141	Lima, Quito, Buenos Aires, Mexico
143	Havana, London
149	Montevideo, Buenos Aires
153	Washington
155	Bogota, Havana
159	Vienna
167	Berlin
181	Costa Rica, Guatemala, Salvador
187	Mexico
209	Salvador, Costa Rica
215	Sofia, Vienna
229	Havana, London
249	Washington
253	Berlin
301	Washington, Berlin, Havana, Mexico, Buenos Aires, Paris, Bogota, Lima, Panama, Costa Rica
303	Berlin

The study and successful attack of twenty-five codes is a very difficult task even though Miss Abbott supplied us with bits of information about the character of their construction. The most important information she gave us was that these twenty-five codes fell into only nine different groups, each code in each group having only a slight difference. The groups are as follows:

1. 9-32-74
2. 131-132-133-123-153-143-141
3. 153-155-159
4. 153-253
5. 167-187
6. 181-141-101

7. 209-229-249-129-149-159
8. 215
9. 301-303-101

Just a few days before we heard from Boyd, the Spanish Foreign Office in Madrid had sent out a circular telegram to Washington, Costa Rica, Panama, Santo Domingo and Lima. We knew this to be a circular telegram because each one bore the same number. This circular telegram of identical text was sent in four different ways: to Washington and Costa Rica in code number 301; to Lima in 141; to Santo Domingo in 32; and to Panama in 74. This was exactly what we had been looking for! The same message encoded in several codes! And Boyd could furnish us with one of these—Code No. 74.

With Code 74 in our possession, we could decode this circular telegram and by superimposing the decipherment over the code words in the messages to Washington, Lima and Santo Domingo, we would have the correct identifications in three other codes. With a few words identified, all the codes would fall apart.

There was a great deal of excitement when this information was given to the Spanish Department of MI-8. We urged Boyd to photograph this code as quickly as possible and arranged that it should be rushed to us by pouch.

A page of this code is shown in photo section. It is one of the most interesting documents I have ever seen. You can see the picture of string, at the top of the page, which Boyd used to hold open the book as he photographed one page at a time. A close examination will reveal the Spanish Government's method of slightly changing their books. This code is a secondary code. The figure code words opposite the Spanish meanings have been changed from the original by pasting columns of new numbers which have been printed on thin slips of paper. The thumb index has been added by pen.

The numbers, opposite the words on the page, can stand for any one of the various forms of the word. For instance, in the word *"acept-ar-acion-es,"* which occurs next to the last, there are several possibilities. The person who decodes the message, construes the word in its proper form, according to the content of the message.

With this code in our hands we now began the slow but sure solution of all nine groups of codes and their twenty-five different encipherments.

Boyd cabled for instructions as to the disposition of the glass negatives which he had used in his photography and we replied that the film could be washed off with a solution of common lye. Boyd was of course instructed to destroy all correspondence on the subject.

We were anxious to get one of the other groups of the Spanish code and told him to proceed to Bogota, Colombia. He replied that he was leaving on the next boat for Bogota and "will secure the code if it is there."

Miss Abbott's mission was now completed. But she was anxious to continue in the fascinating game with foreign members of the diplomatic corps. We had already broken the Chilean diplomatic code and had been reading all their messages for months, but they had suddenly switched to another code. We were satisfied that the new code was merely a disarrangement of the one we were reading, but before this could be determined by analysis Miss Abbott handed me a photograph of the new Chilean encipherment. (See photo section.)

As is seen by the letter, the Chilean Government had decided suddenly to make their communications more difficult by first encoding messages and then enciphering the code. By means of the enciphering table, this was done. In converting the code into cipher, the figure code word *0000* would become *coco;* similarly *0001* would become *coeb,* etc.

Just how Miss Abbott obtained this encipherment is unknown to me, for she was very secretive about the matter. She never asked for any funds. Whether she was adroit enough to obtain it without giving any consideration or whether she purchased it with her own money, I have no way of knowing.

CHAPTER IX

Ordered Abroad

I HAVE made no mention of the hundreds of personal cipher letters that were sent to MI-8 by the postal censorship for decipherment. Now and then one of these contained military information, but for the most part they were written by persons to conceal clandestine love-affairs. One of them from a trapper to his sweetheart is very amusing. I have retained his spelling and have underlined the words that were not enciphered.

My dearest own,

Received your loving letter o.k. Was more than glad to hear from my love. Oh hun, so he was to stay with you from Sat till Sun night. Well, then, you wasent lonesom or homesick and even asked him to come next Sat and stay till Sunday night. He says he is going and he took you a lot of things for you and babe. And you a new Easter hat. Ge it must have ben a nice day to morrow to want to come so quick again.

Well, love, I dident have very good luck, only 32 rats; that only means 35 dollars.

Hun, shall I use 8 of that for you know what? Love, I am a lot better, am going to fish a while, tho then I am going on the road with Dad.

Hun, when the time coms I will help if I can.

Chear up, for God' sake dont go with him again.

For if you do, it will kill me.

It come near it before.

Oh, love, I wish you were here to trap and fish with me. I think the reason you saw me was those nights you spoke of I praied to see you, that or those nights in my sleep. But I do want to see you <u>afuly</u> bad but nothing any more searus then the longing of my heart. <u>It</u> is not <u>sickness</u> but love. I do pray you will get free for some one to <u>woe and win</u> your love again, Darling. Mother is having a nother one of those times with her stomack. You know when she has those aful pains and vomit so, she is vomating now. Well, so long till I heare from you again. You will find a stamp. Good by, my love, my own. A kiss to you and mine.

The writing of cipher love-letters was not confined to the illiterate. The cipher urge also included the educated in their clandestine love correspondence. However, most of the letters that are interesting would be considered too obscene for publication. All of the cipher letters were very easy to solve, so easy that it rather worried me to see husbands and wives trust their illicit correspondence to such unsafe methods.

Another amusing cipher message was intercepted by our wireless station. It was addressed to a Mexican officer at Piedras Negras from a Mexican General in Mexico, and enciphered in the Mexican Army Cipher Disk.

No. 674 Clave Circulo A. 26 49 56 91 sirvase decir al 15 49 73 31 04 36 75 95 alistar dos 07 27 68 92 17 49 74 de las 12 27 65 70 17 27 74 hoy llegare esa.

Deciphered the message in Spanish read:

Clave 26 49 56 91
Sirvase decir al 15 49 73 31 04 36 75 95
                  p a r i e n t e

alistar dos 07 27 68 92 17 49 74 de las
        h e m b r a s

12 27 65 70 17 27 74 hoy llegare esa
m e j o r e s

Translated this reads:

Key 26 49 56 91.
Please tell *aunt* to have two *women* of the *best* ready. I will arrive to-day in your city.

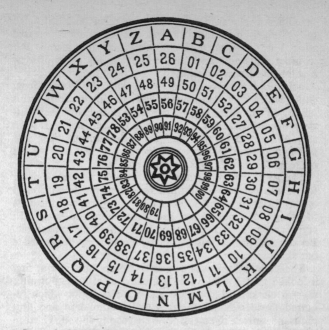

Improvised Cipher Disk of Mexican Army, set to key 26 49 56 91, and used in deciphering the message on page 126.

To make sure that the message would be deciphered, the General even sent the key!

If this Mexican General with his penchant for two girls had been suspected of flirting with German espionage, I have often wondered whether Captain Brown, who boasted that he could supply women for any cause, could have found "two of the best." General, I salute you!

MI-8 was not only the official bureau representing the postal censorship, but also the Department of Justice, the Department of State, and of course the War Department. The Navy Department had insisted on organizing their own Cryptog”raghic Bureau, but in July, 1918, they suddenly discharged all their employees, donated their elaborate secret-ink equipment to our laboratory, and placed a liaison officer in MI-8 to represent them. This came about in a rather startling manner.

In the early part of July, Colonel A. B. Coxe, General Churchill's executive officer, brought Lieutenant Elkins of the Office of Naval Intelligence to my office, and instructed me to show him about. I was not particularly pleased when I was instructed to tell this officer our secrets. But in order that the reader may appreciate my point of view it will be necessary to digress.

MI-8 had been on good terms with the Navy Signal Office which compiled naval codes and ciphers. In fact this office had submitted several messages encoded in their battle codes and asked if, in our opinion, their methods were safe. When the Navy Signal Office transmitted their first problem to me, they remarked, facetiously, that they wished me luck, for they thought I would need it.

The American and British fleets maintained close liaison, for it was necessary for them to communicate with each other during operations. The Navy Department methods for secret communication had been submitted to British cryptographers who had pronounced them indecipherable. Because of this, I was especially anxious to demonstrate our skill.

The Navy system was a most elaborate one, and at first it looked as if I would need a great deal of luck. But after several clerks had compiled elaborate statistics which required thirteen hundred pages and six hundred and fifty thousand entries, the messages were readily solved. Thirteen hundred pages and six hundred and fifty thousand entries, merely to prove that the United States Navy was still controlled by amateur cryptographers!

As a result of this the Navy made some slight changes, but since they obviously knew very little about cryptography their changes were of no value as far as maintaining secrecy was concerned. In fact while I was with the Peace Conference in Paris the Navy Department encoded the President's and the State Department's messages in their system, and though they liked to advertise their indecipherable methods, when I offered to make a substantial wager that the technique I developed while in Washington would still solve their messages, they admitted privately that I was probably right. The fact of the matter is (as we shall see later on), there is no such thing as an indecipherable code or cipher constructed along conventional lines.

The Navy Cryptographic Bureau, which should not be confused with the Navy Signal Office, had absolutely refused to have anything to do with MI-8. And it always seemed curious to me that the Signal Office came to us for advice if their Cryptographic Bureau possessed any skill. I

Photograph of letter from British officer in Turkish prison camp to a girl in London. This shows a clever way for defeating the British Censor. In the original letter the words were of course not underlined.

had tried repeatedly to confer with this section without success. Since they were so secretive it seemed odd that this naval officer wished to be shown about MI-8. I wasn't sure that I wished to reveal our secrets.

"If you don't mind, Lieutenant," I said, "would you tell me just what sort of information you are seeking?"

"No, I don't mind. Frankly, I am on a very unpleasant mission. I know nothing about codes and ciphers and secret inks. I am not from the Navy Cipher Bureau. I am here at the request of the Director of Naval Intelligence. He has asked me to make an investigation of our own Cipher Bureau and MI-8 and report my findings. He is dissatisfied with our own organization. I find that though our Cipher Bureau has been in existence for over a year and has a large personnel as well as an elaborate secret-ink laboratory, it has failed so far to decipher a single cipher or code message or to develop a secret-ink letter."

This was most amazing news. No wonder the Navy Department Cipher Bureau was secretive. They didn't have anything to reveal. This amused me for the Navy Department had refused a year earlier to follow the example of other government departments and make MI-8 a central bureau.

I had just had prepared for the Director a summary or history of MI-8, and showed this to the Lieutenant. It was dated July, 1918, and gave a brief outline of the work that had been done since my arrival at the War College in June, 1917.

Beginning with me and two civilian employees, the personnel had rapidly increased to nearly two hundred men and women.

The Code Compilation Subsection had revolutionized War Department methods and compiled several codes; the Communications Subsection (established to control our own code and cipher messages) was handling over fifty thousand words a week; the Shorthand Subsection could now read documents in nearly any language in thirty different shorthand systems; and our Secret-Ink Subsection was examining two thousand letters a week, and had developed over fifty important spy secret-ink letters.

In addition to personal, military and spy messages, the Solution Subsection had solved over ten thousand diplomatic telegrams of Argentina, Brazil, Chile, Costa Rica, Cuba, Germany, Mexico, Spain and Panama. The codes

Example of personal cipher turned over to MI-8 by censor. The reader may wish to try his hand at decipherment.

of all other Central and South American countries, at the request of the government, were under study.

The report also outlined our duties for training cryptographers for duty in France, examination and report on the safety of codes and ciphers in use by other branches of the government, examination of original cipher methods submitted by the public, etc.

The Lieutenant read the report carefully and returned it. "I'm not surprised that the Naval Director asked me to make an investigation," he said.

I showed him through our various sections and then took him to a separate room where we kept exhibits of some of the more important secret-ink and cipher documents that we had solved.

As a result of his visit the Navy Cryptographic Bureau was abandoned, the elaborate secret-ink equipment turned over to our laboratory, and a liaison officer was placed in MI-8 to represent the Navy Department.

The letter from the Director of Naval Intelligence to the Naval Attaché, London, which was prepared for me as a letter of introduction when I was ordered abroad, contains the paragraph,

"This office has turned over to the Military Intelligence Branch all work along the lines of breaking enemy cipher and code messages, being represented in their office by a Liaison Officer who looks after the interests of the Navy."

For once, the Navy Department, ever jealous of its prestige, admitted failure.

Cryptography seems to do queer things to people. On several occasions I had been obliged to let persons resign on account of shattered nerves. I too felt the strain and though I said nothing about it for several weeks, in July I suddenly knew that I was close to a breakdown and asked to be relieved.

General Churchill was sympathetic, but refused to accept my resignation. Instead he asked that I draw up plans for a Cipher Bureau for the Expeditionary Forces to Siberia which was then being formed. Papers were drawn up ordering me to Siberia with a selected personnel, when a cable came from General Pershing, asking that I be sent to France.

Although I felt some pride in General Pershing's request for my services in France, I was too ill to take a great deal of interest in what was going on. I had nothing to do with the plans that were made for me, but it seems that after an exchange of several cables it was decided that I should go abroad on temporary duty to establish liaison between Allied and American Cipher Bureaus, and to obtain certain information from our Allies on the subject of codes and ciphers.

General Churchill, I know, was looking into the future and was especially anxious that I learn all I could about the methods of our Allies. This would not only help MI-8 and our Cipher Bureau in France, but would also prepare us for a Cryptographic Bureau after the war. General Churchill, as well as other officials, was now convinced that the United States, even after the war, if we hoped to keep informed of the attitudes, purposes and plans of other nations, must maintain a powerful organization for the solution of secret diplomatic code and cipher telegrams. As all the Great Powers maintained such a Cipher Bureau, the United States in self-defense must do likewise.

General Churchill obtained from the State Department, the Navy Department and the French High Commission letters of introduction, and in addition drafted letters to our Military Attachés at London, Paris and Rome, which read:

This will introduce Captain H. O. Yardley, N. A., the Chief of MI-8, who is going to France for temporary duty in order to consult with Colonel Nolan, G. H. Q., on the subject of ciphers and secret codes.

It is to the skill and initiative of Captain Yardley that we owe the present excellent organization of MI-8 and I am sure that as a military attaché who has daily reason to be glad that MI-8 is efficient you will be glad to extend all possible courtesies toward the Chief.

The letters from the Department of State to Ambassador Page in London and Ambassador Sharp in Paris rather amused me for it had not been many months since I was a clerk in the State Department Code Room. The letter to Ambassador Page read:

The bearer of this letter, Captain H. O. Yardley, U. S. N. A., is the officer in charge of the code and cipher section of the Military Intelligence Branch of the General Staff. In this capacity it can be said that he represents the State Department and I should therefore be very grateful if you will lend him every assistance in your power in obtaining any information which may be in the possession of the British authorities and which might in any way assist in the solution of enemy codes and ciphers.

My fourteen months with the Military Intelligence Division had been an unforgettable experience. I had made many new friends and had won the confidence of my superiors. It is not often one has the privilege of associating with men like Van Deman and Churchill.

I had been confident of a measure of success when I went to the War College. The feeling that Captain Manly could carry on consoled me. But I was not very sure of myself now. What would be my experiences abroad? Was I fitted for my mission?

Our convoy took two weeks for its trip to Liverpool, during which, now separated from the problems of MI-8, I quickly recovered my shattered nerves.

With an array of letters of introduction I began the rather uncertain rôle of Military Observer.

CHAPTER X

The British Cipher Bureau

I arrived in London the latter part of August, 1918, and presented my credentials to Colonel Slocum, American Military Attaché. After discussing with me the purpose of my mission, he arranged for conferences with Colonel French of the British War Office, Ambassador Page and the American Naval Attaché.

Colonel Tolbert, American Military Attaché at Copenhagen, was in London on a special mission and dropped in an hour or so later. As Colonel Slocum was engaged, Colonel Tolbert and I had luncheon together. My name was familiar to Military Attachés all over the world, for all mail leaving Washington concerning codes and ciphers and secret inks bore my signature. Colonel Tolbert, as well as Colonel Slocum, seemed pleased with the new secret codes that MI-8 had just published and distributed. By way of conversation I asked about his office in Copenhagen and what precautions were taken to safeguard the secrecy of our new systems of cable communication.

He told me that all employees in his office were American citizens whose loyalty had been thoroughly checked up, and that MI-8's instructions for safeguarding secrets were rigidly enforced. He was alive to the danger of compromising our communications, and laughed good-naturedly when he told me of the repeated attempts of the British to plant secret agents in his office. Van Deman had displayed his shrewd judgment of men when he placed this keen officer at Copenhagen, for Copenhagen lay close to Germany and was the seat of intrigue.

When I returned to the Embassy I asked for the code book, since I wished to report my arrival to Washington.

I was directed to a slender dark-haired young man who, obviously, from his conversation, was English. I was dumfounded when he actually opened the vaults and handed me a code book, a book that had taken months of labor and thousands of dollars of the government's money to compile and publish. Indeed, I was so amazed that for days I made no comment. I had scarcely believed Tolbert's statement that the British had tried to plant secret agents in his office. But here I stood, actually looking at a British subject in our office in London!

I saw Colonel French of the British War Office the following morning and Edward Bell, First Secretary of the American Embassy, in the afternoon. The latter told me that I would have many difficulties in picking up any information on codes and ciphers in London, because through his own secret sources of information he knew that the British Intelligence liaison officer in Washington had warned Colonel French by cable of my mission, and that every obstacle would be placed in my path.

For days I made no progress. I consumed a great deal of tea and drank quantities of whisky and soda with various officers in the War Office. They were affable enough and invited me to their clubs. But I received no information.

I was at a distinct disadvantage for I did not dare communicate with Washington, since the British would decode every word I sent. Not having anticipated that I should find a British subject in possession of our secret codes, I had brought with me no special means of enciphering my cablegrams.

While playing a waiting game with the War Office I quietly investigated the situation in the Military Attaché's office, and finally took a chance on transmitting a secret cable to Washington by a method that I felt certain the British would be unable to decipher. This method, I am sure, is worth describing.

Several months previously the Mexican Government had changed their diplomatic ciphers, and the small group of cryptographers who specialized in MI-8 on Mexican telegrams was unable to break into the new system. Although they had been able to discover the type or method under study, and had followed the usual analysis necessary for the solution of such ciphers, the messages resisted successful attack.

Finally, when I saw that these cryptographers were merely going around in circles, I took a summary of their statistics and analyses home where I could work undisturbed. The analyses before me showed clearly that the messages were enciphered with a mixed alphabet, having for a key a word of five letters. After experimenting for a few hours I discovered why the messages had not been readily solved.

The Mexican cryptographer who had constructed the primary or original mixed alphabet had made an error. Through an inadvertence he had omitted the letter *w* and had repeated the letter *j*. When I recovered the primary alphabet it read:

jilgueroabcdfhjkmnpqstvxyz

Without error it would have read:

jilgueroabcdfhkmnpqstvwxyz

This difference, though seemingly slight, produced a unique behavior of cipher letters in the telegrams that was baffling.

While I sat thinking how I should ever be able to communicate safely with Washington with a compromised code, it suddenly occurred to me that if I would first encode the message in the Military Attaché's code book, then in some manner mutilate these letters by a method that Washington could unravel, I would be safe.

I at last drafted my dispatch, beginning it with a statement that the entire cable was encoded in the Military Intelligence Code, but reenciphered by sliding the consonant alphabet against the vowel alphabet of the Mexican Government's cipher which I had deciphered and reconstructed.

The description was very technical but I took a chance that MI-8, now directed by the genius of Captain Manly, would understand what I meant. If so, no one but MI-8 would be able to read my dispatch, despite the fact that the British must have by now photostated our codes.

I went on to describe the exact situation in the Military Attaché's office. I did this with some trepidation, for although General Churchill had told me to report anything I considered of interest, I still felt some misgivings as to his attitude toward my meddling in affairs foreign to my mission. I doubt if I would have had the courage to draft the cable, had it not been for the fact that Colonel Tolbert told me that the British had made repeated efforts to plant British agents in his office in Copenhagen.

Still I reasoned that as long as we granted British subjects access to our secret means of communication, even in one office, nothing but stupidity could prevent them from reading every message sent and received by our military attachés throughout the world. There would be a squabble among the powers for the spoils of war. We would be helpless in our negotiations with our communications compromised.

In order to save my face, I suggested that Van Deman be ordered to make an investigation. After all, I was nothing more than a Captain.

I managed to escape the scandal my report produced, for Washington was horrified when it learned that our Military Attaché's office in London was full of British subjects. An investigation was made in every Military Attaché's office in the world to the end that all foreigners were discharged and replaced with Americans trained in Washington.

But this did not assist me in my mission, though I did receive the thanks of General Churchill. Discouraged with the British refusal to all my requests, I cabled for permission to proceed to Paris. The matter was taken up with the State Department and I was instructed that they advised that I not try to press the British, but that I should gain their confidence by my silence and discretion, and should establish pleasant personal relations. They told me that the English were cautious about giving confidence until fully convinced of one's trustworthiness and discretion.

This was sound advice but scarcely helpful. Our relations seemed pleasant enough. At least they gave me enough whisky and food to keep me dizzy nearly every night. Perhaps I couldn't drink enough.

Finally Captain Brook-Hunt of the British War Office submitted to me for examination a combination substitution and transposition cipher. The British Army planned to adopt this cipher for the transmission of telegrams along the Western Front. Since such messages carried definite information, such as the disposition of troops and the hour of attack along different sectors, it was vital to the lives of the troops engaged that the messages be indecipherable, for German wireless stations intercepted all telegrams that passed through the air and passed them on to the German Cryptographic Bureau at German headquarters for solution. Readers who are old enough will remember the laconic bulletins issued by the War Offices, such as:

Our troops made surprise attack on —— sector, but were repulsed by superior forces.

Surprise indeed! More likely than not the enemy knew the hour of attack and strength of the forces engaged by the decipherment of wireless intercepts. How many men died for this reason no one knows.

If I could break this cipher the British were about to adopt, and demonstrate that it was suicide to use it for front-line military messages, all my trouble with the War Office would be over. Such an accomplishment would establish me on a professional basis that could not be denied. With these thoughts in mind I asked the Military Attaché for a room where I could study undisturbed. Here for several days I pored over the sample messages that Captain Brook-Hunt had given to me, striving for a solution. Suddenly the whole structure of the messages fell apart and I rushed with my solution to the War Office.

Its doors were now open to me; I could have anything I wanted. That evening I cabled Washington that I was on extremely good terms with the British War Office, due to my lucky decipherment of a double substitution and transposition cipher which they had recommended for use at the Front.

I now spent most of my time in the British Military Cipher Bureau, studying their methods for the solution of different types of codes and ciphers, and collecting pieces of exposition on these subjects. No cryptographer can hope for any great success without both wide experience and schooling. I felt that I was finishing my education.

Through Edward Bell, First Secretary of the American Embassy, and Ambassador Page, I had already approached the British Admiralty Code and Cipher Bureau. Though I discovered that the British decoder was no cleverer than our own, those in power in England considered a Cipher Bureau of such tremendous importance that they placed an Admiral at its head. This man, Admiral Hall, because of the information he obtained from the messages that his enormous bureau deciphered, stood next to Lloyd George in power. The Foreign Office was extremely jealous of his position for it was almost wholly dependent on him for information revealing the secret political intrigues of enemy and neutral governments.

For example, the reader will recall the famous Zimmermann-Carranza note in which Germany promised Mexico the states of New Mexico, Texas and Arizona if she would declare war against the United States. President Wilson was so disturbed about this that when he called a joint session of the House and Senate to deliver his war message, he quoted from this telegram. Admiral Hall had given this message to Edward Bell, who cabled it to the Secretary of State, who in turn gave it to the President. Diplomatic procedure would require that such sensational information be transmitted by the Foreign Office to Ambassador Page, but Admiral Hall did as he pleased. It is no wonder then that he was feared by the Foreign Office.

Edward Bell was on extremely good terms with Admiral Hall, and the little success I had with the Admiralty was due almost entirely to his good offices. The Admiral had been informed by Colonel French of my mission in London and was prepared to give me as little information as possible. He made it clear that he absolutely would not deal officially with the United States Government. He insisted that everything be transacted on a personal basis, and though he remained firm in his refusal to give me any information about the German diplomatic codes used for wireless messages between Berlin and Madrid, he finally consented to give me, personally, several copies of a certain neutral government's diplomatic codes and a copy of a German Naval code in two volumes.

The naval codes he gave me under the most mysterious instructions. He promised to forward them to Washington but they absolutely were not to be turned over to the United States Government. Upon my return to Washington they would be handed to me personally. These codes, so I learned, had been photographed from the original by an English spy within the German Admiralty.

Through various sources I learned a great deal about the Admiralty Cipher Bureau. I did not wonder that England was a great power, for she read practically every code telegram that passed over her cables.

As late as 1921, Clarence H. Mackay, President of the Postal Telegraph Company, testifying before a Senate Committee on cable landing licenses, said, "Since censorship ceased the British Government have required us to turn over all messages 10 days after they have been sent or received. This is a right which they claim under the landing licenses they issue to all cable companies."

There is a very good reason why England controls a majority of the cables: she recognizes the advantage of supervising messages. Many of her cable lines are laid under inducement of large subsidies and guarantees.

Unlike MI-8 in Washington, the Admiralty Cipher Bureau was not founded as a war measure. It had a long and dark history, backed by a ruthless and intelligent espionage. The power, tradition and intrigues of this bureau fired my imagination. MI-8 in Washington must not die at the close of the war.

The British War Office was anxious to have me visit their Cipher Bureau at British General Headquarters in France and offered to take me there by aeroplane. Though I wanted to see Captain Hitchings, who, according to his superiors, was worth four divisions of the British Army, Colonel Van Deman advised against this, for he felt that I could not learn anything there that I had not already picked up in London. Moreover, he was most anxious for me to try my hand with the French Cipher Bureau in Paris.

Colonel Van Deman was leaving London the following day with Secretary of War Baker, and although I disliked going before closing matters with the British Censor, War Office and Admiralty, I felt that his presence in Paris would give me weight. I therefore finally decided to accompany him.

CHAPTER XI

La Chambre Noire

IN Paris I did not experience the same difficulties with the War Office that I had in London, but I soon discovered that the doors of the famous French Black Chamber would never be open to me. I carried a letter (see illustration on page 143) from the French High Commission in Washington that worked like a charm, at least as far as the Military Cipher Bureau was concerned. This letter translated reads as follows:

> HIGH COMMISSION OF THE FRENCH REPUBLIC
> The General Delegate to the
> General Commissioner of the
> Franco-American War Affairs.
>
> Colonel Churchill, Chief of the Military Intelligence Branch, War Department, has especially recommended to me Captain H. O. Yardley, who is being sent to France to study the different codes and ciphers used in the transmission of cables.
>
> I would be especially obliged to you if you would facilitate the mission of Captain Yardley and put him in touch with Colonel Cartier in charge of the cipher section in the Cabinet of the Minister of War. Also with the cipher bureau of the Department of Foreign Affairs.

When I explained my mission to Colonel Cartier, he immediately called in Captain Georges Painvin, the great cipher genius of France. For weeks I had looked forward to meeting the brilliant Painvin, the most skilful cryptographer in all the Allied Governments. The finest tribute I ever heard paid a cipher expert was a lecture given by

HAUT COMMISSARIAT DE LA REPUBLIQUE FRANÇAISE

1864 COLUMBIA ROAD N.W.

WASHINGTON, D.C

IN REPLY REFER TO OUR

Nº 27638

6 Août, 1918.

Le Délégué Général,

à M. le Commissaire Général

aux Affaires de Guerre Franco-Américaines.

Le Colonel Churchill, Chef du Military
Intelligence Branch, du War Department, m'a recommandé
tout particulièrement le Capitaine H.O. Yardley, qui
est envoyé en France pour étudier les différents
codes et chiffres employés dans la transmission des
câbles.

Je vous serais particulièrement obligé
de bien vouloir faciliter la mission du Capitaine
Yardley, et le mettre en relations avec le Colonel
Cartier, Chargé de la Section du Chiffre, au Cabinet du Minis-
tre de la Guerre, et avec le Bureau du Chiffre au
Département des Affaires Etrangères.

Author's letter of credentials from French High Commission in
Washington to French authorities in France.

Colonel Frank Moorman, a Staff Officer at American General Headquarters, who said in part:

Captain Georges Painvin, the chief code expert of the French, an analytical genius of the highest order, was a regular wizard in solving codes. . . . On the basis of this simple message he worked out a complete system of this new code. It is too much to say that the solution of this code changed the result of the war, but it undoubtedly cost the lives of many German soldiers and saved the lives of many of the Allies.

In order that I may keep history straight, I must add that his greatest achievement, although he had just recovered from a long and serious illness (the fate of most cryptographers), was the solution of the difficult ADFGVX cipher, which the Germans suddenly sprang on the Allied cipher experts on the eve of the long-heralded German push of March, 1918.

This cipher was called ADFGVX because only these letters occurred in the cipher messages. The Germans first enciphered a message, one letter at a time, by writing two cipher letters for each German letter. When the message was completely enciphered the cipher message contained twice as many letters as the original German text. The Germans now separated these pairs of letters and mixed them up by a prearranged key. *This key changed every day.* The system, then constituted: first, a substitution; second, a division; third, a transposition. This cipher was so extremely difficult to solve that many have marveled at the brain that *originally* discovered the underlying principles of solution.

When Painvin entered the room, Colonel Cartier was talking over the telephone, and I had an opportunity to study this slender cold-eyed young man, as he stood patiently waiting for his superior to finish his conversation.

Painvin's swarthy drawn face registered zero, as Colonel Cartier introduced me and explained my mission. If anything, he seemed slightly bored at the idea of an American coming to Paris to study French cipher methods. When we were alone in his office, however, and he saw that I followed his analysis of several difficult problems, he gradually thawed out. Eventually we grew to be fast friends. I became an intimate member of his household and spent many quiet evenings there, listening to his brilliant discussion of cryptography.

Painvin gave me a desk in his office and opened his files to me, and I made the most of the opportunity to study under this master, whose instruction and inspiration were to stand me in good stead, when later, from 1919 to 1929, I directed the energies of a group of cryptographers, deciphering the secret codes and cipher messages of foreign governments.

But my experiences with the French were not all so simple. Cables to me from Washington became more insistent in their request for information about the German diplomatic codes in use between Berlin and Madrid. The almost daily question was, "What progress are you making?"

I had made it a point to drop in on Cartier as often as possible without at the same time intruding, so that he would become accustomed to me. Finally one day, when he was particularly cordial, I made bold to ask him permission to study in the department that deciphered diplomatic codes. Colonel Cartier, I think, was prepared for this, for without hesitation he told me that although he had the responsibility for the interception of diplomatic code telegrams, his office did not decipher them. Instead, he forwarded them to the Foreign Office. As I had seen copies of diplomatic code messages on his desk, he could not very well say that he had nothing to do with them.

I had reason to doubt his statement—by now I was alive to the jealousy with which governments guarded the secrets of the Code Bureau that decoded diplomatic telegrams—but there was nothing to do but make inquiries at the Foreign Office.

Hugh Gibson, now American Ambassador to Belgium, was at that time one of the secretaries to the American Embassy. I had known him back in the days when I was a clerk in the Department of State, and he a young budding diplomat. When I went in to see him, he greeted me with his famous Eddie Cantor grin.

I gave him a letter from Edward Bell in London and also showed him a copy of a cable from Washington, suggesting that I call on him for assistance. I explained my difficulty and asked if he could arrange for me to see M. Pichon, French Minister for Foreign Affairs. He advised that I approach the Foreign Office through the Ambassador with whom he arranged a conference.

I gave Ambassador Sharp letters addressed to him from our Department of State, and he immediately telephoned for an appointment with M. Pichon for the following day, and was good enough to accompany me.

I explained my mission to M. Pichon; that I had seen Colonel Cartier, who informed me that the War Office decoded only military messages and sent the diplomatic messages to the Foreign Office, where they were decoded.

He replied without hesitation that that was not the case; that the German Berlin-Madrid messages under discussion were decoded by Cartier before they reached the Foreign Office; and finally that the Foreign Office did not even have a Cipher Bureau.

145

Both Ambassador Sharp and I were uncertain whether he was putting me off or whether he really was unaware of the exact location of the diplomatic Cipher Bureau. Ministers often prefer not to know either how or where the information supplied them regarding other governments is obtained.

When I repeated to Cartier my conversation with M. Pichon, he remarked that it was possible that M. Pichon himself knew nothing definite about the Foreign Office Cipher Bureau; that its location was a mystery, known to only a few men in France—in fact it was referred to as *La Chambre Noire,* the Black Chamber. Cartier either was or pretended to be very angry that M. Pichon had placed him in a false light.

After a conference with our Military Attaché, Major Warburton, and Colonel Van Deman, we decided to address a letter to Colonel Herscher, Clemenceau's secretary. This letter he referred to General Mordacq, Chief of Cabinet, Ministry of War. The General evaded the issue by replying that the Berlin-Madrid messages were encoded in many different codes; that they changed constantly; that the messages were decipherable only by grouping, etc., etc. He *consented, however, to transmit to our State Department, through the French Ambassador in Washington, all messages that seemed of any interest to the United States.* This in itself was an admission that the War Office controlled *La Chambre Noire.* But most amazing of all was the fact that the letter, though signed by General Mordacq, revealed, when closely examined with a microscope and compared with other letters, that it had been prepared and typed in the office of Colonel Cartier! The French seemed always to consider us naïve.

I do not think Cartier had realized the pressure he would have to withstand in keeping me out of *La Chambre Noire.* I said nothing about this letter when I saw him the next day, but he was visibly anxious and asked me repeatedly when I was leaving Paris.

A few days later I saw General Mordacq. He reminded me that the files of the War Office Cipher Bureau dealing with military ciphers had been placed at my disposal, but said that information about diplomatic codes had never been given to any one, and pointed out that our knowledge of them would materially assist us in breaking the French diplomatic codes. He went on to say that inasmuch as France had been saved by the United States, our request could not lightly be refused. However, he requested that the Military Attaché write again, explaining more fully just what was wanted, so that he could take up the matter wih Clemenceau's secretary.

This of course was a mere subterfuge, and we had no intentions of carrying on negotiations by correspondence. Instead, Major Warburton and I went to see Colonel Herscher, Clemenceau's secretary, and explained the whole case. Warburton then requested an interview with Clemenceau which was granted a few days later.

I regret that I was not present at the interview between Major Warburton and Clemenceau, for it must have been very interesting indeed. As Major Warburton tells the story, he recited the facts to Clemenceau as the reader knows them, and concluded with the request that I either be definitely refused admittance or admitted into *La Chambre Noire*. As Warburton unfolded the story, Clemenceau's anger mounted, and at the end he turned angrily to Colonel Herscher and instructed him to order General Mordacq and Colonel Cartier to appear before him the following morning at ten o'clock.

We do not know what was said the next morning, but judging from what followed and from what we know of Clemenceau's character, he must have given them both a fearful tongue-lashing for having admitted that France deciphered the Berlin-Madrid messages. One thing is certain, he told them to wiggle out of the squabble as gracefully as possible, but under no circumstances to permit me to enter *La Chambre Noire*. M. Pichon also must have felt the wrath of *Le Tigre*, for he now, for the first time, repudiated his conversation with Ambassador Sharp and me.

Cartier telephoned the next day for an immediate appointment with Major Warburton, with the request that I not be present.

Cartier told Warburton in effect that Clemenceau had directed him to turn over the diplomatic codes, but that he did not have them, never did have them, and had absolutely nothing to do with diplomatic code messages except their interception by wireless. He said that M. Pichon denied having told me and Ambassador Sharp that the messages reached the Foreign Office from him already deciphered. He was extremely excited, for he had the unpleasant task of discounting General Mordacq's admission that the messages were being deciphered and *the un-*

deniable fact that the French Ambassador in Washington, since my first visit to Mordacq, had transmitted to our State Department information these messages contained.

Two days before this Washington had asked me whether I thought it advisable to ask Colonel House to help, but when I cabled Warburton's interview with Clemenceau and Cartier, they readily saw how hopeless it would be to ask Colonel House to use his influence, for it was by now obvious to every one that France had no intention of permitting me to have even a peek into *La Chambre Noire*. Later, when the reader sees some of the diplomatic messages deciphered by our own Black Chamber, he will better appreciate the impossibility of my entering the doors of the diplomatic Code and Cipher Bureau of a foreign government. However, my negotiations were not wholly in vain, for my failure impressed upon American officials the absolute necessity for an American Black Chamber even in peace times, if the United States hoped to thwart the machinations of other governments.

That Washington was planning for the future I was assured by General Churchill's frequent letters, telling me that he was sure that, with my added knowledge of codes and ciphers obtained abroad, MI-8 would have no equal in the science of cryptography.

CHAPTER XII

At the Peace Conference

AN Armistice was declared between the German and Allied Armies the day of the Clemenceau interview. After cabling a résumé of my experiences with the French authorities and *La Chambre Noire*, I proceeded to General Headquarters at Chaumont and reported to General Nolan. I carried a letter to him from General Churchill which read:

> This will introduce Captain Yardley, Chief of our MI-8, who is leaving in a few days for France in response to your cablegram.
> I know that Van Deman has told you all about Yardley and the very high class work which he has done here. I can add but little to this except to say that we consider Captain Yardley one of our very best officers and we are delighted to be able to send you such a good representative of the Military Intelligence Branch. Please remember, however, that he is going over on temporary duty only and kindly refrain from stealing him.

General Nolan turned me over to his Cipher Bureau. The reader will recall that its personnel was trained in Washington. I haven't the space here to give an account of the accomplishments of this group of cryptographers, but I hope that when the authentic history of the World War is written, this small bureau will receive its rightful share of glory in the part that the American Expeditionary Forces played in the winning of the war.

While at Chaumont I received orders from Washington

149

to report to General Bliss, for "special duty at the Peace Conference." I cabled for further details and was instructed that my special duty was to organize code and cipher communications between the Peace Conference and the Military Intelligence Division at Washington. I was told that my status and allowances as Military Observer ceased when I reported to General Bliss, but that General Churchill, who would soon arrive in Paris, would provide an allowance from special funds.

I immediately left for Versailles and reported to General Bliss in person. He gave me a letter to Colonel Van Deman, who had been appointed Director of Intelligence at the Peace Conference, authorizing anything he considered necessary for establishing a Code Bureau in Paris. Van Deman in turn gave me the same authorization.

I immediately telegraphed General Headquarters for several particular officers and field clerks, demanded two rooms at 4 Place de la Concorde—the general offices of the Peace Conference—and within a short time was well organized. As it was difficult to anticipate my duties, I prepared for both a Communication and a Deciphering Bureau. Eventually we handled the messages of General Bliss, the Secretary of War and Military Intelligence; deciphered intercepted wireless messages of the Entente; and devised codes and ciphers for the House Mission secret agents, who entered Entente and Allied countries to make confidential reports to the President.

When the House Mission called on me to supply secret codes and ciphers for these agents, I cabled Washington full instructions for the particular type of code necessary. For seven days scarcely any one slept in MI-8 in Washington, but within that time they had compiled, proofread and printed a new code, an unheard-of accomplishment. In less that three weeks after my cable, this new code was in my hands.

This request of the House Mission also turned my office upside down, for there were special instructions to draw up, as each agent must have a different means of communication, and each message must be enciphered in a different key.

A stream of agents entered my office for special instruction, then penetrated Europe in every direction, fired with the importance of their missions. Was it not upon their reports of the longings and aspirations of downtrodden peoples that the President would depend for his momentous decisions? So they thought. However, they were soon disillusioned, for to my knowledge none of their reports ever reached the President.

One of these hopeful, courageous agents pulled me out of bed, while I was in Rome a few months later, and forced me to sit up all night while he delivered a bitter harangue. He told me how he had been sent to Montenegro* to discover the true facts of the so-called plebiscite that led to the Serbian seizure of Montenegro, our Ally. According to him, Serbia rushed troops into Montenegro, lined the streets with cannon and machine-guns and shot down any Montenegrin who dared leave his home on the day of the plebiscite. The Montenegrin leaders escaped into the mountains, where after untold hardships this agent had ferreted them out to get their story. Twice the enemies of Montenegro had tried to assassinate him.

Then he almost wept as he told me that he had sent one telegram after another about the rape of Montenegro, our Ally, and had not received so much as an acknowledgment.

"What can I do about it, Yardley?" he begged.

I couldn't see that he could do anything more than he had already done.

"But can't you use your influence with General Churchill?" he pleaded. "Can't you cable my story to him?"

"What good would that do?" I asked. "Your cables reached Paris all right. Don't take your mission so seriously. The President and the others of the Big Four are not playing penny ante. And after all, Montenegro is scarcely a blue chip."

"Then why did they ask me to risk my life?" he fiercely demanded.

That was a difficult question to answer, so I suggested he ask the House Mission. As for me, I was going to bed. If the President wasn't worried about the rape of Montenegro, I couldn't see why any one else should lose sleep over it.

Even if these agents were soon forgotten, at the time they caused us many long and arduous hours of work. The whole background of the American Delegation was fired with the desire to prepare our War President for his difficult task. And he was already on his way to Paris.

* Montenegro is today a constituent republic of Yugoslavia—Eds.

The work too was enlivened with exciting moments. Extremely important telegrams dealing with espionage came through my own private code, and I was obliged to decipher them personally. There were many such telegrams, for Paris swarmed with Allied and Entente spies. The Big Four were soon to redraw the map of the world, affecting the lives and destinies of millions. With such high stakes, the deck would contain many marked cards.

Though I had presupposed that there would be marked cards, and possibly a cold deck now and then, for I was already hardened to ruthless espionage as I saw it and read of it from secret reports, my heart skipped several beats as I slowly deciphered a telegram which gave information to the effect that a certain woman, associated with one of our Peace Commissioners before his marriage, was in England under pay from the British Government of twenty-five thousand pounds sterling for services until the end of the Peace Conference. The report stated that if his attitude at the Conference did not satisfy the English Government, they would use this woman to embarrass our Commissioner.

The telegram shocked me, but I soon became accustomed to this sort of thing. There was another report that a certain woman—let us call her Madame X—was in Paris in the employ of one of our Allies for the purpose of influencing the decisions of another one of our Peace Commissioners.

For twenty-four hours Colonel Van Deman had been unable to locate her. Then Captain Robert W. Goelet dropped in, heard the story, quietly slipped out, and within thirty minutes came back with her address.

Colonel Van Deman, who as Director of Intelligence at the Peace Conference had aged ten years, turned his wrinkled brow to Goelet in amazement, and asked how he did it. Goelet smiled good-naturedly and modestly told his story, an extremely clever bit of espionage.

He was, of course, known to almost every one in Paris, not only because of his wealth but also because of his social position. He reasoned that if Madame X was so famous for her beauty there were many men in Paris who knew her and were sending her flowers. He stepped into a fashionable florists', called to the proprietor whom he knew well, and asked him to select flowers and send them to Madame X.

"Ah—h, Madame X!" exclaimed the voluble Frenchman, and the young officer knew that he had reasoned wisely.

While the proprietor selected the flowers and personally wrapped them, Goelet hung about and chatted with him. Then, as the Frenchman without hesitation began to write on the package, Goelet edged closer and watched him slowly spell out the address for which Van Deman had searched in vain!

If I was unprepared for the sort of espionage that engages women to attempt to influence the decisions of our Peace Commissioners (though one should never be amazed at what occurs either during a war, or at the division of the spoils), the reader may well appreciate the shock I received as I deciphered a telegram which reported an Entente plot to assassinate President Wilson either by administering a slow poison or by giving him the influenza in ice. Our informant, in whom we had the greatest confidence, begged the authorities for God's sake to warn the President.

I have no way of knowing whether this plot had any truth in fact, and if it had, whether it succeeded. But there are these undeniable facts: *President Wilson's first sign of illness occurred while he was in Paris, and he was soon to die a lingering death.*

After the President arrived and the excitement subsided, there was not a great deal to do. In fact, except for a few overworked clerks, and the Commissioners themselves, the whole Peace Conference now developed into one grand cocktail party. Every one with the Mission received stacks of tea and dinner invitations. And in typical American fashion it was the general custom to blackball any French host or hostess who failed to serve champagne. No wonder the French dislike our manners!

Messages trickled in now and then from Washington about the status of MI-8. We were all dreaming now of a powerful peace-time Cipher Bureau, and at last, late in March, when it was obvious that MI-8 was rapidly disintegrating, General Churchill ordered me to proceed to Rome to see what information I could pick up there about codes and ciphers, and then to hurry to Washington to draw up plans for a peace-time organization.

In Rome I learned very little. The Italians were reported to be clever at cryptography, but I soon was convinced that they were not to be classed with the French and British.

The day I sailed for the United States from Genoa, a cable was forwarded to me from The Hague, stating that the German diplomatic codes I had failed to obtain from the British and French could be purchased there from a German for six thousand dollars. The Military Attaché had cabled me after I left Paris requesting that I proceed to The Hague in order to have the benefit of my judgment. As this would delay my arrival in Washington, it was finally decided that I proceed at once and send some one else to examine the codes.

CHAPTER XIII

Soviet Spies

WHEN I reached Washington in April, 1919, I found MI-8 in a sad state. There were no funds available to hold the civilian cryptographers and clerks, and a great many of the officers were anxious to return to civilian life.

However there was determination on every hand to continue the bureau during peace-time, for officials in all the departments recognized that in no other manner could the United States obtain an intimate knowledge of the true sentiments and intentions of other nations. They recognized that all the Great Powers maintained Cipher Bureaus, and that if the United States was to be placed on an equal footing it would be necessary to finance a group of skilled cryptographers.

After several conferences with responsible officials of the State, War and Navy Departments, we decided to demobilize the Shorthand Subsection; demobilize the Secret-Ink Subsection; transfer the Code Compilation Sub-Section to the Signal Corps (the reader will recall that Army regulations required the Signal Corps to compile codes); and restore Military Intelligence Communications to the Adjutant-General of the Army.

This then left only the Code and Cipher Solution Section.

My estimate for an efficient Cipher Bureau called for one hundred thousand dollars per annum. The State Department agreed to turn over to Military Intelligence forty thousand dollars per annum out of special funds, provided the Navy Department was entirely excluded, for they refused to share their secrets with the Navy. This left a deficit of sixty thousand dollars, which Military Intel-

155

ligence managed to obtain from Congress after taking some of the leaders into their confidence. I was told that there was a joker in the Department of State special funds: they could not legally be expended within the District of Columbia.

Since it seemed that we could not remain in the District of Columbia I was commissioned to go to New York and find a suitable place where the famous American Black Chamber could bury itself from the prying eyes of foreign governments.

Following the reasoning in Poe's "Purloined Letter" I selected as a home for the Black Chamber a four-story brownstone front in the East Thirties, just a few steps from Fifth Avenue—the very heart of New York City.

I returned to Washington and selected a group of the most efficient clerks and skilful cryptographers of MI-8, and packed up the necessary accessories of the successful Cipher Bureau—language statistics, dictionaries, maps, reference books, and our own *Who's Who* which included newspaper clippings dealing with international affairs.

I had, during the war, made many close friends with responsible business men and had been offered several attractive positions in the business world. My heart, however, was with codes and ciphers; so when the government offered to pay me seven thousand five hundred dollars per annum and assured me a future in cryptography, I agreed to direct the activities of this group.

Accordingly, after being demobilized (I had been promoted to the rank of Major), I led this small group of men and women to the brownstone front in New York City—the new home of the American Black Chamber.

Practically all contact with the government was now broken. All the employees, including myself, were now civilians on secret pay-roll. The rent, telephone, lights, heat, office supplies—everything was paid for secretly so that no connection could be traced to the government.

We were to read the secret code and cipher diplomatic telegrams of foreign governments—by such means as we could. If we were caught, it would be just too bad!

We employed guards, replaced all the locks and were ready to begin our secret activities. But there were now no code and cipher telegrams to work on! The cable censorship had been lifted and the supervision of messages restored to the private cable companies. Our problem was to obtain copies of messages. How?

I shall not answer this question directly. Instead I shall tell you something of the Soviet Government's type of espionage as revealed by documents that passed through my hands. After you read these, you can draw your own conclusions as to how the United States Government obtained the code and cipher diplomatic messages of foreign governments.

Not long after we took up quarters in the brownstone front, I received an unexpected call from one of my minor correspondents in Washington.

"How do you like the place?" I asked.

"All these locks give me the creeps."

He was nervous, as were many others after they entered the brownstone front. When I asked what he was doing in New York, he pulled out a sheaf of papers and handed them to me. There were seven sheets of cipher letters.

"Where did you get these?" I asked.

"They were turned over to us by the State Department," he told me, "and were originally taken from the occupants of a German aeroplane which was forced to land in Latvia while en route to Soviet Russia."

I studied the documents, three of which are shown below, for several moments.

Fortsetzung 4.		27001.	enere	donea	zneie
stuna	ittft	velds	henrs	304.	ptlzz
tnadm	nsdti	uikgt	vrpit	eschs	agert
levwi	otnis	edsai	ahnao	tdoiu	ngctn
reros	anmrc	heeeg	nennn	etkkv	iucit
osbic	eiren	keaof	iehtg	ungsr	omtre
rnpie	esoek	eruhu	nlben	tdlkk	lotte
eoiae	lrasn	eeson	rerlh	rdtrs	rrbra
hhrpn	knlnr	zdmhe	tisri ·	drdes	ieebl
tanta	sehge	enare	uiish	gkdrh	gamio
rlhha	ebrac	gnaei	baikl	eces.	

Fortsetzung 5.		27003.	intnt	eroci	tthhl
mtprn	rarde	ehsnb	eosnt	nhgzi	loioi
herar	easme	uantr	340.	eseec	keeij
elrtn	naece	ronsl	tvirg	bkhos	ncaei
zanta	rnrmn	esoha	ilaki	tirct	wanwv
lsgeh	egimn	obshd	nshro	pngfm	ecieu
sbrsp	irger	wirui	eelah	eekos	perwt
duthm	cegdu	ebabu	dasie	eavef	dierm
tsaai	rgoss	ohbne	eraet	omhti	dttni

brarm	rnnfs	zsnur	dsrda	bekiv	crelw
tlobe	athnl	onheu	scans	fhhbi	viubr
laeir	aioaj	ruigk	cafcc	tmntf	laatj
27003.	ksffr	remib	tuane	sgneo	eiscc
ebhee	etnee	ntize	940	apnze	eipic
dohua	elzun	ghgnr	mreri	etfeg	oiati
esetr	etndu	tedin	rnthh	nudek	laakw
vzgnk	llems	heser	rnncw	enehe	encne
eregu	rttrg	iotae	eaeee	oipmr	redsa
gkhlg	aleet	ntlat	uahke	tehad	lllse
gtesz	ihree	ginei	aeimi	eamlh	ecldu
srnkr	gthov	baies	raoei	iudrn	gwdsm
ssner	ntssu	gihsu	nnhii	eehol	euatu
deedn	nagej	zdtre	abebh	etrml	uimre
lireo	aabrc	iggie	gbeut	nclel	ucrpo
rugac	oreto	zuams	oleso	dlcoi	ottri
nonvu	iikid	wxten	aeruo	onwgr	gneen
meiil	hegkl	toscz	isuua	esdbi	dcbne
oeiie	nrgen	geeta	rdeai	tense	errhd
tctim	wbrzr	iilem	ithhf	tflon	skzum
eorle	eposi	ztmrc	efebh	eieki	cckia
dglrd	ietka	aefht	goeca	bssee	ifwte
cfleu	iihir	rvwxv	ghnhe	egrru	reucd
aeest	iihak	uarne	nricr	litef	deeen
braes	theim	garlh	sehin	ugnie	vunai
rkvhe	bssmb	inuau	ewdrn	ntaer	uibdv
nrone	ugile	uwbtb	essdm	dtnif	etaec
ianse	ndiyp	fmvre	nhbac	srnti	nnnub
nrnri	vauer	oerog	hnsnc	kaarn	ieees
gsemi	fnrui	rnths	ngtno	aeviu	lheru
nitte	agnhu	icggh	nraar	hddgr	tnuev
thort	aencl	oylms	maera	nnnke	efnre
rlgmf	hleln	hkonw	nslhl	snedu	ntaat
gltmh	ihmln	gukra	hciea	tgeut	tseal
nwtbb	neent	iatri	eane		

"I was instructed to tell you that the State Department wanted a decipherment at the earliest possible moment," he said.

"Yes? How do you suppose we go about deciphering a jumble of letters like this?"

"I haven't the faintest idea," he admitted. "I'm only repeating my instructions."

"You fellows in Washington are always in a terrible

rush to know the contents of a secret document. We'll do our best, but don't give them the idea that all we have to do is to go into a trance to reveal hidden secrets."

I showed him about the place, and got rid of him, for I was myself anxious to see what the messages said.

The Latvian Government, I later learned, had tried to decipher these messages and, after failing, had asked the American Consul at Riga to send them to the United States in order to see what the American cryptographers could do with them.

By the same analysis as that followed in the decipherment of the Waberski document we discovered that these ciphers were transposition, and written in German. I shall not go into the details of decipherment, for I am not sure that all readers will care to follow the method. However, for those who wish to try their hand at cryptography, I suggest they follow the analysis of the famous Pablo Waberski cipher.

I warn the amateur cryptographer, however, that these ciphers are much more difficult to solve, for the analysis will show him that the columns of the rectangle in which they were enciphered are of uneven length. He will require a great deal of ingenuity to place all the columns in their proper order. However, since he will be given the translation of the decipherment, he may be able to do this successfully.

The messages are of course from a Soviet secret agent, probably in Berlin, to his superiors in Russia—the aeroplane was en route to Soviet Russia. It seems obvious that all the names are aliases, for the second message ends with "My name is now Thomas. Regards, James." He is obviously directing Soviet espionage throughout the world. Note especially near the end of the messages the phrase, "GURALSKI arrived here with money on his way to America." The italics in the following messages are mine.

Translation of German Decoded Text
December 23, 1919.
Send money. Italy and France are urgently in need. *Large pearls sell well here; sapphires in England.* The Secretariat asks urgently for material. Money should be distributed through this Zentrale before the conference. In November, Secretariat elected PAUL LEVI, BRONSKI, ZETKINISH. Secretary is in touch with

Holland. The Communistic is issued here and I am also publishing the Russian Correspondence.

A branch has been installed in Vienna. At present no news from CARLO; he works extremely well. ABRANOWITCH, Paris, was there. Contact already established from here with all countries. Good progress is being made. Congress will meet surely January, February. RADEK will make detailed report to you. RADEK or BUCHARIN is absolutely needed here. Please send larger sum, as soon as ready. KOPP is really not able at present. My name now is THOMAS. Regards, JAMES.

The conference in Holland turned out a fiasco owing to the carelessness of the fellows there. KLARA and SYLVIA were arrested. The Dutch Press speaks of the sale of diamonds and of the executive decision of twenty millions. Increased activities by the police against the Secretariat is also noticeable. BRONSKI'S photos have fallen into their hands in an inexplicable manner. We suspect through Poles who are with you. LEVI and ALEXANDER have been arrested recently. Advise if you have the shorthand system of Stolze Schrei or Gabelsberger; in that case I would send shorthand notes. I have prospects of seeing you as a member of a medical mission or as a member of an emigrants' delegation. Please advise if satisfactory to you. *Radio station finally finished. Expert engaged. Next week we start in receiving. We need sums of money urgently for Bulgaria, Serbia and France.* The delegates are waiting here. *The fellow from Triest arrived with money from Italy.* He had been arrested in Vienna. *Money will shortly be sent from here to Italy. GURALSKI arrived here with money on his way to America.* German Government permits exchange of journalists from here. The "Frankfurter Zeitung" is taking advantage of the opportunity. Urgently needed capable talent.

These messages created a sensation among officials in Washington, for they were the first authentic documents that came into the government's possession dealing with international Soviet activities.

MI-8 also received original telegrams that Lenin sent to Bela Kun during the White revolution in Hungary. But these are too long to publish here.

There is one Soviet document, however, that is too revealing to pass over. I have always regretted that I was not employed by a government, such as the Soviet Government, that understood and practised espionage in the same ruthless and intelligent manner.

The following document to me is unique. Although espionage as practised by the Great Powers is no different from this, it is seldom that one comes into possession of a document that is so clear and frank in its instructions to secret agents.

Instructions to Agents for Hiring Spies in Legations

INSTRUCTIONS

When enlisting the Chinese servants and employees in the legations of Japan, England and America you must pay the utmost attention to the following subjects:

a) The man you enlist for our work, as a spy, must be first of all some use to us, that is he must be in touch with the people who carry on the most important and secret work in the Legation (the head of the Legation, the military attaché, the secretaries, etc.), or he must be in the employ as a translator, typewriter, or a boy in the offices of the Legation.

b) You must be certain that the man you enlist is not a traitor and that his reports may be relied upon.

c) He must not know that he works for the Russian Legation. You must make him believe that he works for a certain political party of China.

d) The man you enlist must inform us of the prominent Chinese and foreign gentlemen who frequently visit the Legations, the purposes of their visit, the conversations they hold with the responsible members of the Legation, etc.

He also must find out the people who are in charge of the secret military detective work in the Legation and the Chinese and foreign spies who are in the employ of the Legation.

He must find out where the secret documents and confidential correspondence are kept and find ways and means to steal or copy some of them, remembering that for this work we shall pay him a special premium besides his regular salary.

The striking thing about this document is that Soviet espionage plans so well that its minor spies do not even know that they are working for the Soviet Union!

The Soviet authorities in Moscow will be loud in their denial of the authenticity of this document, but they will recognize it; and having recognized it, will know that I must also possess other Soviet documents of a more sensational character. For instance, instructions for the massacre of foreign nationals, etc.*

---

* *Soviet agents, please note.* Yes, I once had copies of these documents, but I don't care to have my throat cut and do not plan to publish them. In fact they have been destroyed. So be reasonable.

CHAPTER XIV

Japanese Secret Codes

By July, 1919, we were all comfortably seated behind bolted doors, and had begun the work of attempting to make ourselves indispensable to the United States Government. I had assigned the diplomatic code and cipher telegrams of various governments to different groups of cryptographers, and had for myself selected the most difficult task of deciphering those of the Japanese Government.

The reader will recall that back in 1919 there was a great deal of anti-Japanese feeling throughout the world. The American people were especially concerned because Japan had brought up the question of race equality at the Peace Conference, and when Japan absolutely refused to restore the Chinese province, Shantung, which she had seized by conquest from Germany, there were loud recriminations in all newspaper headlines. Aside from this we feared the Anglo-Japanese Alliance which was still in effect. In fact we were suspicious of all nations, for were we not reading in the papers nearly every day of some secret agreement between the Allies which was unknown to us when we declared war against Germany?

It is therefore not difficult to understand why my superiors were especially concerned about the Japanese codes. They begged me to turn all my efforts to the unraveling of Japanese secrets, and I, in a moment of enthusiasm, had promised them either a solution or my resignation within a year.

I had before me about one hundred Japanese diplomatic code messages from and to different Japanese posts throughout the world. The following from the Japanese

Foreign Office in Tokio to the Japanese Ambassador in Washington will serve as an example:

From Tokio
To Koshi, Washington.   Sept. 15

60427	pkxpm	berimacaem	puupemceda
yotomatoma	naugdyikna	detogoisuf	kemaettoik
ovajneisuv	upuemiegto	yuxomakuar	maulonedzy
upoymapalo	tiirgoetsu	miabikuexo	yuwakydape
ugantoemkn	otdecatude	arpulivuzy	siufovetur
etdaseozyo	fyiskunaug	toemkunauf	ovucdexiuw
ofzuevozne	zuununigro	ogupolerze	upotulizto
gocaotdeca	tydearkuli	kulokutoda	kufexedeis
reoziyanow	xedeozneoy	maeljazyab	upuggeyoty
deofkuchfa	heuptosuog	suetkyyoiy	gozyfuirum
ikxetoempu	upkewuetaw	yootoeyoup	upbupeliik
etyuwaupow	mimukukyek	lepeokoyma	pyokmoemis
ikmozetoda	mietweowpu	sizysizyog	izuykuyaoz
peugannaku	wudeogliup	—culiikku	ugofdaewty
nenakyiyem	maumtonego	Uchida	JA: 8041

About all that a superficial study of this message discloses is that the code letters are sent in groups of ten, and that if we consider the letter y both a vowel and a consonant the letters are formed in either a vowel-consonant or a consonant-vowel combination.

During my absence abroad several unsuccessful attempts had been made to decipher these messages, and although I always have assumed that any code or cipher can be solved, during the next five months I was to regret many times that I had been so sanguine in my promise to reach a solution within one year. Since my return to the United States I had worked over these messages at odd moments, but it was not until July that I began a serious and methodical analysis.

I shall not of course attempt to give all the details of the decipherment of the Japanese codes, for these would be of interest only to the cryptographer, but when I tell the reader that the Black Chamber sent to Washington, during the Washington Armament Conference held two years later, some five thousand deciphered Japanese messages which contained the secret instructions of the Japanese Delegates, I am sure he will wish to know how it was possible for the Black Chamber to take such an important

164

part in the making of history. Let the reader therefore, for the moment at least, put aside his natural desire to listen to the whisperings of foreign diplomats as they lean closer together to reveal their secrets, and I shall try to tell a few of the tremendous discouragements that I had to overcome in the decipherment of this code, written in the most difficult of all languages, Japanese.

At the time I began this enormous task I knew nothing about the Japanese language. Before we begin to analyze these code telegrams, let us therefore see just how the Japanese language is formed.

Japanese differs in grammar and in vocabulary in its spoken and written forms, but here we have to deal with the written form only. From about the ninth century on, the classical language was expressed by the use of Chinese ideographs. These ideographs, as of course the reader knows, are either pictorial or arbitrary symbols. We might call ⊙ a pictorial ideograph, which, though expressing no sound, might symbolize and be pronounced *sun* in our language, while in another the sound would be quite different, the idea *sun* however remaining the same. In our language we have such symbols as *1, 2, 3, ?, !,* etc. Though pronounced differently in other languages they mean the same thing.

The method adopted by the Japanese of expressing their language in Chinese ideographs proved very cumbersome, and in the course of time it became necessary to resort to abbreviations which finally took the form of *kana.* The *kana,* which might be termed the Japanese alphabet or syllabary, is expressed in seventy-three or more ideographs representing Japanese and Chinese sounds. Later, in order to express Japanese in Roman letters, these ideographs were Romanized.

The *kana* ideographs and the Romanized *kana* are both given on the following page.

イ I	マ MA	カ KA	ド DO	ザ ZA	ム MU
㋺ RO	ケ KE	ガ GA	チ CHI	キ KI	ウ U
㋩ HA	グ GE	㋵ YO	ヂ JI	ギ GI	ヰ WI
パ BA	フ FU	タ TA	リ RI	エ YU	ノ NO
パ PA	プ BU	ダ DA	ヌ NU	メ ME	オ O
二 NI	プ PU	レ RE	ル RU	ミ MI	グ KU
ホ HO	コ KO	ソ SO	ヲ WO	シ SHI	グ GU
ボ BO	ゴ GO	ゾ ZO	ワ WA	ヂ ZI	ヤ YA
ポ PO	エ E	ツ TSU	ヱ YE		セ SE
ヘ HE	テ TE	ヅ DZU	ヒ HI		ゼ ZE
べ BE	デ DE	ネ NE	ビ BI		ズ SU
ペ PE	ア A	ナ NA	ピ PI		ズ ZU
ト TO	サ SA	ラ RA	モ MO		ン N

Let us see how far the Japanese have gone in order to express their language by Roman letters, taking the word *independence* as an example:

"Independence:"　　獨　立　(Chinese ideograph)

　　　　　　　ド ク リ ツ　(Japanese *kana* ideograph)

　　　　　Do ku ri tsu　(Japanese Romanized *kana*)

The *kana*, of course, has its drawbacks, because without the inflection of voice the meanings can be determined only by the text. Thus, a single *kana* may have as many as fifteen different meanings. Aside from this the Japanese did not use the Roman letters *l*, *q*, *v* and *x*, because these sounds do not appear in Japanese. Thus, when they wish to spell a foreign word they render the most curious phonetic spelling. For example, *Ireland* in Japanese *kana* is spelled *a i ru ra n do*—the *ru ra* being their closest sound to the letters *rela* in the word *Ireland*.

The reader has now had a glimpse of a Japanese code message and an outline of the formation of the Japanese language itself, and recognizes, I trust, the seemingly impossible task I had assumed, when I lightly boasted that within a year I would expose the Japanese secrets. In any case, I felt the heavy hand of despair. If I was to succeed I would indeed need all the careful training and experience that I had received over a period of seven long years.

If there was any hope at all of succeeding, I must first collect elaborate statistics of the letter, syllable and word formation of Japanese. Fortunately, I had available about twenty-five telegrams written in Romanized *kana*. The following will serve as an example:

From Peking
To Gaimudaijin, Tokio.

04301 beisikan nankinjuken kaiketu nikansi toohooen yeikanjisi ronpyoogaiyoo sanogotosi sinshoo . . .

My first step was to split these Japanese words into *kana* and turn over all the telegrams to a corps of typists to rewrite on special sheets, numbering the pages consecutively and giving each line a letter reference. The telegram already quoted would then appear thus:

Page 1

From Peking
To Gaimudaijin, Tokio.

line	a	04301	be i si ka n	na n ki n ju ke n	ka i ke tu
	b			ni ka n si	too hoo e n	ye i ka n ji si
	c			ro n py oo ga i yoo	sa no go to si	si n shoo

The Japanese plain language telegrams gave me in all about 10,000 *kana*. After the typists had recopied all the telegrams, I instructed them to index each and every *kana* on a separate three-by-five card. The information on each card contained the particular *kana* under study in capital letters, the page and line reference, and the 4 preceding and the 4 following *kana*.

To illustrate the method: each of the following horizontal lines shows just what was typed on each card.

.	.	.	.	BE	i	si	ka	n	1-a
.	.	.	be	I	si	ka	n	na	1-a
.	.	be	i	SI	ka	n	na	n	1-a
.	be	i	si	KA	n	na	n	ki	1-a
be	i	si	ka	N	na	n	ki	n	1-a
i	si	ka	n	NA	n	ki	n	ju	1-a
si	ka	n	na	N	ki	n	ju	ke	1-a
ka	n	na	n	KI	n	ju	ke	n	1-a
n	na	n	ki	N	ju	ke	n	ka	1-a
na	n	ki	n	JU	ke	n	ka	i	1-a
n	ki	n	ju	KE	n	ka	i	ke	1-a
ki	n	ju	ke	N	ka	i	ke	tu	1-a
n	ju	ke	n	KA	i	ke	tu	ni	1-a
ju	ke	n	ka	I	ke	tu	ni	ka	1-a
ke	n	ka	i	KE	tu	ni	ka	n	1-a
n	ka	i	ke	TU	ni	ka	n	si	1-a
ka	i	ke	tu	NI	ka	n	si	too	1-b
i	ke	tu	ni	KA	n	si	too	hoo	1-b
ke	tu	ni	ka	N	si	too	hoo	e	1-b
tu	ni	ka	n	SI	too	hoo	e	n	1-b

When the work was completed there were about 10,000 cards. These cards were now assorted according to the *kana;* that is, all the *ba*'s were collected together, all the *be*'s, *bi*'s, *bo*'s, etc. All the *ba*'s were then arranged in the alphabetic order of the immediate preceding *kana,* and so on with the *be*'s, *bi*'s, etc.

Now 10,000 cards are cumbersome to examine. I therefore instructed my typists to type the statistics contained on these cards on legal-size sheets of paper. If we take the 20 cards already quoted and arranged them in the foregoing manner and then type the result on one sheet of paper, we would have the following:

.	.	.	.	BE	i	si	ka	n
.	.	.	be	I	si	ka	n	na
ju	ke	n	ka	I	ke	tu	ni	ka
na	n	ki	n	JU	ke	n	ka	i
n	ju	ke	n	KA	i	ke	tu	ni
i	ke	tu	ni	KA	n	si	too	hoo
.	be	i	si	KA	n	na	n	ki
ke	n	ka	i	KE	tu	ni	ka	n
n	ki	n	ju	KE	n	ka	i	ke
ka	n	na	n	KI	n	ju	ke	n
ke	tu	ni	ka	N	si	too	hoo	e
be	i	si	ka	N	na	n	ki	n
ki	n	ju	ke	N	ka	i	ke	tu
n	na	n	ki	N	ju	ke	n	ka
si	ka	n	na	N	ki	n	ju	ke
i	si	ka	n	NA	n	ki	n	ju
ka	i	ke	tu	NI	ka	n	si	too
.	.	be	i	SI	ka	n	na	n
tu	ni	ka	n	SI	too	hoo	e	n
n	ka	i	ke	TU	ni	ka	n	si

Now if the reader will picture 10,000 lines instead of 20 lines, he will have some idea of the statistics that I had before me of the Japanese language. Even in these 20 lines we see that there are 5 N's and that in 2 of the 5 occurrences *ka* is the preceding *kana*. In other words, we find that *kana* N has the highest frequency and that the highest 2-*kana* combination is *kan*.

The cards were now all rearranged according to the suffix of each *kana* and typed on sheets, so that I had before me graphic charts of both prefix and suffix, or in all 20,000 lines.

Next, the beginnings and endings of all telegrams were copied one beneath the other so that I could discover similar endings and beginnings if there were any.

These charts produced too many queer behaviors for me to attempt to record them all here, but a few examples are of interest. I discovered that the order of frequency of single *kana* is:

n	o	wa
i	ni	ru
no	shi	to etc.

These charts also told me that the most common syllables and words are:

ari	hyaku	koku	migi
aritashi	hyoo	kooshi	moshikuwa
daijin	jin	kore	mottomo
denpoo	kai	koto	narabini
gai	kaku	kyoku	nen
gyoo	kan	kyoo	nichi
hon	ken	kyuu	nikanshi
honkan	kiden	man	etc.

I also learned that Japanese has many repeated sounds that produce such curious doublets as:

ruru	mama	daidai	wawa
gogo	shishi	kokukoku	kiki
nono	kaka	sasa	toto
tsutsu	oo	tata	
koko	momo	kaikai	etc.

The prefix and suffix tables showed me exactly what

169

letters can precede and follow any given *kana*. Let us take *no* as an example and see what the prefix and suffix charts tell us:

	Prefix		Suffix
mo	no	no	kan
to	no	no	go
kyooyaku	no	no	ji
dan	no	no	do
go	no	no	ki
seifu	no	no	shu
ryoo	no	no	to
koo	no	no	i
suru	no	no	gen
etc.			etc.

The exact number of occurrences of these behaviors and just where they occurred in the telegrams (line and page number) were, of course, carefully recorded.

Now while all this work was going on, no small task I assure you, I received a great many good-natured but pitying smiles from my subordinates, for the job of deciphering Japanese code telegrams had already been given up as hopeless. The reader, however, has already seen how I proved that Japanese has its peculiar letter, syllable and word behaviors just as any other language has. Of course, without the assistance of a corps of typists this work would have been too enormous even to contemplate.

But what about the *code* telegrams!

Let the reader again examine the code message on page 164. Now that we have our Japanese language charts, how shall we go about deciphering these telegrams? How indeed! Since April, and this was now July, I had pored over these code messages at odd moments trying to discover what type of code or cipher the Japanese were using. I finally made up my mind that these messages were encoded with a two-letter code. If I should go into the labyrinth of analytical details showing why I finally arrived at this opinion, I am afraid that we should never get to the Washington Armament Conference, or at least not in this book.

Whether right or wrong I had to start at some point. I turned the telegrams over to my typists with instructions to divide the ten-letter code words into two-letter groups and copy them in the same manner as they had the Japanese language telegrams. They selected approximately 10,000 two-letter groups and carded each group on a separate card, showing the four-code-group-prefix and the four-code-group-suffix, just as they had done with the Japanese *kana*. These cards were sorted according to prefix and copied on sheets, then sorted according to suffix and again copied. I now had before me not only 20,000 lines of Japanese language data, but also 20,000 lines of code data.

The typing and indexing, the retyping and reindexing, in all 60,000 lines, as well as the compilation of reduced statistical charts, together with other miscellaneous data—all this work, done by a corps of typists, is the background of the scientific cryptographer. The reader will now better appreciate the difficulties I experienced as a clerk back in the State Department when I was deciphering our own diplomatic codes, for, since I was working alone, I was obliged to do all this drudgery.

As I had anticipated, the indexing of these code words, both by their prefix and suffix, revealed in graphic form repetitions of varied lengths. My first step then was to go through all the messages and underline in different colored pencil all the repetitions of four or more letters. This work I did myself, in order to familiarize myself with the text. My typists also compiled tables of these repetitions, taking great pains to add the references (page and line) so that I could instantly refer to the exact position in which they occurred in the messages.

One of the most striking points that these charts revealed was that the code group *en* occurred only 11 times, and that its position was, in most cases, in the last ten-letter code group of the messages. Now one of the reasons that I had been uncertain of the possibility of a two-letter code was the fact that the last code word *always* contained 10 letters. As the reader can see, in a two-letter code there is only one chance in five of the message ending in letters divisible by 10. How would it be possible to encode a message in a two-letter code and still always have 10 letters in the last group? Only in one way. The group *en* must mean *stop* and the letters following are to be disregarded, being used merely to fill out the ten-letter group so that the foreign decipherer would be uncertain as to the type of code in use. My first guess then was: *en* = Stop?

In order to show you how very clever the Japanese were,

171

it is interesting to note that although the message actually ended with *en,* as we discovered after the code was solved, *en* did not mean *stop* in the Japanese code. It stood for the Roman letter *p.* The code word *ab* equaled *stop!* This is a very important point indeed, for had I immediately identified *ab,* which I could have, had the Japanese used this group at the end of messages, I would have been able at once to indicate throughout all the messages just where each sentence began and ended.

The Japanese language charts before me showed that a very frequent word-ending of Japanese telegrams was the Japanese word *aritashi*—a grammatical verb construction. This word, if encoded one *kana* at a time, *a ri ta shi,* would require 4 code words or 8 letters. It therefore followed that somewhere near the end of some of these telegrams I should find the same repetition of 8 letters. I say *should.* As a matter of fact there were no such repetitions. I did discover however that the code word *yu* occurred very frequently before *en (en = stop).* Perhaps *yu* meant *aritashi.* This later proved correct, but at the time I had no proof.

My first two cards (all guesses were placed on separate cards) read:

"EN = Stop?—see message endings"
"YU = Aritashi?—see YU-EN near message
          endings"

This was very discouraging. I was obliged to give up my theories, though partly correct, as to the identification of *stop* and *aritashi.* Perhaps it was not a two-letter code. Perhaps the language was not Japanese. It might be English or French. The old Russian Government had used French for diplomatic correspondence; Soviet telegrams were often in German; the Chinese Government codes were in English. I must confess that I was discouraged.

For inspiration for this task (I pored over these messages every day and long into the night), I received the constant encouragement of my government, but that was of no definite aid. I also wrote long letters to Dr. John M. Manly, who had returned to his work at the University of Chicago, for I sadly missed his originality of mind. His replies of warm sympathy and assurance that I was on the right track kept me at it.

I can't tell you how delighted I am to hear that you have yourself begun to work on those important messages [he wrote], and that you have made so promising a beginning. . . . The agreements you found are very striking . . . your method is fine and your results are probably right . . . there isn't one chance in ten thousand that you haven't hit the meaning of the differential group. . . . How I wish I were with you. . . .

And how I wished he were with me! These letters kept up my courage though I still worked mostly in circles. Finally I made several trips down to the Japanese Consulate in New York to look the ground over and make up my mind as to the possibilities of getting into the Consulate's safe for a peep at his code book. If I could only be *sure* that I was on the right track. But this would be too dangerous to try in New York. Why not try it in some other country, where, if caught, we would not be suspected! I must see Blank about this, and get his opinion. One think was certain. Washington had given me a job to do— the decipherment of the Japanese codes. If I couldn't do it one way, I'd have to do it in another.

I took up again the history of the decipherment of the Rosetta Stone, which led to the reading of the Egyptian hieroglyphics on the ancient monuments of Egypt. The problem here was not unlike my own, but the method of attack used by scholars was so primitive and elementary that I did not get much encouragement. Their idea as to what constitutes evidence in the correct identification of any given ideograph was so vague that for centuries they had published solutions that later proved to be mere nonsense. Even Champollion, who in 1822 finally arrived at a correct solution, had as late as 1821, twenty-two years after the discovery of the Rosetta Stone, published decipherments which a year later he was forced to admit were pure imagination. Now it is one thing for a scholar to startle the world with such fantasies, only later to repudiate them; but it is quite another thing for the cryptographer to hand his government an incorrect solution of another government's diplomatic secrets. The first merely amuses the public; the second might well lead to war.

However, no matter how elementary their methods of attack, no matter how often they published their fantasies, there is one thing to be said about these scholars—they kept at it and after twenty-three years arrived at a correct solution. And if it took them this long, was it not silly of me to be so quickly discouraged? Thus, I kept closely at my task, disproving one theory after another.

In this labor I received the quiet but confident encouragement of my wife. I worked long into the night, yet when I climbed the stairs to our apartment on the top floor, I always found her, no matter at what hour, reading, studying or sewing. She never asked any questions and listened in silence to my long stories of failure while she prepared me something to eat. And while I ate, and drank quantities of black coffee for I could not sleep without it, I told her, over and over again, that I would never succeed.

"The damned stuff may not even be Japanese," I complained. "I don't believe it is a two-letter code. What do you think?"

"I think you ought to go to bed."

"I doubt if I'll ever solve this code. Do you think so?"

"Of course you will."

"Why, of course? The whole thing is an absolute blank."

"You always talk that way when you are close to a solution. Don't you think you should get some sleep?"

I would go to bed, and two hours later wake up with a brilliant idea and rush down the stairs to my office, open the safe, and start all over again, for now I knew I had the solution. No, just another false lead. And so on, month after month.

During my struggles, General Churchill made frequent trips to New York City. He usually came up on the midnight train, and I met him at Robert W. Goelet's home on Fifth Avenue, where he always took breakfast.

In one of my darkest moments, and they were many, I suddenly thought of a plan to outwit the Japanese. I asked General Churchill whether the Japanese Military Attaché at Washington ever served as an intermediary for the exchange of communications between the Military Intelligence Division and the Japanese War Office.

When he told me that such was the case, I asked whether he would be willing to hand the Japanese Military Attaché a memorandum for transmission by cable to the latter's government. I explained that if we knew the contents of a telegram, we might be able to identify a few words by superimposing the plain text on the code groups.

"I get your idea, Yardley," he told me, "and I must say it is a very ingenious one. But I doubt if our memorandum after translation into Japanese would be sufficiently close to the English original to be of much help."

"I can explain that," I said eagerly, for here was an opportunity not to be lost. "To begin with we must draft a memorandum of sufficient importance to require the Military Attaché to cable. We can mark the memorandum urgent and even request him to cable for our information. Proper names he will be obliged to spell out for his code will not contain them. If his cable, even after translation into Japanese and encoded in his code, still retains the proper name, I'm sure I can find it, though I have only the code message to examine."

He smiled at me good-naturedly.

"That may sound simple to you, but I still don't quite understand."

"Well," I tried again, searching desperately for an example, "suppose we dig up the name of some one who has recently come to the United States from Tokio, a Russian for instance. Now draft a cable something like this. 'Any information that you or the Japanese War Office may have regarding the political activities while in Tokio of one Herbert Charley or Hubert Yardley, a Russian subject, reported as sailing from Yokohoma to San Francisco on November first, is urgently requested.'

"The ideal repetition is one where the difference is between similar beginnings and endings. Can't you see how simple it would be for me to find these names in the code message? I'm sure a telegram along these lines would enable me to break into the code. Do you think a bona fide case can be found?"

This idea intrigued Churchill for he was born for espionage. Later, however, he told me that they had been unable to find a real case that would fit. It might take some time; we must make no error that would lead the Japanese to believe that they were being duped.

General Churchill, in my opinion, was the greatest executive produced by the General Staff during the war. He knew what he wanted, but when he told his subordinates to do a job he was ready at all times to lend them any aid at his command.

The reader must not get the impression that I had given up all hope of deciphering the Japanese codes without aid. I had not. Nor were any of my plans fulfilled, for as we shall soon see I had no need of them. But I was preparing myself for failure. I *might* need assistance.

By now I had worked so long with these code telegrams that every telegram, every line, even every code word was indelibly printed in my brain. I could lie awake in bed and in the darkness make my investigations—trial and error, trial and error, over and over again.

Finally one night I wakened at midnight, for I had retired early, and out of the darkness came the conviction that a certain series of two-letter code words absolutely *must* equal *Airurando* (Ireland). Then other words danced before me in rapid succession: *dokuritsu* (independence), *Doitsu* (Germany), *owari* (stop). At last the great discovery! My heart stood still, and I dared not move. Was I dreaming? Was I awake? Was I losing my mind? A solution? At last—and after all these months!

I slipped out of bed and in my eagerness, for I knew I was awake now, I almost fell down the stairs. With trembling fingers I spun the dial and opened the safe. I grabbed my file of papers and rapidly began to make notes.

WI	UB	PO	MO	IL	RE	(code)
a	i	ru	ra	n	do	(Ireland)

The word *independence* should follow Ireland, for Ireland was then fighting for her freedom.

WI	UB	PO	MO	IL	RE	RE	OS	OK	BO	(code)
a	i	ru	ra	n	do	do	ku	ri	tsu	(Ireland independence)

The only proof here of a correct solution is the repetition: *re re.*
    do do

Now, one of the frequent repetitions in the code messages is *re ub bo.* I already have *ub, re* and *bo.* By filling
                 i do   tsu
these out in their correct order, I have:

RE	UB	BO	(code)
do	i	tsu	(Germany)

I had suspected for a long time that *as fy ok* (code) which occurs several times in the messages means some word for *stop*. The Japanese word must end in *ri,* for I

176

have already identified *ok* in the word for independence.

I try the Japanese word *owari*, which means *conclusion:*

	ri		
AS	FY	OK	(code)
o	wa	ri	(stop)

This looks very good indeed, though of course is not absolute proof.

I make a chart now in order to see how nearly correct I am, or at least to see in how many places the same meanings occur.

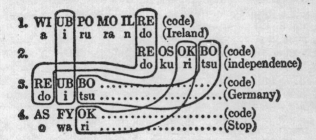

1. WI UB PO MO IL RE (code)
   a i ru ra n do (Ireland)

2. RE OS OK BO (code)
   do ku ri tsu (independence)

3. RE UB BO .... (code)
   do i tsu .... (Germany)

4. AS FY OK .... (code)
   o wa ri .... (Stop)

Even this small chart convinces me that I am on the right track. For an hour I filled in these and other identifications until they had all been proved to my satisfaction.

Of course, I have identified only part of the *kana*—that is, the alphabet. Most of the code is devoted to complete words, but these too will be easy enough once all the *kana* are properly filled in.

The impossible had been accomplished! I felt a terrible mental let-down. I was very tired.

I finally placed my papers in the safe, locked it and leaned back in my chair, checking up my blunders, and at the same time wondering what this would mean to the United States Government. What secrets did these messages hold? Churchill would want to know of my accomplishment. Should I telephone him at this hour? No, I would wait and dictate a letter.

I was unbelievably tired, and wearily climbed the stairs. My wife was awake.

"What's the matter?" she asked.

"I've done it," I replied.

"I knew you would."

"Yes, I suppose so."

"You look dead."

"I am. Get on your rags. Let's go get drunk. We haven't been out of this prison in months."

CHAPTER XV

A Missionary Cryptographer

THE next morning, or rather the same, I dictated a long letter to Churchill, outlining in detail what the reader already knows. I did this for two reasons. General Churchill was always interested in the details of my bureau, and besides I had no small measure of pride in having solved the Japanese codes and wished a record in the War Department files. Churchill had been especially anxious to have a few Japanese telegrams in his possession when we went to Congress for Military Intelligence appropriation. These I promised him in ample time.

I shouldn't wonder but that this letter sounded a bit youthful. Even yet, the memory of those exciting days thrills me.

When General Churchill received my letter he did not wait to write, but telephoned his congratulations, and told me that those in authority would hear of the new success of my bureau. Judging by the tenor of his voice and words, he was more excited than we were.

After dictating the letter I instructed my secretary to tell my cleverest cryptographer, Charles Mundy (I shall call him this for want of a better name, for he now holds a position that might be jeopardized were his past history known), that I wanted to see him.

When he came in I knew by the expression of his small eyes that looked at me through thick lenses that he already knew of the breaking of the Japanese diplomatic codes. In fact I had sensed an air of excitement throughout the office. Every one had anxiously been awaiting the breaking of this code and no doubt had guessed of my success by my manner.

When I showed him a part of my analysis, he smiled his pleasure.

"How are the Russian codes progressing?" I asked.

"We're still working on the manuscript," he said. "The code doesn't look very difficult."

"I may be wrong," I told him. "But I have the feeling that these Japanese codes will make history. I need a Japanese scholar to read them. I have already canvassed the United States for one without success. I'll find one somehow or other. But you know how translators are. It's one chance in a thousand that he will ever develop cipher brains. In my opinion it may be easier for a cryptographer to learn Japanese than for a Japanese student to learn cryptography. I'm going to give some one here an opportunity to study Japanese. I'll give him a year, or two years if necessary, to learn the language. I'll get a fund from Washington for this purpose. Now the person I select for this job need no longer have any strings attached to him. He need report to me but once a month to convince me of his progress."

I could see his little eyes burn with desire. I have never seen a man who was so intrigued with the intricacies of strange languages.

"How would you like the job?" I asked.

"I can't imagine anything more interesting," he replied without hesitation.

"All right, you are elected to become our Japanese specialist. I'll turn the Russian codes over to some one else, and have a desk moved in for a while and we will both complete the decipherment of this code while I see if I can't find a Japanese scholar for you to study with."

Since August I had been making a canvass of American Japanese students through the American International Corporation, Standard Oil, American Military Attaché at Tokio, Diplomatic and Consular Service, Foreign Mission Board in the United States, and various other organizations.

I had already written some five hundred letters; most of the replies came from foreign missionaries:

Though I lived in Japan fifteen years, I have only a slight acquaintance of the language. Bishop Blank's daughter, I understand, speaks the language fluently.

The Bishop's daughter wrote:

I speak Japanese fluently but have no knowledge of the written language. I understand Bishop Blank reads Japanese readily.

This Bishop wrote me:

I am leaving for Japan next week. Reverend Blank translated the New Testament into Japanese.

The Reverend Blank wrote:

Am slowly recovering from a recent operation and can undertake no work that will take me away from Blank. All the men I know who could do the work hold rather important positions and I doubt if you can secure their services.

I was planning ahead for a translator in case I finally broke the Japanese code, but I met with difficulties on every hand. The truth of the matter was that the men who really knew Japanese were missionaries and hesitated to attach themselves to the United States Government, even temporarily (I told them they were to act merely as translators), because the Japanese Government already believed that a Government Intelligence was behind the ten million dollars spent each year for missionary work in Korea and Japan. I was told that no missionary could hope to succeed in either Korea or Japan if the Japanese Government learned of their connection, no matter how slight, with the United States Government.

I had already discussed with General Churchill the advisability of subsidizing the Oriental Language Department of some university, giving a four-year language course to about ten students, then sending the best students to Japan for three years, and from the remainder selecting two or three and offering them a future in the American Black Chamber.

But this plan would take seven years, and I wanted the job done in seven months!

All this looked rather hopeless, but I kept at it and finally discovered a retired missionary of some sixty years of age who I was told was one of America's best Japanese scholars. I paid his expenses to New York and after sizing the man up put all my cards on the table and tried to intrigue his mind with the mystery of codes and ciphers.

He demurred at first and I thought he was afraid to attach himself to an under-cover organization that was prying into the affairs of foreign governments. But I suddenly learned that he was just a good horse-trader and was holding out for more money than I had at first offered. We finally came to an agreement, and he immediately moved his family to New York.

I now regrouped my cryptographers, and selected the most rapid and accurate clerks (accuracy on the part of clerks will often save months of futile investigations in the decipherment of a code) for the Japanese Department.

I selected the largest room available, placed our long-whiskered missionary and thick-spectacled cryptographer at adjacent desks, and changed the locks and keys.

The Black Chamber, housing as it did so many persons of queer sorts, seemed almost like a menagerie, but I never failed to laugh to myself every time I went into the Japanese Department and saw this benevolent-faced, whiskered, old missionary as he puzzled over Japanese words, *kana* and code groups. He was instantly the favorite of the whole office. He was so gentle and so very frightened at the mystery and secrecy. I had never expected to live to see a missionary engaged in espionage. I don't think he ever quite realized what he was doing.

However he was a good translator and in February, 1920, I sent to Washington the first translations of Japanese decipherments. When General Churchill received these messages he took them at once to the Chief of Staff and to officials of the State Department, and told me personally that he considered their decipherment the most remarkable accomplishment in the history of code and cipher work in the United States. He told me to extend to my assistants his personal regards and official congratulations.

I do not make these statements to magnify the accomplishments of the American Black Chamber. History alone will decide those things. I cite them as a tribute to the fine general officer under whom we served. He knew and understood that men and women to succeed at cryptography must be inspired both by a passion for the science and by sympathetic leadership. Certainly, no human being would burn up his heart and brain without the latter.

On June 12, 1920, our missionary made the following translation of a Japanese code message from the Japanese Foreign Office in Tokio to the Japanese Ambassadors to Washington and London. The italics are mine.

A cabinet council has decided on a partial evacuation of the Japanese army from districts of Siberia. The substance of the decisions reached is given in circular No. 104 [No. 309].

In the withdrawal from the respective districts serious thought must be given to the future of the *Semenoff* administration which *has had special relations with the Japanese army.* If the policy of withdrawal is carried out heedlessly and hastily the Semenoff administration may be reduced to desperation and extreme dissatisfaction and engage in a course of action which would cause anxiety for the safety of our troops. *In view of this the possibility of establishing a provisional buffer nation of the far eastern provinces has been advocated as a temporary expedient on the part of our army alone.*

An endeavor is also being made to secure a neutral zone by negotiation with the Verkhneudinsk council. In addition to representatives of the army, Matsudaira, the chief of the administrative section, has been sent to negotiate this.

A partial leakage to foreign governments about these proceedings might produce complications for the whole plan, and you will keep this information extremely confidential to yourself alone.

The last paragraph beginning, "A partial leakage to foreign governments about these proceedings might produce complications," weighed heavily upon the gentle soul of our missionary. For the first time he seemed to realize that he was engaged in espionage, and at last asked to be relieved. He had been with us just six months.

Although the Black Chamber missed the friendliness and kindness of this gentle old fellow, his resignation did not disturb the steady flow of Japanese translations, for in six months Mundy had accomplished the unheard-of thing of mastering the reading of the Japanese language. He had done well in six months what it takes army officers in Japan three years to do poorly. He had the greatest capacity for languages of any one I have ever known. Even back in 1917 when he came to MI-8 he had this facility, but cryptography had sharpened his intellect. He had no originality of mind as a cryptographer, however, and needed assistance when a new cipher problem confronted him; but as a sponge for absorbing languages he had no equal.

The code I had broken, I designated *Ja* for reference purposes—the *J* standing for Japanese, the *a* an arbitrary designation. The next code we solved would be termed *Jb*, the next *Jc*, etc.

Now the Japanese had no intention of permitting us to rest on our laurels, for from 1919 until the spring of 1920 they introduced eleven different codes.

We learned that they had employed a Polish cipher expert to revise their code and cipher systems. It took all our skill to break the new codes that this man produced, but by now we had developed a technique for the solution of Japanese codes that could read anything. Theoretically the Japanese codes were now more scientifically constructed; practically they were easier to solve than the first code, although some of them contained as many as twenty-five thousand *kana*, syllables and words.

The Polish cryptographer seemed to specialize on army codes, for the Japanese Military Attaché's codes suddenly became more difficult than those of any other branch of the Japanese Government. This new system was elaborate and required ten different codes. The Japanese would first encode a few words of their message in one code, then by the use of an "indicator" jump to another code and encode a few words, then to still another code, until all ten had been used in the encoding of a single message.

Messages encoded in this manner produced a most puzzling problem, but after several months of careful analysis, I discovered the fact that the messages were encoded in ten different systems. Having made this discovery, I quickly identified all the "indicators." From this point on it was not difficult to arrive at a solution.

The Japanese Government must have received information of our successes, because they not only employed a Polish cryptographer to revise their codes, but also began a series of well-planned and secret inquiries at the Cable Companies as to whether it was possible for the United States to obtain copies of their code telegrams after they had been filed for dispatch.

Information of this type always reached me, for as Chief of the Black Chamber, I was not only executive and cryptographer, but was obliged to maintain my own espionage system as well.

Early in 1921 there were rumblings of an Armament Conference for the limitation or reduction of arms. No doubt anticipating this, the Japanese again launched a new type of code that was destined to give us a great deal of trouble. Our quick decipherments had largely depended on the fact that their routine manner of composing telegrams gave us hints of words or phrases to expect either at the beginning or ending of telegrams. This made the identification of a few groups in a new code comparatively easy.

But they suddenly switched their method and for several weeks we were in despair. This change required us to develop a new technique to arrive at a solution.

I am sure the Japanese, or Polish, method is worth describing. When a telegram was handed to a code clerk for encoding, he first split the messages in two, three or four parts, depending upon its length. These parts were now given a letter of the alphabet. If there were only two sections they were lettered Y and Z; if there were three sections, they were lettered X, Y and Z; if four, W, X, Y and Z.

Then the code clerk transposed the sections, placing the last section first and the first section last. Y Z now became Z Y; X, Y, Z, became Z, Y, X; W, X, Y, Z, became Z, Y, X, W. After arranging the message in this order he encoded it as well as the section letters, and sent it to the cable office for dispatch.

This arrangement destroyed the beginning and ending! And the beginning and ending are the most vulnerable points in any code or cipher message!

However we finally solved this code, and having made the discovery of the transposition of sections, we used this arrangement to our advantage in the solution of other codes of this type. In new codes we now almost instantly discovered the groups that meant W, X, Y and Z. This method, seemingly very clever, actually played into our hands! And so it often happens that an apparently ingenious idea is in fact a weakness which the scientific cryptographer seizes on for his solution.

The papers were full of news of the approaching Armament Conference. I added a missionary's daughter to our force and another man for translation work, increased the clerical personnel, and sat back waiting for the stream of diplomatic telegrams that we knew would soon clog the cables.

General Churchill, now very ill, was relieved, much to the distress of the Black Chamber for every member knew him personally, admired and respected him, and counted upon his wise leadership.

General Nolan, our new executive, came to New York to look us over. He was already familiar with code and cipher work for he had been Chief of Military Intelligence in France during the war. Diplomatic codes and ciphers, however, were something new to him. He was amazed at the development of the science of cryptography even since the war, and took particular pains to tell every member of the Black Chamber that the value of our work to the government could scarcely be overestimated. Washington, he told us, was anxiously looking forward to the part we would play in the Armament Conference.

CHAPTER XVI

The Washington
Armament Conference

THE first telegram we deciphered which pointed definitely to the opening of a Pacific Conference between the Great Powers to settle disputes in the Far East was telegram No. 813, dated July 5, 1921, from the Japanese Ambassador in London to his home government in Tokio. The Japanese Ambassador and Lord Curzon were discussing the Anglo-Japanese Alliance that was of such tremendous concern to the United States. Lord Curzon suggested that if Japan, America and Great Britain would agree, they might open a Pacific Conference and discuss pending questions. Lord Curzon wished first confidentially to obtain the Japanese views, after which he could communicate with the American Ambassador. He expressed the hope that China, France and the countries of South America would also participate.

The Japanese Ambassador reported to his government that he thought Lord Curzon's views were those worked up in government circles, since a few of the points resembled the view of Winston Churchill. He went on to say that the attitude of America was not yet clear, but if the Japanese Government made no objection to the British proposals, he thought America would naturally express the purpose of participating.

Japanese London-Tokio telegram No. 825, dated three days later, reported another interview with Lord Curzon. The latter had had an interview with the American Ambassador and had suggested that it was proper to arrange to have the United States sponsor the Pacific Conference and send invitations to Japan, Great Britain, France and China and have the conference in America. The telegram went on to state that it is desired to have the invitations appear to proceed from the American Government and not to have it appear as the plan of the British Government. Just why the British Government desired this I have never understood.

The following Japanese telegram No. 386 from Washington to Tokio, July 10, 1921, is the first definite word we have of the American Secretary of State's plans for a conference for the reduction of armaments.

From Washington
To Tokio
When I interviewed the Secretary of State on July 9th with regard to the Siberian question, he told me that he had that day cabled instructions to America's representatives in Japan, England, France, and Italy that it was desired to hold in America a conference on the question of reduction of armaments, but before issuing formal invitations to these various countries, he wished to know the attitude of these countries on this matter, and therefore they should ascertain unofficially the views of the countries to which they were attached, and send in reports.

He said it would be unpleasant to let this matter become known to the general public, and so give rise to complications in discussion. It was therefore being kept secret, but he said he was giving it out to me for my personal information.

During the conversation HUGHES used the words "reduction of armament," and I asked him if this also included reduction in the army.

After a short pause he said his instructions were general ones.

As this was still vague, I pressed him further, and he said it did include the army.

The Japanese Government was taking its time to make up its mind whether it would join in such a conference. The Japanese Ambassadors at Paris, London and Washington urged an immediate decision, and requested instructions over and over again. The two following telegrams explain Tokio's point of view, and give us a clear picture of the negotiations so far which finally led to the conference in Washington. *The italics in all the messages in this chapter are the author's.*

From Tokio
To Washington.

No. 283, July 13, 1921.

VERY CONFIDENTIAL.

Referring to your cablegram No. 281, on July 12 I reported to the Cabinet and the Diplomatic Advisory Council the details of my conversation with the American Chargé d'Affaires, and said that, judging by the explanation of the Chargé and the fact that the Secretary of State in his conversation of July 9 with Ambassador SHIDEHARA had referred solely to the question of limitation of armaments, the original American initiative aimed principally at the limitation of armaments, and at the same time the British Foreign Minister had suggested to Ambassador HAYASHI a Pacific conference in connection with the Anglo-Japanese Alliance and had suggested that Chinese and American representatives should participate in the conference.

Putting together all the facts, it appeared that after the American Government had sent its first instructions, it had received this British proposal, and had used it to send the second instructions combining Far Eastern questions with the question of limitation of armaments. The British proposal besides Great Britain and Japan included France, America and China, and suggested that the South American countries might participate if this were desired. The American proposal omitted South America and added Italy. These were the points which deserved attention.

Finally the decisions given in the accompanying cablegram No. 286 were adopted as the attitude of the Japanese Government toward the American invitation. During today an answer to this effect will be given the American Chargé d'Affaires.

This and the accompanying cablegram have been cabled to China.

The message referred to, No. 286, follows.

From Tokio
To Washington.

No. 286, July 13, 1921.

VERY CONFIDENTIAL.

See covering message No. 283.

The Japanese Government wishes the subjects of discussion to be limited to the limitation of armaments questions, but in case it is necessary to discuss also Far Eastern and Pacific problems, this discussion should be limited to questions of general principles such as the territorial integrity of China, the open door, equal commercial opportunities, etc., and accomplished facts and questions concerning merely China.

The foregoing in haste for your information.

Two more telegrams from Tokio bearing the same date add to our understanding of Tokio's point of view.

From Tokio
To Washington.

No. 287, July 13, 1921.

VERY SECRET.

Please call upon the Secretary of State, and say that the Japanese Government gladly agrees to a discussion on the question of reduction of armament; but as to a discussion in this connection of Far Eastern and Pacific questions, it would mischievously complicate the situation and rather make it difficult to attain the object of the conference if deliberations are carried on in regard to all related questions; therefore *the Japanese Government desires first of all to know the unreserved opinion of both Great Britain and America regarding the kind and scope of these questions.*

Please ask the Secretary's opinion. *If he lets it appear as his opinion that deliberations will take place on all pending questions, please make reply as indicated in my cablegram No. 286 and cable me the result.*

From Tokio
To Washington.

No. 289, July 13, 1921.

VERY CONFIDENTIAL.

The British and American Government authorities have recently manifested their approval of the principle of limitation of armaments, and are agreed that it is urgently necessary to have an international agreement in regard to the limitation of armaments in general, and particularly a naval agreement among Great Britain, America and Japan. In this state of affairs, if the Japanese Government does not accede to the American proposal for a discussion of this question, it cannot avoid the blame of obstructing a plan for guaranteeing international peace. It is therefore considered the best policy from the point of view of the general situation to reply to America that the Japanese Government will willingly participate in a conference.

On the other hand, if Pacific and Far Eastern problems are considered in the conference, and the views of all the Powers are discussed among the Powers, the result will be to confuse the situation. *What course the discussion might take is unknown, but it would open the possibility of our policy towards China and towards Siberia receiving a check from the Powers. The Japanese Government, therefore, for the reason that the success of the conference will be facilitated by limiting its purposes as closely as possible, considers it appropriate that the discussion be limited to the limitation of armaments,* and finds it difficult to declare its definite views on the American proposal until the American Government has tentatively made clear the nature and scope of the Far Eastern and Pacific problems. We wish to know the details of the real attitude of that Government towards the discussion of these questions, and we shall therefore reply that we wish to arrange first for an unreserved exchange of views among Great Britain, America and Japan on the nature and scope of these questions.

It is interesting to note at this time that although Tokio wishes only the question of limitations of armaments discussed at the approaching conference, our government finally obtains consent to the settlement of such disturbing questions as the Anglo-Japanese Alliance, Yap, Shantung, Pacific defenses and final disposition of the German cables.

At this stage of the discussion, the Japanese suddenly switched to a new code for a few of their telegrams. By references in other telegrams we could still decipher, we discovered that the most secret and important messages were in the new code. This discovery threw the Black Chamber into a panic, for although this had been foreshadowed by an earlier telegram stating that a new code, termed *YU,* would soon be used, we had anticipated no difficulty in its decipherment. But to our consternation, the code was of an entirely new type. The Japanese Government, anticipating the discussion of subjects of world-wide importance, had not only constructed new codes, but had adopted a new principle in their construction. We all dropped everything we were doing and concentrated on its solution.

Our difficulty in breaking this code was due to its scientific construction. Although the code messages were on their face the same as others (they were all in groups of ten letters) we could not discover the real length of the code words. Heretofore the code words had been of two-letter and four-letter length. We divided the ten-letter groups of these messages in all their various combinations without success.

Finally we discovered that three-letter code words were interspersed throughout the messages. The code words in all other codes had been divisible by two. This new element of three so confused us that we could not even set about solving the code.

However, once we had discovered the three-letter elements, we quickly solved the messages, and within forty days after their receipt were reading current telegrams almost as rapidly as the Japanese themselves. Momentarily, at least, all those in the Black Chamber gave a sigh of relief. This new code we designated as *Jp*, the sixteenth code we had broken since my original solution.

It is of interest to note that Japan and the Soviet Union are the only nations which attempt to take advantage of the construction of code words of uneven lengths. It is a powerful weapon with which to confuse the cryptographer, and I have repeatedly urged this upon our own government, with not a great deal of success, I am sorry to say.

The following telegram (in the new *Jp* code) is from Tokio to London and gives Tokio's reactions to the London-Tokio telegrams which reported conversations with Lord Curzon.

From Tokio
To London.

No. 436, July 15, 1921.

VERY CONFIDENTIAL.

As you know in a general way from our successive cablegrams, we are giving careful consideration to Lord CURZON'S proposal for a Pacific Conference. We suppose that this proposal must have been tentatively made as the result of full consideration by the British Government, which must therefore have some general concrete plan for the organization of the conference, the scope of the subjects to be discussed, etc., and it is not hard to imagine from the cablegrams sent by the Ambassador at Washington, the American proposal to the Japanese Government, etc., that there is already some understanding with the Americans.

Be the case as it may with regard to America, it must be said that the inclusion of China by the British Government without first consulting Japan was improper in view of the existing understandings between Great Britain and Japan with regard to China. Please observe and report in detail whether there is not an underlying purpose to produce a new situation and to solve the question of revising the Anglo-Japanese Alliance by abolishing it instead. In view of the importance of the interests affected especially for Japan, we are considering the matter solicitously from every side. Please thoroughly understand this, and *during your conversations with the British Government, work especially to sound out their views, without committing us beyond the scope of your instructions.*

The following are our present views, solely for your information.

1. We are in general agreement with your observation that when no decision on the renewal of the Anglo-Japanese Alliance was reached in the Dominions Conference, the British Government in order to reserve the question for future consideration, suddenly reversed its original legal views. We believe that the Pacific Conference proposal was finally hit on as a means of solving this situation. If this is really the case, the nature and scope of the Pacific Conference will not only produce an important effect on the position of Japan and especially on the future of the Anglo-Japanese Alliance, but it may practically destroy the value of the Alliance, and regardless of names, may entirely abolish it.

2. From your cablegrams it appears that the British proposal was concerned in the first place with Pacific problems while the American proposal was especially to have a conference on the limitation of armaments, and at the same time to discuss Pacific and Far Eastern problems.

With regard to the discussion of the question of the limitation of armaments, the Japanese Government has no objection to participating, but in view of the situation of the Powers and our previous declarations, etc., it will willingly announce its wish to participate. With regard to the other questions, however, a necessary preliminary to our decision as to participating is to know the nature and scope of the subjects for discussion. It might be possible to bring up for discussion by the Powers questions of sole concern to a single Power, or at least questions disadvantageous to Japan. This would be entirely unacceptable to Japan.

After consideration by the Cabinet and the Diplomatic Advisory Council it has been decided that we have no objection to discussing the disarmament question or questions of general interest to the Powers such as the open door, equal opportunities in China, etc., but it is the attitude of Japan that it could not readily participate in the discussion of accomplished facts, nor of questions pending solely between Japan and America, or between Japan and China (such as the position of Japan in Manchuria, the twenty-one demands, the Shantung question, etc.).

Please use the foregoing in connection with the last part of our cablegram No. 435.

The following telegram reveals Lord Curzon's plan for a preliminary conference in London. It also shows Anglo-Japanese secret understanding.

From London
To Tokio.

No. 872, July 21, 1921.

VERY CONFIDENTIAL.

By urgent invitation of Lord CURZON I called on him at one o'clock the afternoon of July 21.

Lord CURZON said that on Friday of last week he had proposed to the American Ambassador at London that a preliminary Pacific Conference might be held at London. No reply had been received up to to-day. It was reported in the newspapers that the Japanese Government was exchanging views with the American Government. *He hoped that prior to the sending of a reply to the American Government, its contents might privately be communicated to the British Government.*

I am cabling this in haste, and will report the details of my interview with Lord CURZON by a later cablegram.

Afternoon of July 21.

London-Tokio No. 874, July 21, reports a long conversation between Lord Curzon and the Japanese Ambassador, regarding Anglo-Japanese secret understanding. One paragraph is especially interesting.

. . . Then Lord Curzon said that if, before the Japanese Government made any proposal to the American Government concerning the Pacific Conference, the contents of the proposal could be confidentially communicated to the British Government, it would be much appreciated. If the Japanese Government wished the agenda made clear beforehand, plans for this must be devised.

Two other telegrams also deal with Anglo-Japanese secret understanding.

From London
To Tokio.

No. 882, July 23.
URGENT. VERY CONFIDENTIAL.
Referring to the last part of my cablegram No. 874, on the 23rd *Curzon again asked to be informed of the Japanese answer before it was sent to America. . . .*

From Tokio
To London.

No. 884, July 23.
VERY CONFIDENTIAL.
. . . His Lordship [Curzon] then said that in this posture of affairs, the British Government must be informed of the substance of the Japanese reply before Japan replied to America. There were press reports that Japan had decided to give an answer of unconditional acceptance, and he must again bother me to lay this suggestion before the Japanese Government. Great Britain had encouraged the Americans to take the initiative in issuing invitations to the conference, but she had not imagined that America would plan the agenda. In view of the above-described proposals, it must be said that America did not understand the situation. Not only would the holding of the conference at London be convenient for the Premiers of the self-governeing Dominions, but he thought that London would be a more suitable atmosphere for the place of meeting than America. . . .
Lord CURZON says that the purpose of the Pacific

Conference is the wish to make peace-guaranty agreements parallel to the Anglo-Japanese Alliance, but after all he must have invented this after the question of the scope of the discussion had been brought up. If it were true, he would have told me of it from the first. Hitherto His Lordship has not plainly described the purposes of the conference, and now it is suddenly in his mouth. First and last there is a contradiction here and room for question, but after all if it related only to another's past error, I would not venture to speak of it. The position of the British Government, however, is almost the same as ours, and they urgently need to keep in touch with us. I invite your special consideration to this.

In this spirit, *I think that it would be an opportune policy to inform Great Britain of the substance of our answer to America, and to work to secure a complete understanding between Great Britain and Japan before the conference.*

On July twenty-eighth the Japanese Ambassador at Washington called upon Secretary Hughes and discussed Lord Curzon's proposal. His report to Tokio of this conference covers six pages. The last few lines, I think, fairly indicate the Secretary's reactions to the Curzon proposal:

From Washington
To Tokio.

No. 443, July 29.

. . . On my way out, I met the British Ambassador in the corridor of the State Department. I asked him whether he had yet laid this British proposal before the American Government.

The Ambassador replied that he had handed it to the Secretary of State the previous evening as a written memorandum.

I said that it did not look as if HUGHES would accept the proposal.

The British Ambassador whispered that he saw himself that there was not the least prospect of getting his consent.

When the United States received coldly Lord Curzon's views for a preliminary conference in London, he suggested a preliminary conference outside of Washington, but some place in America, and asked the Japanese Ambassador to

196

ascertain the views of his government. The Tokio-London reply is very long. Only the last two paragraphs are quoted.

From Tokio
To London.

No. 464, July 30, 1921.

URGENT. VERY CONFIDENTIAL.

You will therefore reply to Lord CURZON that the Japanese Government has no objection to holding informal preliminary conversations between representatives of Japan, Great Britain and America at some place in America outside of Washington provided that America consents and that the purpose of the conversations is to agree on the agenda. *At the same time you will say that the Japanese Government wishes to effect the close cooperation of Governments of the two countries for which Mr. LLOYD-GEORGE expressed a wish,* and that in the first place it wishes to have as unreserved as possible an exchange of opinions between the two countries regarding the agenda, and that it wishes to be informed if the British have any plan in regard to the agenda and the Pacific agreements.

You will try thoroughly to penetrate the ideas of the other party. If unexpectedly they should still have no plan, you will say that you are sure that Lord CURZON can of course have no objection to our negotiations with America, the details of which you have heretofore confidentially communicated to him. You will ascertain his views and report the result by cable.

On July 30, 1921, Tokio-London telegrams gave Japan's consent to Lord Curzon's proposal for a preliminary conference in the United States some place outside of Washington, but by this time America had replied that such a preliminary conference was not desirable. The newspapers criticized England for this move. The American view seemed to be that if the three great powers came to a secret agreement before the conference American opinion would be greatly irritated.

London-Tokio telegram No. 909, August 4, 1921, gave a three-thousand-word résumé of the negotiations so far. Three of the paragraphs are of especial interest in their discussion of American reactions to an Anglo-Japanese understanding.

2. As I see the situation, the principal parties to this conference, Japan, Great Britain and America, are at present regarding one another with mutual distrust.

Thus the Japanese Government appears to imagine that the original British initiative in calling the conference was due to some negotiations between Great Britain and America, as if there was a plan for these two Powers to agree to oppress Japan, and the Japanese Government appears to interpret the British proposal for an informal exchange of views as a secret plot to force the adoption of some definite plan which Great Britain already has.

On the other hand, it appears from cablegram No. 443 from the Ambassador at Washington to Your Excellency that the Americans suspected that Great Britain and Japan had combined against America for an informal exchange of views, while in Great Britain it was thought that Japan and America were conducting negotiations from which Great Britain was left out. . . . *That America thought Great Britain and Japan had united in the plan for an informal exchange of views must I think be clear from the course of events up to the present time.*

London-Tokio telegram No. 916, August 5, 1921, gives a clearer picture of Anglo-Japanese understanding.

I called on Lord CURZON on the afternoon of the 5th by request.

I took the opportunity to ask about later developments in this matter.

Lord CURZON said that there had been no further developments. He said that he thought that it was a great mistake for America to have rejected the British proposal, *and that perhaps America would shortly come asking his opinion about the agenda of the conference.* He thought that in that case he might reply that as America had rejected his proposal to have an informal meeting, exchange views and decide on the agenda, America must decide on the agenda.

He then said that he had cabled to the British Ambassador at Tokio a résumé of this matter since the proposal for the conference was made, and had instructed the Ambassador to explain thoroughly to the Japanese Government that the British Government had from the first revealed the whole matter to the Japanese

Government, and that it was anxious to maintain close touch with the Japanese Government.

His Lordship asked whether I could attend the meeting of the Supreme Council to be held on the 8th. When I replied that I would, His Lordship said that this would be very convenient. *The French Government was rather nervously excited about the Upper Silesia question, and the question was one of considerable difficulty. He hoped that Great Britain, Japan and Italy would take an identical attitude on this question.*

In Paris-Tokio No. 1204, August third, we see France bidding for Japan's support on the Silesian question:

On August 3rd I called on Premier BRIAND at his request. . . . The Premier alluded to the Pacific conference. He repeated that the chief purpose of France in this question was Japanese-American friendship, and that France would work to soften the feelings of both sides, hinting indirectly that he hoped that we would exercise the same friendship with regard to the Silesia question. . . .

The following telegram, London-Tokio No. 923, August 7, 1921, gives an intimate picture of Lord Curzon's real views of the American proposals.

Referring to your cablegram No. 469:

1. As CURZON is to go to Paris tomorrow, his affairs today would be in a state of confusion and there would be no opportunity to talk with him, so I sent a member of the Embassy staff to the house of his private secretary to say that the American Chargé d'Affaires at Tokio had called on Your Excellency on August 5 and had inquired the views of the Japanese Government in regard to opening the conference at Washington on Nov. 11, and we wished to know whether the British Government had already accepted the proposal.

The private secretary said that the councillor of the American Embassy [Note: Name garbled] had called on Lord CURZON on the evening of August 5 and had orally communicated the same proposal of the American Government, but in any case as the American Government had rejected the British proposal for an informal exchange of views, *the determination of the agenda, the*

*date of the conference, etc., were entirely the "business"
of the United States,* and Lord CURZON had merely
listened to the proposal. He had of course not replied
in writing and the secretary thought that he in no way
committed himself in regard to the proposal. He himself, however, had not been present and did not really
know precisely what had been Lord CURZON'S answer.
I could ascertain this direct from Lord CURZON to-
morrow when I would accompany him to Paris. For the
sake of certainty, inquiry was also made of the chief
of the Far Eastern Section, who gave the same answer.

I shall inquire again tomorrow when I go to Paris
with Lord CURZON and shall cable the facts from Paris,
but *I think that although the British have indulged in
more or less sarcasm about the American proposal, they
have not opposed it.* From appearances, I think that
there is no objection to the Japanese Government replying that it accepts the proposal so far as Japan alone
is concerned. . . .

The reactions of the Japanese Government at Tokio to
the negotiations that have now been conducted over a
period of a month are fairly well summarized in the following telegram. Japan also outlines the course that her
Ambassador must pursue at the conference.

From Tokio
To London.

No. 470, August 7, 1921.
VERY CONFIDENTIAL.
Contrary to expectation, it appears that there has
been no definite understanding from the beginning between Great Britain and America in regard to the conference of the Powers, and, especially in view of the
course of the informal meeting proposal as reported in
your cablegram No. 902, and in cablegram No. 443 of
the Ambassador at Washington, it may be conjectured
that the relations of the two countries lately have not
been pleasant. The conduct of the Japanese Government between them requires careful consideration.

In matters like the proposed informal meeting, the
policy of the Japanese Government was neither to reject
the British plan nor to echo the American attitude, as
you know from our successive cablegrams. Under the
circumstances it will be the best policy to stand in the

exact middle leaning to neither side, but rather *it will be best to maintain an impartial attitude and quietly watch the progress of events. In the conference, however, during discussion of Far Eastern and South Sea questions, etc., there will be many cases in which we will have mostly to keep step with Great Britain with regard to our acquired rights.* We should therefore exchange opinions unreservedly with Great Britain and hope for a smooth harmonious course of affairs.

It need not be said that it would be undesirable if in spite of our always simply and frankly working for the objects of the conference, and working to maintain perfect harmony among Great Britain, Japan and America, the feeling should come to be entertained by the British and American Governments that we are trying to practise a double policy, and you will make every effort in your contact with the authorities of the country to which you are accredited to carry out the Japanese policy under favorable conditions.

All the negotiations up to this time, and even later, present a very confusing picture. But I can explain this. The British cryptographers in London are of course turning over to the Foreign Office decipherments of all these messages. But England doesn't seem to realize that the United States is also receiving decipherments of the same messages. As a consequence, England reads the conversations held in Washington, and America reads the conversations held in London. Here is an enigma for the historian to romance about.

Tokio-Washington No. 358, August twelfth, again refers to Anglo-Japanese understanding:

Referring to the last part of our cablegram No. 349, *as you are aware, the Japanese Government wishes constantly to keep in touch with the British Government during the conference, and especially to have an unreserved exchange in regard to the nature and scope of the agenda.* You will bear this point in mind in arranging the agenda with the American Government, and to prevent us from being pressed for time you will give attention to doing everything possible to leave enough time to reach an understanding with the British Government also. . . .

Curzon is again piqued at the Americans as shown in Paris-Tokio No. 1288, of August fifteenth.

> While Lord CURZON was here I had two conversations with him about the Pacific conference which I report as follows.
>
> He said that the American authorities did not know how to use the opportunity Great Britain had given them. . . . Under the circumstances, Great Britain was no longer in a position to open its mouth. For this reason when the American Ambassador had asked his opinion about the agenda, he had said positively that as America was managing the affair, she should also decide the agenda to please herself. . . .

November eleventh is the date for the Armament Conference. There is much discussion of a preliminary informal talk to arrive at an agenda, but nothing comes of it. Newspaper men, specialists, statesmen, spies, now begin their journey to Washington.

Washington writes the members of the Black Chamber letters of congratulation and appreciation at our speed and skill, and begs us to maintain an even flow of messages. A representative arrives to arrange for daily courier service to the capital.

"Every one happy in Washington?" I ask.

"Sure," he smiles. "They all read the messages before they have their morning coffee."

Thousands of messages pass through our hands. The Black Chamber, bolted, hidden, guarded, sees all, hears all. Though the blinds are drawn and the windows heavily curtained, its far-seeking eyes penetrate the secret conference chambers at Washington, Tokio, London, Paris, Geneva, Rome. Its sensitive ears catch the faintest whisperings in the foreign capitals of the world.

At Rome, after a dinner party, two Ambassadors draw aside and discuss in low whispers the famous journalist, Frank Simonds, and the effect of his penetrating articles upon the outcome of the Armament Conference. Both fear his power as a writer.

At Geneva, an Ambassador is frantic at the popularity of Louis Seibold's cabled dispatches. This famous journalist is also feared.

At Paris, during a state dinner the French Minister of

Marine leans closer to the Japanese Ambassador and whispers that France and Japan must stand to the last ditch on the submarine question.

At London, Lord Curzon still pouts because America has stolen the conference from him.

At Tokio, in secret Advisory Councils, Japanese leaders gather to draw up their demands.

At Washington, spies swarm from the four corners of the globe. Here America awaits the opening date of the conference with serene confidence.

At New York, the Black Chamber trembles lest new codes be suddenly installed. It establishes swift courier service to and from Washington, and awaits the opening gong.

On November eleventh, before a distinguished gathering of the leading statesmen of the world, at the Pan-American Building, Secretary of States Hughes formally opened the Armament Conference. Although the Secretary urged the examination of the Far Eastern questions which were of vast importance and pressed for solution, he devoted most of his speech to the question of reduction of armaments. His speech was very attentively listened to from beginning to end, and frequently evoked enthusiastic applause. The vehement applause of the Congressmen and Senators who were in the hall attracted especial attention. His speech made a deep impression on all.

In regard to naval limitation, the Hughes plan called for parity with England and a ten-to-six ratio with Japan. On the morning of November fourteenth the Committee on Limitation of Armament held its opening meeting in the Pan-American Building. Kato from Japan, Hughes from America, Balfour from Great Britain, Briand from France, and Schanzer from Italy were present. With Hughes presiding the discussion opened. It was agreed that committee meetings in the future were to be secret, but the chief secretaries were to draw up a communiqué and publish this after obtaining the approval of the presiding officer and the plenipotentiaries of each country.

On November sixteenth the Committee on Limitation of Armament discussed the American proposal. Although there is no indication of what transpired at this meeting, Admiral Kato, the Japanese plenipotentiary, cabled his government on the same date that Japan had decided as a middle plan to advocate a ten-to-seven naval ratio as the minimum ratio of American-Japanese strength. Delegate Kato also gave an interview to Japanese newspaper correspondents, in which he laid great stress upon the fact that the seventy-percent ratio was absolutely necessary for the national defense of Japan and that this was the policy which had been already laid down by the naval authorities.

The newspapers now carried column after column of discussion of the American ten-to-six proposal and the Japanese counter demand for a ten-to-seven ratio. On the occasion of Secretary Hughes' interview on November eighteenth with American and foreign newspaper correspondents, one of the correspondents asked the Secretary's opinion on the Japanese proposed amendment. With the promise that his name should not be quoted, at least so the Japanese secret messages represented, the Secretary stated in effect, in very carefully guarded words, that the American proposal gave fair consideration to the present naval strength of each country, and that the proportion of tonnage allotted to each country was settled on this basis, and therefore in regard to all proposed amendments to make a substantial change in this proportion, America would put up a strenuous fight.

The newspapers of the nineteenth published the substance of these words of the Secretary of State as the views of America, and they were all one in declaring that the conference had encountered a barrier.

All this of course was quickly reported to the Japanese Government, and on November 22, 1921, Tokio, uneasy at the turn of events, instructed Admiral Kato to work for the ten-to-seven ratio "without any change." The message reads:

From Tokio
To Washington Conference.

No. 44, November 22.

VERY CONFIDENTIAL. URGENT.

Referring to your No. 28, importance is attached to the fact that at the meeting of the Diplomatic Advisory Council, Minister of the Navy Kato said that the ratio of 10 to 7 between the American Navy and our Navy should be the limit. We understand that you will *work to maintain this limit without any change.*

Although the newspapers freely predicted that no agreement could be reached, and there was no sign of weakness in the inscrutable eyes of the Japanese Delegates, the secret messages themselves of Admiral Kato to his government in Tokio showed definite signs of weakening, though in the conference room and to the newspapers he still insisted on the ten-to-seven ratio. The Japanese Government in Tokio remained silent to Kato's request for further instructions.

However, the Japanese had definitely won a victory in the discussion of land armaments when Briand of France refused to consider the reduction of the French Army. Briand's remarks to Saburi, outlined in the following telegram, are especially enlightening.

From Washington
To Tokio.

Conference No. 77, November 25.
Armament limitation committee No. 2.

The committee on the question of limitation of armament convened on the morning of the 23rd, and a committee composed of delegation heads met the afternoon of the same day.

The question of naval armament was discussed. Great Britain, America, and Italy explained the necessity for discussion of the whole question of armament. Italy was particularly earnest in advocating this, but BRIAND reiterated his explanation of the standpoint of France. He opposed it flatly, going to the length of saying that if the question of limitation of land armament was one which affected France alone, coercion by other countries would constitute an infringement of sovereign rights and could by no means be tolerated. He said there was no objection to a discussion of poison gases and aircraft as proposed by HUGHES; and if France did not wish to be spiritually isolated, she could not oppose a general declaration in regard to land armament; but he claimed there should be added in this declaration a statement to the effect that the condition of France made reduction impossible.

Since he persisted in the attitude that he would not take part in a discussion of general limitation, it was resolved to reserve this question from the subjects announced, and to create three boards of experts with respect to aircraft, poison gases, and rules and regulations of war, and to discuss these questions in the committee of delegation heads, after the boards had made their reports.

You will be informed of the circumstances of the discussion from the report of Major-General TANAKA.

At a luncheon today BRIAND addressed Secretary SABURI, with some statement that the old adage "Speech is silver, but silence is golden" could not be limited only to . . . [Note: Text is "ousoo"], *hinting that Japan in her silence was attaining the greater part of her aims. Our delegates noticed that the atmosphere of the conference tended to treat the land armament question as an "ousoo" question, and took no part in discussion.*

Major-General Tanaka's report of this incident, enciphered in the most difficult of all the Japanese codes, is as follows:

From Washington
To Tokio.

Army Conference No. 15, November 24.
After the session Briand told the other delegates goodbye and will return to France in a day or two. That through his strong efforts a general discussion of the limitation of land armaments was avoided must be considered a great success for France.

On the 2[?]th Briand said jestingly to Councillor Saburi that the old proverb "Speech is silver but silence is golden" was not limited to . . . alone. *It is the feeling that through Briand's fight Japan without an effort has achieved a large part of its objective.*

While all of this is going on, we see Lord Curzon in London on the same date still discussing the Anglo-Japanese Alliance:

From London
To Tokio.

Cablegram No. 1204, November 24.
After the conversation reported in my cablegram No. 1203 [Note: Probably J-6102, of which only the second section has yet been received], I said to Lord CURZON

206

with reference to criticisms of the Anglo-Japanese Alliance, that the attacks on the alliance found here and there in the American and British press, and especially in the NORTHCLIFFE newspapers were subtle falsehoods, but while every one recognized the past good results of the alliance, in view of the changes in the world situation the nature of the alliance was not the same as at the time when it was originally made. The alliance must become principally a pledge of moral cooperation and mutual support, but if Great Britain and Japan continued to respect it, it would be mutually advantageous.

The idea of saying that the original purposes of the alliance have been extinguished and immediately dissolving it and abandoning it because it is unpopular in the United States was an unthinkable procedure to which I could not assent. If there were no objection to dissolving the alliance, it would be proper to have negotiations between the two parties in the spirit of preserving the existing friendly relations, and it would be necessary to be careful not to leave any bad results on the two peoples. This I properly amplified and explained, sounding Lord CURZON'S intentions.

Lord CURZON replied that the attitude of the British Government towards the alliance was the same as heretofore and would not change in the near future. The attacks of the Times faction appeared to proceed from the policy of the paper. If there were any decision on something to take the place of the alliance, it was a matter of course that there would then be negotiations beween the two parties.

At last on November 28, 1921, the Black Chamber deciphered what I consider the most important and far-reaching telegram that ever passed through its doors. A photograph of the code message itself and the Japanese decoded text are shown in the photo section. It is from the Japanese Foreign Office to the Japanese Plenipotentiary in Washington. It is the first sign of weakness on the ten-to-seven Japanese demands. This telegram was definitely to determine the respective strength of the fleets of Japan and the United States. It shows that if America presses Japan vigorously, Japan will give up proposal 1, then proposal 2, and that provided the status quo of the Pacific defenses is maintained, she will even accept a ten-to-six naval ratio.

From Tokio
To Washington.

Conference No. 13. November 28, 1921.

SECRET.

Referring to your conference cablegram No. 74, we are of your opinion that *it is necessary to avoid any clash with Great Britain and America, particularly America, in regard to the armament limitation question.* You will to the utmost maintain a middle attitude and *redouble your efforts to carry out our policy. In case of inevitable necessity you will work to establish your second proposal of 10 to 6.5.* If, in spite of your utmost efforts, *it becomes necessary* in view of the situation and in the interests of general policy *to fall back on your proposal No. 3,* you will *endeavor to limit* the power of concentration and maneuver of the Pacific *by a guarantee to reduce or at least to maintain the status quo of Pacific defenses* and to make an adequate reservation which will make clear that [this is] our intention in agreeing to a 10 to 6 ratio.

No. 4 is to be avoided as far as possible.

With this information in its hands, the American Government, if it cared to take advantage of it, could not lose. All it need do was to mark time. Stud poker is not a very difficult game after you see your opponent's hole card.

Admiral Kato now began to report the hopelessness of obtaining his demands for a ten-to-seven naval ratio. One of his telegrams, too long to quote for it contains over a thousand words, gives a résumé of the situation. One paragraph is especially interesting:

From Washington
To Tokio.

No. 131, December 2.

VERY CONFIDENTIAL. URGENT.

The conference of naval experts concluded without reaching an agreement and reported the day before yesterday, November 30th. As a result of this, on yesterday, the 1st, I was asked for an interview by Mr. BALFOUR and met him at a hotel at noon. Mr. BALFOUR *was in a state of extraordinary anxiety and even his words trembled.* He began by saying that it was reported that the navy specialists had not reached a consensus of opinion. *He was unbearably anxious for fear that unless some agreement on this question was reached, the whole armament limitation would be overthrown.* He thought that this would result in making the quadruple agreement impossible and would also affect the Pacific questions. He asked whether there was not something he could do to help. . . .

Mention in the foregoing telegram is made of the Quadruple Agreement. Other questions at this time were also being discussed, such as the Pacific Defenses, Yap, Shantung, etc. It is of course impossible to go into all the phases of the Armament Conference, but one message about Shantung will be quoted. Shantung, it will be recalled, is the German possession in China ceded to Japan by the Versailles Treaty. The Chinese Government had refused to sign the Peace Treaty because Japan refused to restore the province, and America was attempting to bring about a settlement between Japan and China by the restoration of Shantung, a Chinese province.

Japan had unwillingly permitted this question to be discussed. The following telegram gives us an idea of what they think of the negotiations:

From Washington
To Tokio.

Conference No. 150, December 6.
URGENT. VERY CONFIDENTIAL.
. . . We consider it extremely advisable and necessary to push the Shantung question to a solution as quickly as possible.

Now the knottiest point in the question of the disposition of Shantung is the proposal for the joint administration of the Shantung Railway. Not only did the Chinese Delegates in our second meeting express and emphasize opposition to joint administration, but, as you are aware, from the first the United States also have refused their approval to it. Judging also by the remarks of the British secretary reported in our cablegram No. 130, these two countries are not favorably impressed by our joint administration proposal, and perhaps if the negotiations come to a standstill, the British and Americans may not limit themselves even to proposing a compromise plan supporting the Chinese contentions.

On the other hand, when we consider the matter maturely, the attempt to carry out in fact as well as in name a thorough joint administration would be attended with not a few practical difficulties. Thus as in the example of the .... the putting of Japanese and Chinese in practically the same positions not only increases expense but blocks the smooth and harmonious movement of the work, and there is no reason to expect good results from it.

We therefore think it is advisable not to persist in nominal questions, but rather to adopt the policy of throwing away the name and keeping the fact, and to facilitate the solution of the whole question by not refusing, as circumstances may demand, to withdraw with a good grace the joint administration proposal. We earnestly hope that you will consider this and will ask for a decision by the Cabinet Council.

But the whole success depended upon an agreement between Japan and America with respect to the relative naval strengths of the two fleets. Apparently both Japan and America refuse to concede one point. But the Japanese messages have already told us that they have weakened. Admiral Kato again on December eighth urgently requested Tokio to send instructions.

From Washington
To Tokio.

No. 168, December 8.

VERY URGENT.
VERY CONFIDENTIAL.

Your instructions with regard to our cablegram No. 142 have not yet been received, and on this account the conference is making absolutely no progress on the armament limitation question. Every one here is waiting for our answer, and there is a gradual tendency to attribute the responsibility to us, and to turn the tide to our disadvantage. . . .

At last, all hope of success gone, Tokio on December tenth capitulated, and instructed Kato to agree to the ten-to-six ratio. The cable in part reads:

From Tokio
To Washington.

Conference No. 155, December 10.

VERY CONFIDENTIAL. URGENT.

Referring to your Nos. 142 and 143, . . . We have claimed that the ratio of strength of 10 to 7 was absolutely necessary to guarantee the safety of the national defense of Japan, but the United States has persisted to the utmost in support of the Hughes proposal, and Great Britain also has supported it. *It is therefore left that there is practically no prospect of carrying through this contention.*

Now therefore in the interests of the general situation and in a spirit of harmony, *there is nothing to do but accept the ratio proposed by the United States.* . . .

America at last had won her point.

Christmas in the Black Chamber was brightened by handsome presents to all of us from officials in the State and War Departments which were accompanied by personal regards and assurances that our long hours of drudgery during the Conference were appreciated by those in authority.

CHAPTER XVII

I Receive the Distinguished Service Medal

DURING the Armament Conference the Black Chamber had turned out over five thousand decipherments and translations. Nearly every member of the organization was a nervous wreck from overwork, and as for myself I suddenly found that I was too ill to get out of bed, where I remained over a month. Even after I got up I did not regain my strength. Walking only a few steps completely exhausted me. Finally in February, the doctors ordered me to Arizona.

I was too ill to be of any value to the Black Chamber, but my secretary tried to keep me cheered with long memoranda. Our new Director, Colonel Heintzelman, had relieved General Nolan, and had just visited the office in New York. I think parts of my secretary's letter to me while I was in Arizona will give some of the background of the Black Chamber.

Colonel Stuart Heintzelman, the Director, called this morning at nine o'clock. He was here until noon and, I think, went away with a very favorable impression. He seemed to be greatly interested in the work we are doing and is very desirous of helping us in every possible way. He seemed to be especially interested to know whether every one here is happy and contented and whether the organization is functioning smoothly.

[Here follows a description of his
visit to each of the departments]

Colonel H. and I then came down-stairs where we spent

another half-hour. He said he and the others in Military Intelligence as well as the State Department were very much concerned about your health. He was most fearful lest you should have tuberculosis. I reassured him and told him of your interview with Doctor Evans who had diagnosed your case as a run-down condition due to overwork. I assured him that after a few weeks out there you would come back a new man. He felt very much relieved to know this. He asked me to send his regards and best wishes for your full recovery.

. . . He asked about the building and whether there was any one here while you were gone and whether people in the neighborhood knew of the nature of the work done in this office. . . . He said that if I ever got into any kind of trouble, I should telephone him immediately and he would get the first train up here.

. . . As he was leaving he said he was very much pleased with the work we are doing here, and assured us that it is highly appreciated by all concerned in Washington. He thanked us for the extra efforts we had made during the Conference and told us we could always count on his cooperation in every way possible.

. . . Col. H's visit made a very favorable impression on all. Every one found him a very human and likable man, who not only is keenly interested in this work, but also appreciates its importance and difficulties.

. . . He emphasized the necessity for guarding the building and keeping everything secret. . . . The idea in the back of his head seemed to be that it would be a good plan to move at frequent intervals so that people in the neighborhood would not get wise to our activities. I explained to him that I felt sure that no one in our neighborhood suspected the nature of our work, especially in view of the fact that there are almost a half-dozen other offices in the same block in private homes conducted in the same manner as this office.

. . . He asked whether I would experience any difficulty in cashing checks during your absence. I told him there would be no trouble at all.

In June, 1922, I returned from Arizona in excellent health, but found my most valuable assistant in a frightful condition. He had been working sixteen hours a day for so long that he talked incoherently, with a strange light in his eyes. I kept close watch over him for a week or more, for cryptography steals into the blood stream and does curious things to people.

I myself had already had trouble in this respect. Then there were the cases of two girls who were near a nervous breakdown and asked that I let them resign. One dreamed constantly that a bulldog was loose in her room. For hours she chased it under and over the bed, behind the chair, under the dresser, and finally when she caught it, she found written on its side the word *code*. The other girl dreamed each night of walking along a lonely beach, weighed down by an enormous sackful of pebbles. She struggled along for miles with this heavy burden on her back, searching for pebbles that matched those in the bag. When she found one that exactly matched she could take the duplicate from the bag and cast it into the sea. This was her only method of lightening the burden that weighed so heavily upon her shoulders.

It was therefore with some concern that I observed my assistant. Finally he came to me of his own accord and told me he was becoming afraid of himself. I told him to go away for a couple of months and try to forget codes and ciphers. Upon his return he said that he wished to give up cryptography and try something else. We finally found a good position for him in another field. I suspect that he does not now regret his step.

Not long after I returned from Arizona I was ordered to Washington for a conference which Colonel Heintzelman. He had just been promoted to a Brigadier-General and would shortly be relieved, because the Director of Military Intelligence is not a general officer. When a Director is promoted to a General he is relieved by a Colonel. Colonel Nolan had been relieved because he too had been promoted to a Brigadier-General.

"Yardley," General Heintzelman began, "I have talked about you to the Chief of Staff, General Pershing, and the Secretary of War. You are to receive the Distinguished Service Medal."

I could only connect this in my own mind with the part played by the Black Chamber during the Armament Conference. It was a surprise to me, for no matter what may be said about my organization, it can never be charged that any of us ever played politics, either for promotions or for honors. In fact, we were happy to remain unknown, hidden behind curtains, as long as our work was useful to the United States Government.

I thanked him for his interest in my behalf. It is not too much to say that in my opinion the Black Chamber had a great deal to do with the promotions of both Nolan and Heintzelman to general officers, for it was well known that the Chief of Staff and the Secretary of War were vitally interested in the translations from the Black Chamber, and both officers were in a measure responsible for our successes.

"In awarding you the D. S. M.," the General began again, "we find it difficult to draft a citation that will describe your distinguished services, and at the same time keep the nature of your activities secret, for of course all citations are published. Have you any suggestions?"

"I naturally have never given the matter any thought."

"Well, we'll draft something, so that your successes will not be revealed. The only regret is that the real reason for conferring the D. S. M. can not be given."

We were of course well aware that if our activities were discovered there would be no protest from foreign governments, for we knew that all the Great Powers maintained Cipher Bureaus for the solution of diplomatic telegrams. This was a sort of gentlemen's agreement. Just as in warfare armies do not attempt to bomb each other's headquarters, so also in diplomacy statesmen do not protest against the solution of each other's messages. However, if foreign governments learned that we were *successful* they would immediately change their codes, and we would be obliged after years of struggle to begin all over again. For this reason the War Department would need to draft the wording of my citation in a manner that would not lead foreign governments to suspect the skill of the Black Chamber.

After discussing with him some of the new problems of my office, I returned to New York, and within a few weeks was again ordered to Washington.

I was to appear before Secretary of War Weeks at two P.M. to receive the D. S. M. On the way to his office I asked General Heintzelman if Secretary Weeks really knew why I was being awarded the D. S. M. He assured me that the Secretary was one of the most ardent supporters of the Black Chamber.

I felt rather silly standing before the Secretary of War, as he read my citation that seemed to have very little to

215

do with the breaking of codes of foreign governments, but I was relieved when he pinned the medal on my lapel, for with a twinkle in his eye he winked at me. The wink pleased me immensely.

The vague phraseology of my citation and the note from my secretary to me while I was in Arizona gave some idea of the fear on the part of Washington that our activities would be discovered. We were not only asked to move our office from time to time, but many other so-called precautions were taken to keep our identity secret.

As Chief of MI-8 my name was known in every corner of the earth, for I had to sign all letters dealing with codes and ciphers. Aside from this I was well known to English, French and Italian cryptographers during the war, as the Chief of MI-8. If a foreign government wished to find out whether the United States still maintained a Cipher Bureau, the first thing their secret agents would do would be to locate me, and of course my address was on file with the Adjutant-General of the Army.

It was really useless to attempt to hide my whereabouts, but as the attempt seemed to please Washington, I made no protests. My name was not permitted in the telephone book, mail addressed to me was through a cover-address, etc.

Washington was especially concerned that I keep away from congressional investigations. During the investigation of Secretary of Interior Fall, my correspondent in Washington telephoned me for God's sake to lie low for if I was called upon to decipher the Fall messages we would be ruined.

During the Senate's investigations of the authenticity of the Mexican cipher telegrams published in the Hearst papers that produced such a scandal, I was in Washington and had a good laugh with one of my minor correspondents. Why, I do not know, unless the Navy still advertised itself as it did during the war, but in any case the Senate appealed to the Navy for its opinion as to the genuineness of these Mexican cipher messages. We in New York had already analyzed the telegrams and could, at a moment's notice, have given an incontestable opinion as to their authenticity, for we had deciphered thousands of Mexican code and cipher diplomatic and consular messages. The Navy, however, came around to my correspondent for his opinion, but was told that the War Department had no Cipher Bureau, and did not know a thing about the subject! The situation was especially ludicrous, for the Naval officer knew that my correspondent was lying, but there was nothing he could do about it.

It certainly amused us both to see so-called Naval experts give their opinion about the Hearst documents. How did they become expert? The last I had seen of a Navy Cryptographic Bureau was when they closed up their office and placed a liaison officer in MI-8 because of their failure to decipher a single message.

This morning, and I am now writing of February, 1931, I was informed by a friend just back from Washington that the committee investigating Soviet activities had one thousand Soviet code messages which had been turned over to "Government experts" to decipher, but they couldn't be solved by these experts. This was very enlightening, for it had been my impression that the Black Chamber had a monopoly on experienced cryptographers, and the Black Chamber had long ago been closed by the government.

In spite of all the precautions to maintain secrecy regarding our activities, we were once nearly given away through our kindness in giving a helping hand to Bruce Bielaski while he was conducting under-cover investigations of rum-runners off the Atlantic coast.

He was intercepting by wireless a great number of cipher messages to "mother" ships along the coast, which lay beyond the twelve-mile limit, waiting for opportune moments to discharge their cargoes of fine wines and liquors to rum-runners. Bielaski, with whom I was closely associated during the war when I was Chief of MI-8 and he Chief of Investigations of the Department of Justice, knew of my present activities and asked if I minded if one of my assistants deciphered these messages. I said no, so long as it did not interfere with our work. He gave my cryptographer two hundred dollars per month for this, and often when the latter needed help I assisted in the decipherment of these bootleg cipher messages.

Finally Bielaski decided he could win a case for conspiracy by presenting as evidence several messages we had deciphered that showed conclusively the nature of the activity of a mother ship off the coast of Atlantic City. He sent his coast guard out to haul in the vessel, which, as I remember, contained about a half-million-dollar cargo.

He was all ready for the trial, and called me up to tell

me that he would need expert testimony on the decipherment of the messages. I nearly dropped dead when he made this request, and told him emphatically that I could permit no one connected with my office to give such testimony. To do so would disclose our secret activities. The newspapers would be full of the activities of the Black Chamber. Foreign governments would change all their codes and years of labor would be erased. Needless to say, this ended our connection with bootleg cipher messages.

Despite all our precautions, however, some one, or some government, suddenly became interested in our secret activities and went about learning what they could in the manner I knew they would follow, for I had not been connected with espionage all these years for nothing.

For several weeks now I had known I was under observation. Whenever I ventured on the street, which was no more than once or twice a day, I sensed this shadow behind me. But to make certain I employed a private investigator. After this when I appeared my unwelcome friend sprang from nowhere and strolled along well behind me, and behind him too ambled my investigator. We were of course now certain that I was being watched. For what purpose? My man endeavored to discover this by following my shadow after I returned to the office, but he was too clever. He also sensed that he was covered and at the proper moment eluded pursuit.

Nearly every day late in the afternoon I dropped in at a speakeasy in the West Forties for a cocktail or two before dinner. As the bar was always jammed, more often than not one engaged a stranger in conversation without formality. One afternoon a likable young chap and I became friendly. He seemed to be an importer, and as I had introduced myself as the publisher of a public code for the use of importers and exporters, the conversation naturally turned to the economical use of commercial codes. We had arrived at the pleasant stage of "Let's have just one more," when a waiter whispered that a lady wished to see him. He excused himself, but in a moment was back again, his face wreathed in smiles.

"My girl just showed up," he proudly explained. "Won't you have a drink with us?"

As this seemed reasonable enough to me, I followed him into the adjoining room through which one passes from the street entrance to the bar itself. A dozen or more couples reclined in deep, comfortable, wicker chairs, which sprawled before small glass-topped tables; and scattered about the room here and there one glimpsed a girl drinking moodily alone. One gorgeous creature smiled bewitchingly as we approached. She had removed her hat, better no doubt to display the golden hair which curved in an intriguing manner about her ears. At our introduction she offered a slender hand in a warm friendly manner. After a few moments of casual conversation and another cocktail I excused myself. As I left they waved me a friendly good-by.

A few days later on my way back to the bar I heard some one say:

"Oh, hello there!"

I turned and recognized my friend with the golden hair and infectious smile. She was nervously twirling the stem of her cocktail glass.

"Waiting for some one?" I asked.

She shrugged her shoulders and, while I stood rather uncertain, begged me to sit down.

I presume it is a good sales point for a woman in any surroundings to reveal her charms, but it did seem to me that she showed a bit too much of her legs as she nestled in the deep cushions. Very beautiful legs too, I reflected, at the end of the third cocktail.

I could not place her, for her friendliness was a bit forced; it did not seem reasonable for one of her beauty and charm to possess such warmth for a bald-headed man. Perhaps it was the liquor or perhaps her deep blue eyes, too far back and too close together, that produced that invitingly dissolute air.

The conversation finally turned to my commercial-code business and how I happened to publish a commercial code, and with each drink the questions turned to the more intimate side of my code and cipher past. I had always been uneasy about my secret work. But being shadowed for several weeks, and now this lovely creature with her amorous eyes and strange inquisitiveness! I must confess I did not like it.

She opened her purse, took out a small gold compact and disappeared into the ladies' room. I immediately took advantage of her absence and searched her purse, but discovered nothing except about fifteen dollars, a key and two or three perfumed handkerchiefs.

She had given me her address and telephone number.

If I could only search her room perhaps I might find the answer to my uneasiness. I might be mistaken, but it seemed to me that she was doing her best to get me drunk. Why not reverse matters?

When she returned I ordered straight whisky and a ginger-ale chaser. She still preferred cocktails. I might have been slightly drunk, but I was sober now and watched carefully that she actually drank her cocktails instead of pouring them on the floor. She too watched me, I thought. We were past the stage of wanting anything to eat, so for several hours consumed one drink after another; that is, she did. As for me, I was reverting to the very old trick of taking a sip of straight whisky, then pretending to sip ginger ale. But while I held the ginger-ale glass to my lips, instead of swallowing whisky, I let it run slowly through my lips into the ginger ale. After each drink, then, I had an empty whisky glass, but most of the liquor was now mixed with the ginger ale.

Although she possessed a most unusual capacity for alcohol, yet she watched me in amazement as I ordered one drink after another without any apparent sign of weakening. Finally when I saw she was quite drunk, I ordered a taxi and drove to her address in the East Eighties. On the way she fell into a quiet stupor and leaned heavily on my arm as I helped her from the cab. From the mail-box in the vestibule I learned the location of her apartment and helped her as best I could up the first flight of stairs. I fumbled for her key, and in another moment we were in a beautifully furnished two-room apartment. Once inside she lay down on the couch and instantly fell into a deep labored sleep.

I quickly searched the apartment and discovered what I was looking for in the handkerchief drawer of her dressing-table. It was a typewritten note that must have been delivered by messenger the day before. It read:

Have tried to reach you all day by telephone. See mutual friend at first opportunity. Important you get us information at once.

The message was unsigned, unaddressed.

I bent over to see if she was still asleep, gently took off her slippers, covered her with a blanket and quietly let myself out.

The next day she disappeared and left no trace of her

whereabouts. Who employed her, just what information her employers wanted I have no way of knowing. However, whatever they wanted they must have wanted badly, for the next night the office door was forced, cabinets rifled, and papers scattered all over the place. I took it for granted that they had photographed the important documents which they required.

CHAPTER XVIII

The Secretary
Sees the President

THE Black Chamber did not deal solely with the diplomatic codes of Japan. We solved over forty-five thousand cryptograms from 1917 to 1929, and at one time or another, we broke the codes of Argentina, Brazil, Chile, China, Costa Rica, Cuba, England, France, Germany, Japan, Liberia, Mexico, Nicaragua, Panama, Peru, Russia, San Salvador, Santo Domingo, Soviet Union and Spain.

We also made preliminary analyses of the codes of many other governments. This we did because we never knew at what moment a crisis would arise which would require quick solution of a particular government's diplomatic telegrams. Our personnel was limited and we could not hope to read the telegrams of all nations. But we drew up plans for an offensive, in the form of code analyses, even though we anticipated no crisis. We never knew at what moment to expect a telephone call or an urgent letter demanding a prompt solution of messages which we had never dreamed would interest the Department of State.

Among these preliminary studies were the code telegrams of the Vatican. But our analysis of the Vatican code nearly got me into trouble, and was abandoned under rather rare circumstances.

A new Director—I shall not give his name—had been appointed, and I was ordered to Washington to outline the history of the activities and accomplishments of the Black Chamber, and to give him my plans for the future.

The new Director, his executive officer and I were

lunching at the Army and Navy Club, when the Director asked:

"Yardley, what code do you plan to solve next?"

"I don't know, but the Vatican code telegrams rather intrigue me. Our preliminary analysis shows that they can be read. . . ."

I noticed with amazement that the Director's face went very white. At the same moment the executive officer gave me a vicious kick under the table. It scarcely needed the injury to my skins to make me realize that the Director was a Catholic, but it gave me an opportunity to cover up my confusion.

My voice was a bit tremulous, but I began again:

"Our preliminary analysis shows that they can be read, but I personally feel that it is unethical for us to inquire into the Vatican secrets. I hope you concur with my view."

The word unethical sounded a bit strange in its association with the activities of the Black Chamber, but in this case it was effective, for the blood slowly returned to the Director's face.

"You are quite right, Yardley," he said. "I wouldn't bother with the Vatican code telegrams. I'm glad to see that you recognize that there are certain limits that we can not exceed in the espionage necessary for the successful operation of your bureau."

Though the Black Chamber made preliminary analyses of many codes that it was never called on to solve, it was on the other hand required to solve all the codes of certain countries even though they gave our government no information of any value, since at the moment there were no important questions being discussed. This was done of course with only a few governments, and was necessary, for only by continuity is it possible to keep up with the changes that the codes of all governments gradually undergo. In fact the success of a Cipher Bureau in breaking new codes is often dependent on continuity. If we read a particular government's messages over a period of years, when the code is suddenly changed, it is less difficult to break the new one, because, having observed this government make slight improvements from year to year, we are familiar with the line of reasoning of the expert who is compiling the codes. Each government has pet theories about codes and ciphers, and as long as the same man compiles them, we assume, when confronted with a new code or cipher, that we are dealing with his particular type.

Let us take the Mexican Government as an example. In 1917 they enciphered their messages in simple substitution ciphers, of the *Gold Bug* type. Shortly afterward their cryptographer evidently thought these unsafe, for he adopted multiple substitution ciphers.

The type of multiple substitution adopted by the Mexican cryptographer is a modification of the *Beaufort* cipher. This type is almost identical with systems known as *Sliding Alphabet Cipher, Tableau de Porta, Tableau de Vigenère, Système de St. Cyr.*

It is about systems of this type of cipher that Voltaire expressed the opinion that people who boasted of their ability to read secret messages without knowing the key word and the system employed were mountebanks and liars, to the same degree as men who boasted of their ability to understand a language which they had never studied. Voltaire was not always right.

The full details of the technique required for the decipherment of messages enciphered in this system would be of interest only to the cryptographer, but having mentioned Voltaire's caustic remarks, I shall indicate briefly how the cipher expert approaches this problem.

The Mexicans adopted the most complicated form of the Beaufort cipher. The first step in its construction is the selection of a word on which the alphabets are based. One of the many used by the Mexican Government is *repulsion*. This requires nine letters of the alphabet. The remaining seventeen letters are now written after the word REPULSION. This gives a mixed or disarranged alphabet:

repulsionabcdfghjkmqtvwxyz

This cipher alphabet is now used to construct a rectangle of 26 alphabets, by sliding it one letter at a time:

FIGURE 1

```
REPULSIONABCDFGHJKMQTVWXYZ
EPULSIONABCDFGHJKMQTVWXYZR
PULSIONABCDFGHJKMQTVWXYZRE
ULSIONABCDFGHJKMQTVWXYZREP
LSIONABCDFGHJKMQTVWXYZREPU
SIONABCDFGHJKMQTVWXYZREPUL
IONABCDFGHJKMQTVWXYZREPULS
ONABCDFGHJKMQTVWXYZREPULSI
NABCDFGHJKMQTVWXYZREPULSIO
ABCDFGHJKMQTVWXYZREPULSION
BCDFGHJKMQTVWXYZREPULSIONA
CDFGHJKMQTVWXYZREPULSIONAB
DFGHJKMQTVWXYZREPULSIONABC
FGHJKMQTVWXYZREPULSIONABCD
GHJKMQTVWXYZREPULSIONABCDF
HJKMQTVWXYZREPULSIONABCDFG
JKMQTVWXYZREPULSIONABCDFGH
KMQTVWXYZREPULSIONABCDFGHJ
MQTVWXYZREPULSIONABCDFGHJK
QTVWXYZREPULSIONABCDFGHJKM
TVWXYZREPULSIONABCDFGHJKMQ
VWXYZREPULSIONABCDFGHJKMQT
WXYZREPULSIONABCDFGHJKMQTV
XYZREPULSIONABCDFGHJKMQTVW
YZREPULSIONABCDFGHJKMQTVWX
ZREPULSIONABCDFGHJKMQTVWXY
```

The method employing the table is as follows:

A key word which has been agreed upon by the correspondents (in this instance, "now") is written under the text of the message, letter for letter, and is repeated as often as may be necessary.

Text: ThisI sTheM essag eEnci phere dInTh eBeau fortC   ipher
Key: nowno wnown ownow nowno wnown ownow nowno wnown ownow
Cipher: pwpff epwxr nefjb   anl*qf* yxnwa qpjec akxkb ahojq *fyxnw*

The cipher letters are found in Figure 1 at the intersection of the text and the key letters. *P* (cipher) is found at the intersection of *t* (text) and *n* (key); *w* (cipher) is found at the intersection of *h* (text) and *o* (key), etc.

225

After enciphering a message in this manner, the Mexicans added a numeral in clear language to indicate to the receiver the particular key word which had been used. They had sixty key words for use with each rectangle, which they also changed frequently.

This message to the cryptographer, who has no knowledge of the key or the table or the system involved readily falls into the substitution class, for the frequency of such letters as *x, j, w*, which seldom occur in any language, indicates that it can not be a transposition cipher such as the Pablo Waberski document.

Note the repetitions of *qfyxnw* and *pw* which I have italicized. The interval between the first is 21; between the second, 6.

The factors of 21 are 7, 3.

The factors of 6 are 2, 3.

The common factor of both 21 and 6 is therefore 3. The number of alphabets employed, then, unless these repetitions are coincidences, is 3. Assuming that this is correct, we next arrange the cipher message in 3 columns.

p	*w*	*p*		a	q	p
f	f	e		j	e	c
p	*w*	x		a	k	x
r	n	e		k	b	a
f	j	b		h	o	j
a	n	l		*q*	*f*	*y*
q	*f*	*y*		*x*	*n*	*w*
x	*n*	*w*				

Note how the repetitions fall into the same columns. If we insert the message itself above these letters we will better understand why this is true.

Key	**n o w**		**H E R**
			x n w
	T H I		E D I
	p w p		a q p
	S I S		N T H
	f f e		j e c
	T H E		E B E
	p w x		a k x
	M E S		A U F
	r n e		k b a
	S A G		O R T
	f j b		h o j
	E E N		*C I P*
	a n l		q f y
	C I P		H E R
	q f y		x n w

The first repetition is caused by *th* in the words *this* and *the* falling in the same columns. The second repetition, *cipher* and the same letters in the word *enciphered*, is caused by the same reason.

We have now reduced a multiple alphabet cipher, considered insoluble not many years ago, to three single alphabets. We already know from reading Poe's "Gold Bug" that single alphabet ciphers can be readily solved, if they are long enough to pile up frequencies.

For the sake of brevity, therefore, let us assume that we have a longer message before us and have solved it, and after solution, have consolidated the cipher alphabets in the following manner:

```
text    A B C D E F G H I J K L M N O P Q R S T U V W X Y Z
cipher  k m q t a v w x g y z d r j h b e n f p c u l s i o
                                                   1st Alphabet
cipher  j k m q n t v w f x y c z h g a r o d e b p u l s i
                                                   2nd Alphabet
cipher  s i o n x a b c p d f r g l u y h w e j z k m q t v
                                                   3rd Alphabet
```

The last three lines are the secondary alphabets. They will decipher this particular message, but they are not the original or primary alphabets used by the Mexicans. Examine them carefully. They seem to have absolutely no resemblance to the primary alphabet made from the word *repulsion*.

Now since we will encounter more messages in this system it is important to recover the primary alphabets, so that we can decipher them as easily as the Mexican. We must take advantage of the solution of the first message.

How shall we go about this? Note the underlined sequences f g h Both *fgh* and *vwx* are normal sequences of letters found in our alphabet. Now if we invert these, we find opposite *vwx* in the upper alphabet, the letters *uls,* and opposite the letters *uls* we find the letters *cdf.* Let us continue in this manner and make a table of our findings:

(text)		(cipher)
fgh	equals	*vwx*
vwx		*uls*
uls		*cdf*
cdf		*qtv*
qtv		*epu*

Now by joining *epu* and *uls* in the last column we have the sequence EPULS. Let us begin over again, using this sequence to start with.

(text)		(cipher)
epuls	equals	*adcdf*
abcdf		*kmqtv*
kmqtv		*zrepu*
zrepu		*onabc*

Zrepu and *epuls* in the first column may now be joined together, which gives us *zrepuls*.

Z is the last letter in the alphabet and if it has not been disturbed from its normal position, *repuls* is the beginning of the word from which the alphabets were constructed. We may continue the analysis already followed or try to guess the word. Either method gives us the correct word, *repulsion*.

From the word *repulsion*, we now construct the same table as that used by the Mexican Government and when the next message comes to us for decipherment, we have only the key word to discover.

In long messages this will not be difficult, but we wish to decipher even short messages. For this we must develop still another technique. Such a method is too lengthy to discuss here. Suffice to say, we learned more about this type of cipher than the Mexicans themselves knew. In fact often they got their key words mixed and telegraphed that the message could not be deciphered. If they had asked us we could have given them the key, and told them that the message had been deciphered by us and sent to the State Department!

The clashes between the United States and Mexico as revealed by the decipherments of messages in this system are too numerous to quote, but there was one amusing case that has a direct bearing on this particular type. The translation of the decipherment reads:

Please do not be surprised at some telegrams I am sending you without encipherment and which might appear indiscreet but which purposely are sent in plain text in *order to have the State Department learn their contents.*

The message was from the Mexican Embassy in Washington to the Mexican Foreign Office in Mexico City.

Now the Mexican attempt to mislead the Department of State was, curiously, the one method that would have no effect, for *plain text messages were never intercepted!* We had always assumed that plain text messages did not contain information worth considering. Therefore no attempt was made to obtain copies. Had the Mexican Embassy sent these misleading messages in cipher, they would have reached the State Department. By sending them in plain text, the Embassy defeated its own purpose.

The Mexican Government used modifications of the Beaufort cipher for a number of years, then suddenly decided that it was unsafe. They then constructed tables containing twenty-six *different* mixed alphabets. The old table had contained twenty-six alphabets, but they were all based on the same word. This new system presented a much more difficult problem, but we finally developed a technique that would quickly solve messages even in this more advanced form.

Then in 1923, or thereabouts, the Mexican Government

must have employed a new cryptographer for they suddenly switched to codes. These were not very difficult to solve, since they were constructed alphabetically. Their solution followed the same line of attack as explained in Chapter VI, which told of the decipherment of the two code telegrams from the German Foreign Office to the German Minister at Mexico City.

These codes now began to show improvement in their technical construction, until finally the sequence of the code words and the plain text words for which they stood was thoroughly mixed. In Chapter VIII there is quoted a page from a German trench code that shows how a thoroughly disarranged code is constructed. The last illustration in the photo section also shows a thoroughly mixed code in use by the British Foreign Office during the Washington Armament Conference. The latter is what we call a "skeleton code." At this stage about thirty-five hundred words had been identified. The British Government seemed to prefer small codes of only ten thousand words and phrases.

We have now watched the slow development of Mexican means for the encipherment of their diplomatic messages. They had started with simple single substitution ciphers and had gradually reached the stage of the disarranged code. It was by continuity that we were able to solve them so readily. Over a period of years we learned not only their pet theories on so-called indecipherable codes and ciphers, which assisted us immeasurably, but also became familiar with their stock expressions or phraseology. No cryptographer can hope for rapid solutions unless he has this background to assist him. Aside from this, if no attempt is made to decipher messages during quiet periods when there seems to be no likelihood of important issues arising, the true aims and intentions of a government can not possibly be ascertained. One never knows at what moment another government will start a movement prejudicial to our interests.

The importance of continuity of decipherment of messages is even better emphasized in the case of still another government, for although there was no international question of any consequence at the time, we deciphered in the regular routine course of business a most amazing message. Had we not been practising continuity, we would never have stumbled on it.

This sensational code message was from a certain Ambassador in Washington to his home government and concerned a case of bribery. The episode had to do with the Ambassador, a high American government official, and the latter's secretary. One is now dead. The other two will at once recognize themselves. However, they may ease their minds, for under no circumstances will I reveal either their names or the exact nature of their intrigue.

It was in the summer of 192—. I had sent the decipherment of the message to Washington the night before, and was not surprised when I received a long-distance call.

"Hello, hello, Yardley; can you hear me?" came a voice suppressed with excitement.

"Yes, go ahead."

"Refer to your number——." The documents from my office to Washington were numbered consecutively for reference purposes.

"All right," I said. "I know what you mean."

"Come down on the midnight train and be at the State Department at nine A.M." He spoke rapidly.

"I'll be there," I promised. "But why all the fuss?"

"We are in a hell of a mess," he shouted. "Now listen carefully. Bring enough material with you to prove that this document is correct." The telephone was silent for a moment. "It is correct, isn't it?" he almost pleaded.

"Hell, yes," I assured him.

"Then come prepared to prove this to the State Department. Can't explain any more over the telephone." And with this he hung up.

I did not wonder at his excitement. Still it had been many years since our decipherments had ever been questioned. There must be more to this case than I realized.

I arrived at the State, War and Navy Building the next morning a few moments before nine, and made my way through the long corridors to the office of an important Department of State official who dealt directly with the Secretary on matters that affected my bureau. I was prepared for almost anything. I did not know him very well; in fact had not seen him since I was at the Peace Conference. But on the few occasions that I dealt with him he had been frank and aboveboard, a most unusual practise for a member of the diplomatic corps. For this reason I did not anticipate any great trouble with him.

His secretary showed me in at once. As I hung up my hat, I noted an air of tenseness about him. I could understand his worried look well enough, for this telegram concerned the very foundation of our government. Still, I mused, how do I fit into the picture?

He asked me to sit down, scooted his chair a bit closer and, leaning forward, began with, "This message you sent down night before last. You, of course, realize the seriousness of this telegram."

I made no comment. I had seen so many sensational telegrams of both American and foreign governments that I was long past the stage of being surprised at anything.

"Are you sure you have the correct decipherment?" he asked.

"Of course."

"Why do you say *of course?* You could have made an error."

"An error in spelling, an error in typing, an error in translation—yes. An error in decipherment that would garble the meaning—no." I thought for a moment. "Have you ever had an occasion to doubt any of our decipherments?" I asked.

"No."

"You have had plenty of opportunities to check up on us." When he made no reply, I continued: "Every day or so you receive the decipherment of a telegram of an Ambassador that starts off with something like this, 'Have today interviewed the Secretary of State. I told him so and so, and he replied, etc., etc.' Now I suppose the Secretary himself reads these telegrams I send down. He knows what is actually said at these conferences with foreign Ambassadors. Has the Secretary ever found any discrepancies between our decipherments and what actually went on that would lead him to believe that our solutions are ever incorrect?"

"Certainly not that I know of," he readily admitted. "But I have been instructed to satisfy myself in this particular case. There is some talk of demanding the recall of this Ambassador. You can see how very important it is that there be no mistakes."

I opened my brief case and took out a sheaf of papers and spread them on his desk.

"Suppose I show you just how we solved this telegram," I said. I then led him, step by step, through the solution. He followed me closely, asking intelligent questions as we progressed. At the end of an hour or so I said: "You can now see for yourself how utterly impossible it is for us to make an error in decipherment. Either we decipher a

232

message or we do not. Sometimes, of course, we can only decipher fragments of a telegram, and sometimes we place a note at the top of our decipherments questioning the correctness of this word or that one, but in a case like this where a long telegram is completely solved, it is utterly impossible to have anything but the correct solution."

"I'm satisfied," he admitted. "But for the life of me I do not see how you ever got started. It must be intriguing, but I should think you would all go mad."

He had lost his worried expression while following the analysis of the solution of this message, but he was now frowning at me again.

"Now, Yardley, I have a most unusual story to tell you. Yesterday morning, a few moments after this message arrived, the Secretary took it over to show it to the President. The President glanced at your decipherment, then, handing it back to the Secretary, said, 'Yes, the Attorney-General showed that to me a few moments ago. He just left.'"

He paused and eyed me furtively. He waited for some comment. I made none, for I knew now what was coming.

At last he said very slowly and deliberately:

"Now, tell me if you can, *how did the Attorney-General get a copy of this message?*" He said this as if he were exploding a bomb.

Some one, perhaps the Secretary, had tramped on his toes, for he was very angry by now.

"That's easily explained," I answered, "though you may not yourself appreciate the explanation. You see, during the war the department that I organized was the central Code and Cipher and Secret-Ink Bureau for the War, Navy, State and Justice Departments. At that time the Department of Justice had on their pay-roll an agent who had dabbled in ciphers. The Department of Justice contributed his services when we asked for him. He became expert. So after the war, when we moved to New York and organized as a civilian bureau on secret pay-roll, though we severed relations with the Navy Department, we took him with us. But he remained on the Justice Department pay-roll. Your predecessor knew of this and concurred. Am I clear?"

"Yes. Go on."

"Now, he must have an excuse for being on their pay-roll. So now and then I permit him to send to the Attorney-General a message that——"

"But of all messages, why this one?" he demanded.

"Well," I said, "in the first place I happened to turn this particular message over to him for decipherment. In the second place this looked to me like a Justice Department case."

"A Justice Department case!" he exclaimed. "The activity of an Ambassador is never a Department of Justice case."

I was not so sure of that, but made no reply for it was none of my business. I was already in bad enough.

"Have we funds available to employ this man?" he asked.

"Yes."

"Would he be willing to be transferred to your pay-roll?"

"I think so."

"Then transfer him. We don't want a Justice Department agent in your office."

I promised to do this at once and prepared to leave.

"There is one other point in this case that affects my office," I began, walking back to his desk.

"What is that?"

"If you demand the recall of this Ambassador, both he and his government will know that we are deciphering his telegrams. His government will appoint a new Ambassador, install a new code, and one never knows how much difficulty a new code will cause. You must realize that though my bureau is skilful, yet a new code may very well demand months of labor. The new Ambassador will probably engage in the same sort of activities, but we may not be in a position to know just what is going on. Isn't it more desirable to keep this Ambassador here and know what he is up to than to have a new one without being certain that we can check up on his activities?"

"Yes, we have thought of all that. My impression is that the entire case will be dropped. It is too serious to meddle with."

This official planned better than he realized, when he demanded that I transfer this man from the Justice Department pay-roll, for it was not long thereafter that we deciphered a series of messages that concerned the activities of one of the Attorney-General's close associates.

234

CHAPTER XIX

A Word with the State Department

SOMETIMES weeks elapsed without our hearing from Washington, then we would suddenly receive a letter demanding a quick solution. Sometimes I wondered if the government believe we deciphered telegrams by machinery.

In the fall of 1926 I received a telephone call from Washington telling me that one of these letters requesting quick action was on the way. The letter arrived on the eleven o'clock mail. When I opened it I found several sheets of paper containing three hundred and ninety code words. The following are the first few lines of the message:

8453207440	5400000001	19977 NCOTRAL	2116388212
0000178607	4747722681	2212567444	0757021928
2105311032	8151788212	6742358138	4346728381

There was no address, no signature, no date. The note accompanying the sheets of paper apologized for not being able to give us any information as to the origin of the code message but requested a telephone call just as soon as we learned anything.

A glance at the message showed that it was a five-figure code, sent in groups of ten. Note the repetition of 00001 in the second and sixth groups. With the entire message before me, I could see at a glance many other repetitions of several five-figure code words. The fourth group NCOTRAL was probably cipher and spelled a place or a name not in the code book.

235

I immediately put through a call to Washington:

"Just got your note. The message is in code and I suppose we can read it, but why all the mystery?"

"I don't know a thing, Yardley."

"Well, you know where you got it, don't you? You can give us a clue as to the language it is in."

"I haven't the least idea of the language. S. D. gave the message to me under the most secretive conditions, but told me to impress on you the importance of a quick solution. Be sure to let me know what progress you make, no matter how slight."

"All right," I answered, and hung up.

By S. D. he meant the State Department. This was just another one of those problems of opening a safe without the combination. If the Department of State was interested it must be a diplomatic message. The only important controversy at the time was the Tacna-Arica case in which the United States was acting as umpire. This disputed territory had nearly led to war between Chile and Peru, and the United States was attempting to get them to settle their dispute without resorting to arms. The message, then, so I reasoned, must be either Peruvian or Chilean. I had been surprised that the State Department had not asked us to furnish decipherments of both countries' telegrams during this controversy, but I was long past attempting to anticipate the Department's vagaries.

We maintained a clipping bureau of our own, and indexed all articles in the *New York Times* and a few other papers regarding any international controversy, so that we could review what had been mentioned in the newspapers without any research. A perusal of the clippings regarding this controversy showed that one of the questions was the disposition of the City of Arica. We reasoned therefore that the phrase *ciudad de Arica* should occur at least once.

As we had deciphered the Chilean and Peruvian codes during the war and were familiar with their construction, we assumed that this message was encoded in an alphabetical system; that is, one in which the words retain their alphabetical sequence and the code words their numerical order. The codes we had solved during the war were, however, five-letter code words instead of five figures.

Our analysis told us that the code word occurring most frequently was 36166, which we assumed as *de* and inserted this meaning throughout the message. As *ciudad de Arica* should occur, we began to look for a word that followed *de* that would fit for Arica—the code word for Arica should begin with 00 . . . since Arica would occur early in the code book itself. After several hours' search we gave up 36166 as meaning *de* and filled it in as *en*.

As *en* brought no results, we temporarily abandoned the solution of 36166.

We now selected 27359, another high-frequency group, to mean *de*, and again began our search for *ciudad de Arica*, which we finally tentatively identified.

In this manner after the first day we filled in only such words as *de, en, el, que, y, a,* etc., and were rather doubtful of a quick solution, for the problem now, of course, became a great deal more complex, since about 250 out of a total of 390 code words in the message occurred only once.

The next morning, however, we fortunately identified the words *Secretary of State,* and such phrases, translated, as *the Secretary of State said,* etc.

When we made this discovery, I picked up the telephone and told my correspondent in Washington to inform the Department of State that the message was from either the Chilean or Peruvian Ambassador, and that the message reported a conversation with the Secretary of State about the Tacna-Arica controversy. Also that if they wanted a quick solution he should send us a résumé of this conversation. It was the Secretary's custom to dictate résumés of conversations immediately after a conference with a representative of another government. These were often sent to us and were invaluable in the solution of new codes.

The résumé arrived the next morning, and within a few days we had deciphered the entire message, which turned out to be from the Peruvian Ambassador to his home government in Lima. A part of the translation is quoted:

No. 37. 1. Last night I had dinner alone with STABLER. After dinner he told me that the Secretary of State had always had in mind talking with me confidentially on account of my previous connection with the Tacna-Arica affair and also on account of my greater facility in English. I replied that if he wished to see me at any time I should be very pleased to go at once. STABLER had a good deal to say about the good offices of the Secretary and himself for the settlement of the matter in a satisfactory manner. I did not communicate this to you yesterday because I considered it of no greater importance than a casual conversation, but this morning STABLER telephoned to tell me that the Secretary of State wished to talk with me today.

2. I called on the Secretary immediately and had a long conversation with him. The Secretary said . . .

The telegram continues for several pages and gives the substance of the conversations between Secretary of State and a Mr. Ellis, and the latter's reactions.

Now the question arises, why is the Department of State interested in a telegram of this sort? The Secretary of State already knows what took place at this conference. Why is there any interest in the Peruvian Ambassador's report of this conversation?

The answer seems obvious enough. The Secretary was attempting to settle a most difficult dispute, in which not only Peru and Chile were vitally interested, but also Bolivia. He should call in representatives from each country and feel out their demands. He must effect a compromise of some sort to prevent these countries resorting to arms. Unless he knew that his conversations were correctly reported, unless he learned the real impressions of these representatives, how could he hope to settle their quarrel?

When I sent the complete decipherment of this message to Washington, word came back that a certain official in the Department of State wished to see me. This was the same man with whom I had dealt during the war while attempting to solve the Spanish Government's codes.

This would of course be another one of those mysterious conversations. He had something in mind and I thought it well to prepare myself before I saw him. Accordingly, I went down a day early without announcing my arrival, and called on one of the diplomatic secretaries who always knew all of the gossip.

This man knew of my bureau, in fact had visited us frequently, and did not hesitate to discuss any matter freely with me. Although I like to talk about myself, as I presume most of us do, when I met these secretaries of our diplomatic corps, I encouraged their confidences, for often they gave me bits of information that I needed.

This young diplomat had a most pleasing manner and

was a brilliant conversationalist. But this morning he wanted to talk about himself, and I had to listen for an hour to records of his amorous intrigues before the conversation turned to codes and ciphers.

"I think I'll quit the service," he finally said. "It is getting on my nerves. Now we have a report that the Mexican Government is deciphering our messages. There is a terrible scare about it. Imagine—using a code that even Mexico can solve. But you know the Department. Nothing will be done about it. Same kind of codes, and the Department is surprised that another government can solve them. Every day they see what your office can do. Still no attempt to profit by your experiences. Why the Department pays money for the solution of foreign codes and doesn't demand that you direct the kind of codes we should use is a mystery to me. The Department makes me ill. I think I'll resign." And so, on and on.

I made no comment to all this, but I was confident I knew what would be the subject of the State Department official's conversation. He would be very mysterious and ask me vague questions, but I would know what it was all about.

The next day when I went in to see him he congratulated my office on solving the Peruvian code so quickly, and said that he was sending a complete file of the Peruvian telegrams for decipherment and that we would receive current messages each day. He begged me to make an extra effort to get the decipherments to him at the earliest possible moment.

He was rather impressed with the fact that we had solved the code without knowing the language, address or signature. He waited several minutes for me to say something, but I was long accustomed to his manner and sat smoking while he made up his mind to tell me, in his secretive way, what was on his mind.

"Yardley," he finally began, "I have wondered for a long time whether our own codes are safe." Another long pause. "It may be possible for me to get copies of some of our coded messages so that your office can see whether you can decipher them." He would not of course tell me that there was a report that the Mexican Government had already broken the code.

"I should be very glad to look at them, but that isn't necessary."

"Why not?"

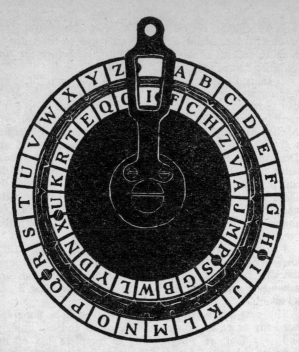

Plett's Cipher Machine, a modification of the famous Wheatstone cryptograph. The inner disk contains twenty-six spaces, the outer twenty-seven. The machine is so constructed that with each revolution of the inner disk it changes its position one space. The alphabet may be changed at will.

"I am familiar with the Department's codes. I can give you my opinion without your sending me the coded telegrams for analysis."

He looked at me for a long time. "What do you know about our codes?"

"I know all there is to know." And I went on to describe their construction and all the intimate details of the Department's secret means of communication.

"How do you know these things?" he asked.

"Well," I said, smiling inwardly, "cryptography is my business. Does it seem odd to you that I take an interest in not only the codes of foreign governments, but also in those of our own?"

"You mean that State Deparement employees discuss these matters with you?"

I said nothing, while he eyed me in silence.

At last he said, "Suppose you give me a memorandum showing how you could solve our codes."

I dreaded this request, for any recommendation I would make would require the Department to revolutionize its entire system of secret communication, and as every one knows, departmental procedure is too cumbersome to permit revolutionary changes.

"I don't think it would do any good," I replied.

"Why not?"

"Well, the question of secret codes goes deeper than you imagine. It isn't a question of a slight change. You see, during recent years cryptography has grown into a definite science. And during this growth, the Department of State has remained stationary. As you are aware, no one in the Department has had any experience, and therefore no one can know anything about the science of cryptography. Its position is hopeless, and I do not see how I can help any."

"Why not?"

"You oblige me to be frank."

"Go on."

"Well, to begin with, let us see who is responsible for the Department of State codes. What does he know about the subject? Nothing. Why was he appointed to his present position? Because he is an experienced cryptographer? No. He was appointed because he is an expert on archives and indices. The construction of codes and ciphers is only incidental to his present position.

"You might point out that since he was appointed he has compiled a number of codes. That is true. But one learns nothing about cryptography by compiling codes. One learns by tearing them apart. Now, if you will call him in here he will tell you that he couldn't decipher the simplest types of codes and ciphers. He doesn't pretend, at least not to me, that he understands the science of cryptography. How could he? He has had no opportunity for experience. This is not his fault. It is the fault of the Department of State. Though you employ experts for every other conceivable subject, you leave the very basis of successful diplomacy, which is safe communication, in the hands of an amateur cryptographer.

"You and I have been closely allied in the game of solution of government codes. It is needless to point out to you that the Great Powers all maintain staffs of experienced cryptographers to solve our, as well as other governments', codes. Isn't it a rather pitiful spectacle to see the Department of State require an amateur cryptographer to compile codes and ciphers that will be torn apart by the best cipher brains in the world?"

"That is exactly why I am asking your advice," he interrupted.

"If the Department of State expects to keep up with the growing science of cryptography, it will require more than my advice," I replied. "Now you ask for a memorandum that will point out just how I would go about solving your diplomatic codes. To what purpose? The memorandum reaches the employee who compiles your codes, and he says, 'Oh, yes, I see how you do it now. I'll make a code that doesn't have this weakness.' But he doesn't see at all. He only knows how this particular problem is solved. No amount of exposition can ever make him realize, simply because he is not a professional cryptographer, that the skilled cipher expert solves a problem by the first weakness he discovers. This doesn't mean that there are no other weaknesses in the system, and it does not mean that his solution is the most rapid one.

"Now he corrects this weakness, and what then? The skilled cryptographer searches for another. To illustrate, I was the first person in the United States to write an exposition on the solution of our own diplomatic codes. What did the Department do? Just what I have already said. It made a few improvements, corrected the weakness by which I solved these codes, but your basic method of communication is the same as it was when I was a youngster in the Code Room."

He was intensely interested and stared at me a while, then said:

"Instead of preparing a memorandum outlining how you would solve our codes, why don't you prepare one telling us what changes we should make?"

I smiled at this, for I knew the situation hopeless.

"I can't do it. I would not care to have the job of trying to make your present methods indecipherable. And if I can't do it, I don't see how an amateur can. As a matter of fact the Department is so far behind in the science of cryptography that its position is hopeless. Your codes, your point of view, belong to the sixteenth century."

"Sixteenth-century codes!"

"Yes. You have made a few improvements, but basically the codes in use are the same as those of the sixteenth century. Aside from this, your codes are just as cumbersome, just as antiquated as the sixteenth-century methods of communication. Though we now have instantaneous communication by telegraph and telephone, and the Department takes advantage of these, you still require your code clerks to fumble around for hours encoding and decoding dispatches when you should have not only instantaneous transmission, but also instantaneous encipherment and decipherment. Aside from this, the State Department should have an indecipherable means of communication."

"Aren't any codes indecipherable?"

"No. Not as the Department understands a code or cipher. *But there is one indecipherable means of communication.* To adopt such a system, however, the Department would be obliged to discard all its antiquated ideas. The means I refer to revolutionizes communications. You could discharge ninety per cent of your code clerks; and your telegrams would be absolutely indecipherable."

"You mean a cipher machine?"

"Yes, but not the type of machine you have in mind. During the war the American Telephone and Telegraph Company invented a machine that automatically enciphered and transmitted a message over the wire by merely striking the letters of the message on a typewriter keyboard, while the machine at the other end of the wire automatically deciphered the message and at the same instant typed it. Had the enemy at any point between these two machines tapped the wire, he would have intercepted nothing but a jumble of letters. In cases where instantaneous transmissions and decipherment was not practicable the operator first enciphered the message by striking the letters on the keyboard and turned the resultant cipher message over to the cable company. When the cipher telegram reached the addressee, he adjusted his machine, struck the cipher letters on the keyboard and the original telegram appeared before him.

"This machine filled every requirement of simplicity of operation, speed and accuracy. *But it was not indecipherable.*

"There have been many cipher machines invented. One in particular was so ingeniously contrived that there is no repetition for four billion letters. Or at least that is what the inventor thinks; for you see, there again you have the amateur attempting to escape repetitions by a series of disks, tapes, electric impulses, etc. These machines fill your needs in simplicity, speed and accuracy, and if you adopted them, you could discharge ninety per cent of your code clerks, but all these machines are invented by people who haven't as yet grasped the fact that there is no method of avoiding repetitions. To the eye these machines, as well as innumerable other ciphers and types of codes, do escape repetitions, but mathematical formula will reveal them."

"If this is true, and I am ready to admit anything you tell me, how is it possible to construct any practicable means of secret communication that is indecipherable?"

"There is no way as long as the attempt is made to avoid repetitions. *The only indecipherable cipher is one in which there are no repetitions to conceal.* Therefore no need to attempt to escape them."

"There is such a method?"

"Yes."

"It can be made practicable by some such machine as the American Telephone and Telegraph machine that you described?"

"Yes, though for small offices the machine need be no larger than a typewriter. If and when the Government of the United States adopts such a system, and not until then, may they have absolute certainty that their messages will never be read by a cryptographer. Sooner or later all governments, all wireless companies, will adopt some such system. And when they do, cryptography, as a profession, will die.

"I hope you now understand why I prefer not to write a memorandum for your Code Bureau. Even with all my experience, I wouldn't know how to go about compiling an indecipherable code or cipher along the conventional lines. There is only one indecipherable means of communication, and its adoption would require the Department to revolutionize its antiquated methods. I'm afraid there is nothing that either you or I can do about it.

"What I have said might have seemed disrespectful to the Department, but I'm sure you appreciate my position. I am not a State Department employee and feel free to say what I believe."

He looked worried.

"I fully understand your position," he interrupted, "and I am grateful for what you have said. This matter must be given serious consideration, but you know as well as I how slowly the Department acts."

I agreed with this, and the conference ended. I rather regretted having gone off on such a tangent, for the situation I knew was hopeless.

Nothing less than an international scandal would wake up the government to the fact that the very basis of all successful diplomacy is safe and secret lines of communication. But my whole life had been devoted to destruction. I should like to leave a monument to constructive cryptography.

As I walked through the wide high corridors on my way to the entrance, I mused how proud one might be to leave to the United States Government a method of communication that would insure the secrecy of her dispatches throughout the ages. Aside from this, of course, was professional pride. Then too it would be fun to laugh at foreign cryptographers as in my mind I saw them puzzling over our secret telegrams, striving in vain for a solution.

But why dream? After all, weren't all diplomatic representatives just funny little characters on a stage, whispering, whispering, then yelling their secrets to the heavens as they put them on the cables!

Well, in any case, I must hurry back to New York. The Department of State wanted to know what secrets the Peruvian Ambassador had been whispering in Washington.

CHAPTER XX

The Black Chamber Is Destroyed

IN the latter part of 1928 the newspapers were full of the Anglo-American naval race. The British in 1927 had walked out on Hugh Gibson at the conference at Geneva, but when President Coolidge recommended the fifteen-cruiser bill which would bring us to parity with England, the British statesmen suddenly changed their tone and decided after all that perhaps it might be well to enter an agreement with America on limitation of cruisers.

Everything pointed definitely to a conference in 1929. We therefore set about to prepare ourselves to play an important part, as we had done in 1921-22 at the Washington Armament Conference.

This was not a simple matter. The Black Chamber had entered a critical period of history. It became increasingly difficult to obtain copies of the code telegrams of foreign governments, and we were forced to adopt rather subtle methods. Our superiors did not always assist us in the measures necessary to maintain the flow of telegrams into the Black Chamber.

I envied the foreign cryptographer, for he had no such problem to worry over. All coded messages were turned over to him as a matter of routine, as they were to us during the war. In fact England, in her license contracts to cable companies, required them, upon demand, to deliver all telegrams to the Admiralty. And it is in the Admiralty that the skilled English cryptographers are hidden. The difficulty in obtaining material worried me considerably, and I planned at one stroke to settle the matter once and for all time.

My plan was a bold one, but for reasons which I can not give, failed.

Momentarily I concentrated on the approaching conference. Both England and Japan would be more aggressive than ever. As late as 1927 during the crisis in China we had seen them still making joint and, so they thought, secret decisions before consulting America. America would need every resource at her command to hold the position she obtained at the Washington Conference. The Black Chamber must again play its part.

The new Secretary of State had already taken office, but it was the custom of my correspondents in Washington to permit a new Secretary of State to familiarize himself with his new duties before bringing to his attention the activities of the Black Chamber.

Finally we deciphered a series of important code messages, and when I sent them to Washington I suggested that this presented an opportune moment to acquaint the new Secretary with our skill.

I accordingly awaited the reception of these messages with the greatest anxiety. I was to receive advance news of the Secretary's reactions. A few days later when I saw a letter on my desk from one of my informants, I studied it a long while in silence before I had the courage to open it.

Finally I ripped it open. The first words spelled our doom. The letter was almost illegible, full of exclamations, and what-not. I put in a telephone call for more details.

My informant told me that the messages I had sent down were given to the Secretary, who wished to know how they were obtained. When informed of the Black Chamber he had totally disapproved of our activities and ordered that all State Department funds be withdrawn from our support, and that the State Department have absolutely nothing to do with our organization. He took the position that we should not supervise the telegrams of foreign governments. This of course spelled the doom of the Black Chamber which was now supported almost totally by State Department funds.

I slowly hung up the receiver and turned to my secretary, who had been with me for ten years. She had gathered the meaning of the conversation. Her face was as white as death.

"I'm sorry," I said inanely. "I guess we'd better call in the others."

When I told them the decision at Washington, they all stared at me with uncomprehending eyes. Most of them had devoted many years to cryptography, working secretively, not even their most intimate friends being aware of their real accomplishments. That cryptography as a profession would ever die had never entered their minds. It was tragic to hear these people, their intellect sharpened by years of original investigation, ask me the same questions over and over again. They did not understand, and were like children seeking an explanation of the unexplainable.

The next day I received official notice of the closing of the Black Chamber, and was ordered to come to Washington at once.

Before reporting to my immediate superior I went the rounds, talking here and there with those who were familiar with the situation. One of these was a member of the diplomatic corps, who, as chief of different bureaus in the Department of State, I figured, had been dependent for his conduct of affairs upon the messages we deciphered.

When I walked into his office he gave me a hopeless smile.

"Have you heard the bad news, Yardley?" he asked.

"Yes."

"It's a terrible mess." Then in self-defense, "You know I'm not the top side." He always referred to any Secretary of State as the top side.

"No, unfortunately not," I said.

We discussed the matter for a few moments, then I arose to go.

"There's nothing we can do, Yardley. The top side simply won't have it. Don't see how we can get along without you."

"Oh, you'll manage," I replied. "Well, good-by. It's been pleasant to work with you."

I at last reached the office of my immediate superior. He told me the story, and expressed his profound regret at the sudden manner in which it had become necessary to close the Black Chamber. We both agreed there was nothing that could be done. The Black Chamber was almost entirely dependent on State Department funds. Aside from this, we both agreed that it was up to the Department of State to define policies. If the Department considered the code messages of foreign governments inviolate, then inviolate they must remain. It would be usurpation of power on the part of the War Department if it engaged in activities against the policies of the State Department. There was nothing to do but close the Black Chamber and dismiss its employees. Its chapter in American history was ended.

My superior gave me letters of appreciation and recommendation addressed to each of my employees, and was kind enough to draft one for me to keep.

I left my superior's office a bit sad, I think, for one does not sever an association of sixteen years without a tug at the heart.

Before leaving I would see still another official of the Department of State, a personal friend of mine, who had been one of the Black Chamber's most ardent supporters. He was out to lunch and would not be back until two-thirty.

I walked through the corridors that I had known so well sixteen years before, out to the street, and sat down in the park across the way.

There would soon be another Armament Conference. It would be held in London, no doubt. How would America fare in the conference room without the Black Chamber? The Department of State still used its sixteenth-century codes. I could see the rush of excitement in the British Admiralty Cipher Bureau, as their skilful, experienced cryptographers prepared for the phalanx of American code clerks and their antiquated codes. I rather envied the British cryptographers.

Would America be defeated at this conference? Would England and Japan force their demands? I felt a bit sorry for the American Delegation, though, of course, I could not then know that it would be so badly defeated in London as to return with six-inch guns, and submarine parity and a ten-to-seven naval ratio with Japan.

America, having abandoned the secret practises of the Black Chamber, must, in self-defense, in order to protect herself from the prying eyes of skilful foreign cryptographers, demand by a new treaty with the Great Powers that diplomatic messages remain inviolate. But would America be shrewd enough to make such demand?

From where I sat I could see the windows of the Code Room where I had received my early training. I felt homesick for code books and telegraph instruments and good fellowship. I must visit old friends in the Code Room. I had been almost twenty-four when I came there. I was now forty. Sixteen long years. To me, a lifetime. To America, an episode. Sixteen years of drudgery, illness, espionage, brain-wearying science, flowery letters and honors. Why? To what purpose?

I must not become reminiscent, but return to see my friend who would now be back from lunch. He had known me as a struggling clerk in the Department of State back in 1913 and had supported me through all these years. I must tell him good-by.

When I returned, his secretary showed me in at once.

He gave me a sickly smile and a limp hand and asked me to sit down. His attitude puzzled me, for he had always gone out of the way to do me favors. While he talked aimlessly about nothing, I tried to account for his manner. Then I put myself in his position. Suppose I myself had employed some one to use embarrassing means to obtain information that I considered vital, would I be anxious to see this person after he had obtained the information I desired, and I had paid him off?

I began to feel sorry for him, too. He was so obviously ill at ease.

"I dropped in merely to pay my respects," I said. "You know of course that we are closing up shop in New York."

"Yes." He was very restless.

"It's rather difficult to give up old friends, old associations, but it can't be helped," I added.

"Yes, we shall miss you. Too bad we can't have you with us."

He was visibly relieved when I shook hands and said good-by. He walked with me across the spacious room and even opened the door for me.

Thus ended the secret activities of the American Black Chamber.

The most fascinating people and events of World War II

Available at your bookstore or use this coupon.

___**ADOLF HITLER, John Toland**　　　　　　　　　　　　　　27533　3.95
Pulitzer Prize-winning author John Toland's bestselling biography of Hitler based on over 150 interviews with the numerous survivors of his circle of friends, servants and associates.

___**A MAN CALLED INTREPID, William Stevenson**　　　　　　29352　3.50
The authentic account of the most decisive intelligence operations of World War II - and the superspy who controlled them.

___**CYNTHIA, H. Montgomery Hyde**　　　　　　　　　　　　　28197　1.95
The incredible, but fully-documented true story of a brave, shrewd sensual woman's contribution to the allied victory — in World War II's most unusual battlefield.

___**PIERCING THE REICH, Joseph E. Persico**　　　　　　　　28280　2.50
After 35 years of silence, top-secret files have been opened to reveal the stupendous drama of the most perilous and heroic chapter of intelligence history.

 BALLANTINE MAIL SALES
Dept. NE, 201 E. 50th St., New York, N.Y. 10022

Please send me the BALLANTINE or DEL REY BOOKS I have checked above. I am enclosing $.......... (add 50¢ per copy to cover postage and handling). Send check or money order — no cash or C.O.D.'s please. Prices and numbers are subject to change without notice.

Name_____

Address_____

City_____State_____Zip Code_____
Allow at least 4 weeks for delivery.

Bestsellers from BALLANTINE BOOKS

Available at your bookstore or use this coupon.

___ **SHADOW OF THE WOLF, James Barwick**   28316 2.75
What is the second most powerful man in Hitler's Germany doing in England? A WWII espionage thriller—"A first-rate 'what-if' novel!"—*Los Angeles Times*

___ **SHIBUMI, Trevanian**   28585 2.95
#1 Bestseller! A stunning espionage thriller set from China to Spain. Hero Nicholai Hel is the perfect assassin...and the perfect lover.

___ **ENEMIES, Richard Harris**   28435 2.75
A startling thriller of pursuit and political espionage—"Grips like a fist from the opening pages!"—*Cosmopolitan*

___ **SS-GB, Len Deighton**   29317 2.95
What if Hitler had invaded England and won the war? The international bestseller by a renowned master of espionage.

___ **VICAR OF CHRIST, Walter F. Murphy**   28371 2.95
The national bestseller about the first American Pope. "If you read one bestselling novel a year, *The Vicar of Christ* is the one."—John Leonard, *The New York Times*

___ **SOLDIERS OF '44, William P. McGivern**   28385 2.50
The national bestseller about the men who fought when to fight meant to save what they loved. "Few readers are likely to stop reading."—*The New York Times Book Review*

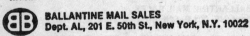 **BALLANTINE MAIL SALES**
Dept. AL, 201 E. 50th St., New York, N.Y. 10022

Please send me the BALLANTINE or DEL REY BOOKS I have checked above. I am enclosing $.......... (add 50¢ per copy to cover postage and handling). Send check or money order — no cash or C.O.D.'s please. Prices and numbers are subject to change without notice.

Name_____

Address_____

City_____ State_____ Zip Code_____
Allow at least 4 weeks for delivery.

AL-39

HISTORY COMES ALIVE

Bestselling and acclaimed true stories of war, peace, rebellion and intrigue.

Available at your bookstore or use this coupon.

____**A DISTANT MIRROR: THE CALAMITOUS 14th CENTURY**
by Barbara W. Tuchman   **29542 8.95**
The #1 bestseller by a Pulitzer Prize winning historian. "A beautiful, extraordinary book!"—*Wall Street Journal.*

____**A RUMOR OF WAR** by Philip Caputo   **29070 2.50**
A true story of Vietnam combat by one who was there. "Heartbreaking, terrifying and enraging!"—*Los Angeles Times*

____**FOUR DAYS OF NAPLES** by Aubrey Menan   **28906 2.50**
An army of children brings the Nazis to their knees in this "stirring story."
—*San Francisco Chronicle*

____**A MAN CALLED INTREPID** by William Stevenson **29352 3.50**
Over 2 million copies sold! The authentic account of the war's boldest superspy!

____**RETURN FROM THE RIVER KWAI** by John and Clay Blair, Jr. **29007 2.75**
The famous story continues in this book hailed as "magnificent."—*Pittsburgh Press*

BB BALLANTINE MAIL SALES
Dept. AL, 201 E. 50th St., New York, N.Y. 10022

Please send me the BALLANTINE or DEL REY BOOKS I have checked above. I am enclosing $ . . . . (add 50¢ per copy to cover postage and handling). Send check or money order — no cash or C.O.D.'s please. Prices and numbers are subject to change without notice.

Name_____

Address_____

City_____State_____Zip Code_____

04   Allow at least 4 weeks for delivery.   AL-29

Military works by
MARTIN CAIDIN
One of the best known and most respected writers of true-life war adventures.

Available at your bookstore or use this coupon.

___**FLYING FORTS**   28308   2.25
The extraordinary story of the B-17 In World War Two. With 32 pages of photos.

___**FORK-TAILED DEVIL: THE P-38**   28301   2.25
More wartime excitement, in the air and on land.

___**THE NIGHT HAMBURG DIED**   28303   1.95
The bomber raid that turned Hamburg Into a roaring Inferno of flame. With 8 pages of photos.

___**THUNDERBOLT**   28307   1.95
Flying the deadly P-47 with the 56th fighter group In World War II. 8 pages of photos.

___**A TORCH TO THE ENEMY**   28304   1.95
The complete story of U.S. air power and the fire raids that destroyed Japan. With 16 pages of photos.

___**ZERO**   28305   2.25
The first overall account—from the enemy viewpoint—of Japan's air war in the Pacific. With 8 pages of photos.

BB   **BALLANTINE MAIL SALES**
Dept. AL, 201 E. 50th St., New York, N.Y. 10022

Please send me the BALLANTINE or DEL REY BOOKS I have checked above. I am enclosing $ . . . . (add 50¢ per copy to cover postage and handling). Send check or money order — no cash or C.O.D.'s please. Prices and numbers are subject to change without notice.

Name_____

Address_____

City_____ State_____ Zip Code_____

06   Allow at least 4 weeks for delivery.   AL-26